LAW AND LIBERTY IN THE WAR ON TERROR

LAW AND LIBERTY IN THE WAR ON TERROR

EDITORS

Andrew Lynch
Edwina MacDonald
George Williams

FOREWORD
The Hon Sir Gerard Brennan AC KBE

THE FEDERATION PRESS
2007

Published in Sydney by:
The Federation Press
PO Box 45, Annandale, NSW, 2038
71 John St, Leichhardt, NSW, 2040
Ph (02) 9552 2200 Fax (02) 9552 1681
E-mail: info@federationpress.com.au
Website: www.federationpress.com.au

National Library of Australia
Cataloguing-in-Publication entry

Law and Liberty in the war on terror
Editors: Andrew Lynch; George Williams; Edwina MacDonald.

Includes index.
Bibliography
ISBN 978 186287 674 3 (pbk)

Judicial power – Australia. Criminal Law – Australia. War on Terrorism, 2001-
Terrorism – Prevention. Terrorism. International offences.

347.012

Text printed on
100% recycled paper

Typeset by The Federation Press, Leichhardt, NSW.
Printed by Ligare Pty Ltd, Riverwood, NSW.

Foreword

The Hon Sir Gerard Brennan AC KBE

> *Any society that would give up a little liberty to gain a little security will deserve neither and lose both.*
>
> Benjamin Franklin

Franklin's aphorism, like many other aphorisms, seems too simplistic in its generality. We continually yield some liberties in order to live in society, respecting the rights and the integrity of our fellows. But the spirit of the comment is surely right. When we yield more than is necessary to achieve social order and harmony, we have denied the worth of liberty – the priceless precondition to human dignity and self-respect. In times when we are threatened by terror which may be achieved, if need be, by suicidal attacks, must we yield up some of those liberties which the law hitherto has been jealous to preserve? Is it right to sacrifice the liberties of those who may be suspect participants in, or supporters of, terror in order to gain some security for those who are not so suspected? The chapters in this book canvass these questions, proponents of the new anti-terrorism laws seeking to justify their provisions and opponents arguing that the laws go too far. These chapters also show the extent of the changes that have been made to our legal and administrative structures.

The debate opens with the Attorney-General, Philip Ruddock, defending the laws which he administers, as designed to prevent terrorism and to define its special criminality. Alex Conte compares the New Zealand laws, largely based on international sources. Ben Saul and Kent Roach debate the justification for inserting a motive in the definition of terrorism and the scope of the statutory proscriptions are discussed by Andrew Goldsmith and Patrick Emerton. At this point it is obvious that the anti-terrorism laws are framed to achieve a purpose that has not previously informed the general criminal law: the laws are designed primarily to forestall the commission of a terrorist crime, not to inhibit its commission by prescribing a penalty for crime committed. One reason for the change is that some would-be terrorists are willing to die for their cause and deterrence by punishment would have no effect, as Robert Cornall, Secretary of the Attorney General's Department, points out. He enters the policy debate, espousing the new laws as 'essential to provide an adequate legal basis to deal with this unprecedented terrorist threat'. Subjection to detention and interrogation is authorised subject to specified conditions. The laws do not permit the infliction of torture, which Sarah Joseph and Neil James reject as both contrary to international law and ineffective.

The preventative purpose of the new laws carries with it serious implications for what has been traditionally regarded as the rule of law. Wide powers to detain or to restrict a person's freedom of movement or to compel submission to questioning are conferred on law enforcement agencies or are ordered on application by them and a wide range of conduct which might assist terrorism or which is peripheral or preliminary to the commission of a terrorist act is swept into the ambit of terrorism offences, exposing to penalty persons who would not otherwise be treated as being a party to an offence or as having attempted to commit an offence.

Commenting on the powers of law enforcement agencies, James Renwick points out that provisions which authorise executive detention run counter to the traditional legal principle, protective of a fundamental freedom, that there can be no imprisonment without formal charges. The new provisions do not fall within the established exceptions to that principle but Geoff McDonald opines that a process of authorisation which requires a judicial order that can be challenged on appeal – or, it can be added, approval by a judicial officer acting as a persona designata – is more acceptable than the process adopted in some other countries. Even so, the process of securing judicial consent is itself problematic. Justice Margaret White, concerned by the absence of a contradictor when an ex parte application is made, and noting the broad and open textured tests to be satisfied in the security legislation, commends the Queensland expedient of appointing a Public Interest Monitor.

The material to be placed before a judicial officer to secure the issuing of a warrant need not do more than show 'reasonable grounds to believe' that the warrant will have a specified anti-terrorism effect. Questions of this kind, affecting the freedom of individuals, are not the ordinary stuff of judicial decision-making. Principles of natural justice and the open administration of the law are, or may be, compromised. David Dyzenhaus and Rayner Thwaites question the significance of such a regime for the rule of law. They analyse the judgments delivered in *Al-Kateb v Godwin* and *Thomas v Mowbray* to illustrate the different ways in which the rule of law might be understood by the judiciary. Is the rule of law upheld by deferring to executive power provided that power is conferred by legislation or must there be an adherence to basic procedures and concepts by which the judiciary protects traditional rights and immunities?

Some of Patrick Emerton's concern about the broad scope of terrorism offences derives from the discretionary power exercised by executive regulation to declare a group to be a 'terrorist organisation' and thus expose persons associated with the group to criminal prosecution. He submits that the discretion has not been exercised even-handedly and Waleed Aly notes that in Australia, unlike other countries, only Islamic organisations have been proscribed. Another concern, discussed by Stephen Donaghue, relates to the inability to adduce evidence for reasons of national security as certified by the Attorney-General.

Even if a sanitised version of such evidence is admitted, its precise terms may not be disclosed to an accused. Non-disclosure may extend to counsel in some instances, unless counsel has a national security clearance. Phillip Boulten claims that the new laws have changed the dynamic of the criminal trial as a battle between prosecution and defence. Security interests are now represented at the bar table and sometimes threaten criminal proceedings against counsel in the trial.

Clive Walker, speaking with the experience of anti-terrorism legislation in the United Kingdom, sees executive-based action that emphasises preventative intelligence gathering leads to 'rather more shaky foundations in legitimacy because of the jettisoning of aspects of due process such as open hearings and evidential standards'. To provide some check, he favours the creation of a kind of Ombudsman reporting directly to a Parliamentary Committee on the operation of anti-terrorism legislation.

Public opinion on the operation of these laws may well be misinformed. Tanja Dreher points out that journalists, restricted in what can be reported, are increasingly dependent on leaks and spin from official sources. Moreover, communal fear of terrorism has been heightened by a discursive linking of national security, immigration and Islam. This is not conducive to that informed public discourse which Katharine Gelber identifies as critical to the democratic legitimacy of a law and as a defining characteristic of Australian democracy.

Waleed Aly regrets the ineffectiveness of a Muslim voice in the debates on anti-terrorism – in part due to the disparate ethnicity, culture and sectarian allegiances of Australian Muslims and in part due to public suspicion of Muslims defending civil liberties after terrorist attacks by Islamic extremists. Muslims are united, however, in their concerns about the vagueness and generality of some of the anti-terrorism laws, especially if they be held to impact on Muslim charity – one of the five pillars of Islamic practice. They have grounds for fearing that the broad discretionary powers conferred by the anti-terrorism laws will be implemented by distrusted law enforcement and intelligence agencies.

Both Andrew Lynch and Clive Walker reject as spurious the notion of striking a balance between human rights and protection from terrorism. Andrew Lynch notes the alarming width of the anti-terrorism laws which 'can easily result in executive overreach'. The scope of the new laws and the investing of courts with powers not only to punish wrongdoers but to protect the community from wrongdoing are working a rapid readjustment in the legal system. Many will agree with his call to preserve individual rights and constitutional constraints on government – perhaps, it could be added, important *traditional* constraints on government and government agencies. He declares:

> Safeguarding our defining civil liberties and the presumption of innocence … is neither a hindrance nor a luxury, but instead the only certain way to ensure that in responding to the threat of terrorism we do not allow those who would do us harm to dictate what kind of people we are and our relationship with the state.

The chapters in this book cannot be dismissed as mere academic analyses. They have to do with the lives and aspirations of all Australians. They ask whether Australia is, and whether it will be, a united, secure, free and confident nation.

Sydney
October 2007

Contents

Part III
Beyond Guilt or Innocence – Preventative Orders and Counter-Terrorism

Part IV
Human Rights and Terrorism: is a Trade-off Necessary?

Part V
Australia's Response Compared

Preface

This book is the outcome of a three-day symposium held in July 2007 to discuss and debate the role of law in responding to the threat of terrorism. Australia has adapted quickly to the new global security climate ushered in by the attacks of 11 September 2001. This has presented numerous challenges and the measures adopted have attracted much controversy. The purpose of the symposium – and now this book – was to bring together as many different perspectives on the relationship between law and security as possible so as to enable ideas and positions to be better understood and challenged. We are enormously grateful to all who participated in that event and to those who have continued this process of engagement by contributing a chapter to this book.

We feel that some mention should be made of the inclusion of the phrase 'war on terror' in the book's title. This expression is widely contested and our use of it is not an endorsement of the adoption of a war paradigm in responding to terrorism. Nor does it indicate unqualified approval of the many political uses to which others have put that phrase. It should be apparent, in any case, that a book featuring over 20 authors cannot be categorised as adopting any one particular view or position. Nevertheless, the expression – for good or ill – is arguably the defining one of our times and we decided that its use appropriately conveyed the context in which Australia's national security law has been rapidly developed. We were content for individual contributors to distance themselves from it as they felt necessary – something which several do.

Last, we wish to thank the Australian Research Council for its support of the symposium through the *Discovery Projects* funding scheme, and Chris Holt and the editorial team at Federation Press for their support and enthusiasm in publishing this work – and particularly the speed with which they did so as to ensure it speaks to current events.

Andrew Lynch
Edwina MacDonald
George Williams

November 2007

Australian Government
Australian Research Council

This project was supported under Australian Research Council's *Discovery Projects* funding scheme (project number DP0556465).

Contributors

Mr Waleed Aly

Waleed Aly is a lecturer in the School of Political and Social Inquiry at Monash University, and also works within the university's Global Terrorism Research Centre. At the time of delivering the presentation on which this chapter is based, he was a director of, and media spokesperson for the Islamic Council of Victoria, the peak representative body for Victorian Muslims. He resigned from this position just over a month later. He was admitted to legal practice in 2005 and worked in private practice until 2007.

Mr Phillip Boulten SC

Phillip Boulten is a Sydney barrister. He specialises in criminal cases – both at trial and on appeal. He has represented a number of people suspected of and charged with terrorist-related crimes. He has acted for people who have been subjected to interrogation by the Australian Security Intelligence Organisation (ASIO) as well as for several people whose cases have been heard in the courts.

The Hon Sir Gerard Brennan AC KBE

Sir Gerard Brennan was born and educated in Queensland. He was a barrister and appointed QC in Queensland, New South Wales, Northern Territory, Papua New Guinea and Fiji. He has been a Judge of the Industrial Court of Australia, the President of the Administrative Appeals Tribunal, a foundation Judge of the Federal Court, a Justice of the High Court of Australia and Chief Justice of Australia. He is a former Chancellor of the University of Technology, Sydney. Sir Gerard has been appointed a Knight Commander of the Order of the British Empire and a Companion of the Order of Australia. He holds Honorary Degrees from Trinity College Dublin, University of Queensland, Central Queensland University, Australian National University, Griffith University, Melbourne University, University of New South Wales and University of Technology, Sydney. He is currently a Non-Permanent Judge of the Court of Final Appeal of Hong Kong.

Dr Alex Conte

Alex Conte is a Reader in Law at the University of Southampton, England. He was the 2004 New Zealand Law Foundation International Research Fellow, undertaking a comparative study of the interface between counter-terrorism and human rights as between New Zealand, Australia, Canada and the United Kingdom. A member of the Advisory Panel of Experts to the UN Special Rapporteur on counter-terrorism, he is also a fellow to the International Policy Institute on Counter-Terrorism. He has acted as a consultant on various projects of the UN Office of the High Commissioner for Human Rights, the UN Terrorism Prevention Branch, and the Organization for Security and Co-operation in Europe. Recent publications include *Counter-Terrorism and Human Rights in New Zealand* (2007) and *Security in the 21st Century: The United Nations, Afghanistan and Iraq* (2005).

Mr Robert Cornall AO
Robert Cornall has extensive experience at a high level in public administration. He is currently the Secretary of the Attorney-General's Department. Before this he was the Managing Director of Victoria Legal Aid and the Executive Director and Secretary of the Law Institute of Victoria. He was also a partner and solicitor at Middletons Oswald Burt Solicitors. Robert completed his Bachelor of Laws at the University of Melbourne. He was appointed an Officer of the Order of Australia in 2006 for his contributions to the public sector.

Dr Stephen Donaghue
Stephen Donoghue is a member of the Victorian Bar, where he practices principally in administrative law and constitutional law. He has been counsel for the Commonwealth in numerous national security cases. Stephen studied law at the University of Melbourne, where he received the Supreme Court Prize. He has a doctorate from Oxford and was a recipient of a Menzies Memorial Scholarship in Law and a Commonwealth Scholarship. He was associate to Justice Hayne at the High Court of Australia, and is a member of the Advisory Board of the Centre for Comparative Constitutional Studies at the University of Melbourne

Dr Tanja Dreher
Tanja Dreher is an ARC Postdoctoral Fellow at the University of Technology, Sydney where she is undertaking a project on News and Community Conflict Resolution. Her research has focused on news and cultural diversity and on experiences of racism and anti-racism work during the 'war on terror'. She is the author of the research monographs *Targeted: experiences of racism in NSW after September 11, 2001* (2006) and *Whose Responsibility? Community antiracism strategies in NSW after September 11, 2001* (2007) and has contributed to many community media interventions involving Arab and Muslim Australians.

Professor David Dyzenhaus
David Dyzenhaus is a Professor of Law and Philosophy at the University of Toronto, Associate Dean, Graduate Studies, of the Faculty of Law, and a Fellow of the Royal Society of Canada. Previously, he served as Assistant Professor and Canada Research Fellow at the Faculty of Law, Queen's University.

He holds a doctorate from Oxford University and law and undergraduate degrees from the University of the Witwatersrand, South Africa. In 2002, he was the Law Foundation Visiting Fellow in the Faculty of Law, University of Auckland. In 2005-2006 he was Herbert Smith Visiting Professor in the Cambridge Law Faculty and a Senior Scholar of Pembroke College, Cambridge.

Dr Patrick Emerton

Patrick Emerton is a Lecturer in the Faculty of Law, Monash University. His areas of research include philosophy of language, political philosophy, and legal responses to political violence. He is an active participant in the policy debate surrounding Australia's new anti-terrorism laws. His evidence has been cited extensively in the reports of parliamentary and expert committees, and he has given expert commentary in the print and electronic media. He is also a member of the Federation of Community Legal Centres Anti-Terrorism Laws Working Group.

Dr Katharine Gelber

Katharine Gelber is a Senior Lecturer in Politics and International Relations at the University of New South Wales with research interests in free speech and hate speech. She is currently engaged in an ARC-funded large research project entitled 'Securing Freedom: Political Speech in Australia'. She has co-edited a book with Prof Adrienne Stone entitled *Hate Speech and Freedom of Speech in Australia* (2007) and has published articles in *Review of International Studies*, the *Australian Journal of Human Rights* and the *Australian Journal of Political Science.*

Professor Andrew Goldsmith

Andrew Goldsmith is Professor of Law and Criminal Justice at Flinders University, Adelaide. He has an undergraduate law degree from the University of Adelaide, a Master of Arts in Social Theory from Monash University, a Master of Arts in Criminology and a Doctor of Juridical Science from the University of Toronto, and a Master and Doctorate of Laws from the University of London. His research interests are in policing and law enforcement from a comparative and transnational perspective, and he is currently engaged in research projects related to transnational policing and security, including the 'Policing the Neighbourhood' study of Australian police missions in Timor-Leste, Papua New Guinea, and the Solomon Islands. He recently completed (with co-editor, James Sheptycki), *Crafting Transnational Policing: Police Capacity-Building and Global Police Reform* (2007, forthcoming).

Mr Neil James

Neil James is executive director of the Australia Defence Association. Before this Neil served for over 31 years in the Australian Army in a range of regimental, intelligence, liaison, operational planning, operations research and teaching positions in Australia and overseas. He was the original author of the Australian Defence Force's interrogation manual and a specialist consultant on subsequent editions. As a senior intelligence officer he has tasked, coordinated and supervised interrogation and its integration with other means of investigation and intelligence gathering. He has also worked as an interrogator, a senior instructor on courses teaching interrogation and resistance to interrogation, and commanded an interrogation centre.

Professor Sarah Joseph
Sarah Joseph is the Director of the Castan Centre for Human Rights Law, and a Professor of Law in the Monash Faculty of Law. She has published widely in the field of human rights, including issues such as commercial law and human rights, terrorism, and the right to be free from torture. She has also published in the area of Australian constitutional law.

Dr Andrew Lynch
Andrew Lynch is a Senior Lecturer in the Faculty of Law at the University of New South Wales and is the Director of the Gilbert + Tobin Centre of Public Law's Terrorism and Law Project. Andrew's research has concentrated on judicial decision-making in the High Court of Australia and the intersection of public law and legal responses to terrorism. He is an author of *What Price Security? Taking Stock of Australia's Anti-Terror Laws* (2006) and *Equity and Trusts* (2nd ed, 2005) as well as journal articles, conference and seminar papers in these and other areas. Additionally Andrew has given evidence to a number of parliamentary, executive and non-government inquiries into Australia's counter-terrorism legislative scheme and writes regularly on public law issues in the media.

Ms Edwina MacDonald
Edwina MacDonald is Senior Research Director at the Gilbert + Tobin Centre of Public Law, Faculty of Law, University of New South Wales. She is the author of a number of journal and media articles, and has also made numerous submissions and given evidence to parliamentary and government inquiries into counter-terrorism laws. Edwina has previously worked in the development of domestic and international criminal law policy in the Australian Attorney-General's Department and has also worked in community legal organisations and as a legal editor.

Mr Geoff McDonald PSM
Geoff McDonald is the Assistant Secretary of the Security Law Branch of the Attorney-General's Department. He has headed the development of a range of security legislation, including the anti-terrorism legislation. Previously, as head of the Criminal Law Branch, he played a central role in the development

of the Model Criminal Code and the federal Criminal Code working closely with State and Territory Governments. He is a Macquarie University law graduate and started his career working in the New South Wales local courts. As part of the Queen's Honours for 2006, he was awarded a Public Service Medal for his work on anti-terrorism and crimes legislation.

Dr James Renwick

James Renwick is a barrister and an Adjunct International Lecturer at the University of Sydney Law School. He has a Bachelor of Laws and Doctor of Juridical Studies from the University of Sydney, where he was also a Parsons Scholar. He established Australia's first National Security Law course in 2003 and continues both to teach it and to be a leading practitioner in the area. He has appeared as junior counsel in half a dozen major constitutional cases in the High Court of Australia. He represented Australia in the 2004 hearings in *US v David Hicks* at Guantanamo Bay, Cuba. He also serves as a Lieutenant Commander in the Royal Australian Naval Reserve. He received the 2007 Fulbright Professional Australia-US Alliance Studies Scholarship, which he will use to undertake research at the School of Advanced International Studies, Johns Hopkins University, Washington DC into the perceived legal impediments to closer joint or complementary Alliance action and information sharing; and the conduct of terrorism trials.

Professor Kent Roach

Kent Roach is a Professor of Law and Prichard-Wilson Chair in Law and Public Policy at the University of Toronto and a Fellow of the Royal Society of Canada. He has written eight books including *September 11: Consequences for Canada* (2003). He is the co-editor of *Global Anti-Terrorism Law and Policy* and *The Security of Freedom: Essays on Canada's Anti-Terrorism Bill* (2005). He teaches and lectures on comparative anti-terrorism laws with articles published in Canada, Holland, Hong Kong, Italy, Singapore, South Africa, the United States and the United Kingdom. He has assisted the Arar and Air India inquiries in Canada and appeared before a working group drafting anti-terrorism laws in Indonesia.

The Hon Philip Ruddock MP

Philip Ruddock was elected to federal parliament in 1973 and has been the Australian Attorney-General since October 2003. The portfolio includes responsibility for the administration of the legal system, but also covers national security, family law, human rights, privacy and copyright. As Attorney-General he has responsibility for counter-terrorism policy, security coordination, critical infrastructure protection and emergency management. Before becoming Attorney-General, he was Australia's longest serving Minister for Immigration and Multicultural Affairs and also had responsibility for Indigenous Affairs. He has undergraduate arts and law degrees from the University of Sydney and, before entering Parliament, was a partner of the boutique commercial and general law firm, Berne Murray and Tout in the city of Sydney.

Dr Ben Saul

Ben Saul is the Director of the Sydney Centre for International and Global Law at the Faculty of Law, University of Sydney. He has published widely on international law and his latest book, *Defining Terrorism in International Law* (2006) is the leading scholarly work on the subject. Ben also practises as a barrister, including in the International Criminal Tribunal for the former Yugoslavia, the Balibo inquest into war crimes in East Timor, and in a challenge to Israel's security barrier in Palestine.

Mr Rayner Thwaites

Rayner Thwaites is a doctoral candidate at the University of Toronto, studying jurisprudence on indefinite immigration detention. He has worked as a solicitor with Mallesons Stephen Jaques and at the Public Interest Law Clearing House in Melbourne. He has also served as an associate at the Federal Court of Australia, and a sessional lecturer at the University of Melbourne.

Professor Clive Walker

Clive Walker is the Professor of Criminal Justice Studies at the School of Law, University of Leeds, where he was also Head of School from 2000 until 2005. He has written extensively on criminal justice, human rights and media law issues, including books on miscarriages of justice, the internet, and libel law. However, his principal research focus has been terrorism and the law. Since his doctorate on terrorism in 1982, he has produced a large volume of papers and books covering all aspects of the subject. In 2003 he was appointed special adviser to the UK Parliamentary select committee which was considering what became the *Civil Contingencies Act 2004* and published a book commentating on that Act, *The Civil Contingencies Act 2004: Risk, Resilience and the Law in the United Kingdom* (2006). He has also assisted in a number of official inquiries, such as the hearings by the Canadian Parliament into anti-terrorism legislation and studies in the UK into control orders and the definition of terrorism.

Justice Margaret White

Margaret White was appointed Justice of the Supreme Court of Queensland in 1992. She was formerly a barrister in private practice and sometime Senior Tutor in Law at the University of Queensland. She was Master of the Supreme Court from 1990-1992; has been a Member of the Senate of the University of Queensland since 1993 and Deputy Chancellor since 2006. She was a Second

Officer in the Women's Royal Australian Naval Service Reserve from 1968 to 1974 and a Commander in the Royal Australian Navy Reserve in 2003.

Professor George Williams

George Williams is the Anthony Mason Professor and Director of the Gilbert + Tobin Centre of Public Law at the Faculty of Law, University of New South Wales. He is the author of 13 books including *A Charter of Rights for Australia* (2007) and *What Price Security? Taking Stock of Australia's Anti-Terror Laws* (2006). He is also the editor of further books including *The Oxford Companion to the High Court of Australia* (2001). He practises as a barrister in courts including the High Court of Australia and is a well-known media commentator on legal issues.

PART I

Law's Role in the Response to Terrorism

1

Law as a Preventative Weapon Against Terrorism

Philip Ruddock

Sir John Latham, a former Commonwealth Attorney-General, liked to quote Oliver Cromwell's statement on security matters that 'being comes before well-being'.[1] It is a good observation to keep in mind. The necessary premise of any constitutional order and system of government is that people are alive. Serious threats to national security must be addressed.

The Commonwealth has legislated in recent times to protect against the threat of global terrorism. I consider that the threat of terrorism is one of the most serious threats we face. The government's counter-terrorism policy has the key elements of prevention, preparedness, response and recovery. Our legislation largely focuses on the first two elements, prevention and preparedness. Relevant measures include control orders, preventative detention orders and enhanced questioning and detention powers.

Preventative measures generally

Before turning to the specifics of Australia's response to terrorism, I would like to emphasise that preventative measures are not, as some critics have suggested, new to Australian law. The most obvious example of an age-old and recognised preventative measure is the denial of bail. Similarly, the executive may take preventative steps with respect to asylum seekers, the mentally ill and people with infectious diseases. (Even Sir Gerard Brennan and Sir William Deane, while justices of the High Court, acknowledged as much.)[2] In the first and second world wars, regulations allowing internment of enemy aliens were upheld by the High Court as constitutionally valid.[3] In recent times, State parliaments have legislated for preventative measures in respect of child sex offenders: from those cases, we now know which kinds of measures are constitutionally permissible[4] and which are not.[5]

The Commonwealth's anti-terrorism legislation was enacted with accepted principles in mind. A recent constitutional challenge as to the validity of parts of the legislation was unsuccessful.[6]

Preventative reforms

The Commonwealth has legislated for two specific preventative measures to deal with the threat of terrorism. They are control orders and preventative detention orders.[7]

Control orders allow limits to be placed on the movement and activities of people who pose a terrorist risk to the community. Control orders are issued by courts on the executive's application. A court can only issue a control order if the court is satisfied that the order would substantially assist in the prevention of a terrorist attack or that the person to whom the order relates has trained with a proscribed terrorist organisation.

Control orders accord with the essential meaning of prevention, which is to contain threats at their source and inhibit the risk of proliferation. If there are reasonable grounds for the police to suspect that a person is training with a terrorist organisation, then the obvious course of action is to apply for a control order to prevent that person from contacting members of that organisation. Similarly, if there are reasonable grounds for suspecting that a person is visiting certain places in order to prepare for a terrorist act, the police are justified in preventing that person from doing so. It is far better to prevent a terrorist act than to pursue perpetrators after an attack.

This rationale does not ignore the proper procedures that must be followed when seeking a control order, and the legislation is explicit in this respect.

Control orders have been criticised on the basis that they do not require a person to be convicted of a criminal offence before they may be subject to a control order. However, it must be remembered that this is protective legislation. It seeks to prevent rather than to react to terrorist offences. This approach is justified in the light of the enormous threat which terrorism poses to our security.

The second preventative measure which the Commonwealth has legislated for – preventative detention orders – is intended to operate at the point where a terrorist attack is imminent or where a terrorist attack has recently occurred. A preventative detention order can be issued if there are reasonable grounds for suspecting a person will either engage in, or is preparing for, a terrorist act and that detaining that person is reasonably necessary to prevent a terrorist act. In addition, a preventative detention order can also be issued if it is necessary to preserve evidence relating to a terrorist attack that has recently occurred.

The rationale for preventative detention orders is the same as that of control orders: if there is credible evidence to satisfy a court that a person would be involved in a terrorist attack in the immediate future, the logical and responsible course of action is to seek to contain and isolate that person to prevent an attack.

Questioning and detention powers

Control orders and preventative detention orders are important measures for preventing suspects from engaging in or facilitating the commission of terrorist acts. Yet these tools are only effective if terrorist suspects and their plans are correctly identified. Reliable intelligence is vital. The questioning and detention powers of the Australian Security Intelligence Organisation (ASIO) help gather intelligence to give prior warning to law enforcement authorities.[8]

Proper procedures must be followed in executing these powers. Before ASIO officers can invoke the questioning and detention regime there must be reasonable grounds for believing that questioning a person would substantially assist in collecting important information relating to a terrorism offence and, most importantly, that other methods of collecting this intelligence are ineffective.

Terrorism is, by its nature, secretive and carried out covertly. If the government is to act preventatively, it is imperative that Australia's intelligence agencies are able to penetrate the barrier of secrecy and uncover information which will assist in investigating terrorism.

Terrorism offences

When legislation was being introduced into the parliament to enact new terrorism offences,[9] some questioned their necessity when existing legislation already criminalised similar offences of murder, serious assault and destruction of government property. It was argued that these existing offences already captured the conduct likely to be perpetrated by terrorists.

Considering the expansive challenges posed by the terrorist threat, such a narrow focus with respect to the law is ill-conceived. Enactment of the terrorism offences serves two very important functions. First, the offences address the combination of violent destruction and political or ideological motivation which is unique to terrorism but which is largely absent from other crimes. The underlying motivation of terrorism provides a compelling, nihilistic drive to terrorists that often trumps their value of the perpetrators' own lives. It would be short-sighted to divorce these motivational contexts from the crimes themselves when they directly inform the gravity of the conduct.

Secondly, and this is particularly relevant to the goal of preventing terrorist acts from occurring rather than simply responding after an attack, the terrorism offences target preparatory conduct – actions undertaken before a terrorist act is committed. If Australia did not have such preparatory offences and a terrorist attack were to occur, the best we could expect from our criminal justice system would be convictions for murder. It would be too late, however, for the innocent victims claimed by the attack. That is too high a price for our society to pay when we are capable of acting sooner.

Australia's preventative focus is already well in train and has seen convictions for conduct preparatory to terrorist acts and others committed to stand trial. Extensive police investigations have led to the arrest, to date, of 28 individuals who have been accused, among other things, of engaging in activities connected with preparation for a terrorist act. Other individuals have been charged with providing funding and support to a terrorist organisation.

The counter-terrorism offences, combined with appropriate powers, enable our intelligence and law enforcement authorities to act pre-emptively where necessary for public safety.

The necessity of specific terrorism offences was affirmed in the independent review of the 2002 counter-terrorism laws, conducted by the Security Legislation Review Committee. The committee was chaired by former Supreme Court justice Simon Sheller AO QC.

Safeguards

The ultimate safeguard of liberty in Australia is the Constitution, along with the popular participation found in it. Australians voted for the Constitution, we are at liberty to amend it (and have done so in the past), and in the meantime we are subject to the system of representative and responsible government, and separated powers, for which the Constitution provides. All action, whether it be legislative, executive or even judicial, is done under the Constitution in Australia. The response to terrorism is no different. That response, as I have said, is done according to accepted principles. Courts are involved in determining whether preventative action is justified. As Chief Justice Gleeson indicated recently, the involvement of courts amounts to a protection of human rights, not an abrogation of them. His Honour said:

> [T]he exercise of powers, independently, impartially and judicially, especially when such powers affect the liberty of the individual, would ordinarily be regarded as a good thing, not something to be avoided. … To decide that such powers are exclusively within the province of the executive branch of government would be contrary to our legal history, and would not constitute an advance in the protection of human rights.[10]

While the primary purpose of the counter-terrorism laws is to act as a tool to assist in preventing terrorist acts, the laws are enacted under the Constitution and accordingly have a role in protecting human rights and civil liberties. I believe that there is an appropriate balance between the preservation of national security and human rights, which is reflected in the range of safeguards that apply to control orders, preventative detention orders and ASIO questioning and detention. However, I would make the point that these matters are not static: the protection must be commensurate with the risk, at all times.

In deciding whether to issue a control order, a court must be satisfied on the balance of probabilities that each of the requirements of the proposed order is reasonably necessary and reasonably appropriate and adapted for the purpose of protecting the public from a terrorist act. In determining what is reasonably appropriate and adapted, the court must consider the impact of each of the control order requirements upon the person's circumstances, including his or her financial and personal circumstances. Consideration of these issues is undertaken by a court, ensuring independent judicial weighing of the merits of the application.

The preventative detention regime sets strict time limits on how long a person can be detained, prohibits questioning during detention, protects a person's right to be treated with dignity and humanity, and provides opportunities for contact with family members and legal representatives. The maximum period of detention is, at a total of 14 days, half that employed in countries such as the United Kingdom – and recent times have seen moves that suggest a further increase is under contemplation. In France, a terrorist suspect may be detained for up to three years without charge. The Australian preventative detention regime strikes an appropriate balance – it provides a period of detention to protect the community from an imminent terrorist act, while providing a time limit on detention and access to a lawyer.

The ASIO questioning and detention regime also sets strict time limits on the period of questioning and length of detention that is permitted. It also requires an independent person with judicial experience to supervise the questioning, and also provides ready access to complaints mechanisms. Access to a legal representative and the right to humane treatment are among the many other safeguards.

The Australian government recognises that overzealous national security measures could undermine public trust in government. That is why our counter-terrorism laws have been modelled on the United Kingdom's long experience in dealing with terrorism in Northern Ireland and, in particular, on the lessons the United Kingdom has learned about maintaining adequate accountability. As a result, the safeguards we have inserted into our legislation are more explicit than in any other comparable country.

Conclusion

The Australian system of government is a strong one. Dicey thought that all federations were weak,[11] and militant Islamists say the same thing about Western democracies generally. In Australia, however, the Commonwealth's defence power waxes and wanes according to the threat which is posed. The power ensures that the Commonwealth can meet its principal duty to protect Australian citizens.

There is no point in having a Constitution and its various protections if nobody is around to live under it. In this decade alone, Australians and Australian property have been, either directly or indirectly, the subject of planned, aborted or actual attacks in every year. The Director-General of ASIO, Paul O'Sullivan, said recently:

> Australia continues to face a challenging and dynamic security environment. We continue to be a terrorist target and the threats of attack are likely to be with us for many years. An attack in Australia remains feasible and could well occur.[12]

There has been much misunderstanding about the counter-terrorism laws and the effect they will have on ordinary people. That is why the government, together with law enforcement agencies, is engaging with the community and explaining the operation of the laws, their intended targets, and people's rights and obligations under the laws. These initiatives help to strengthen public trust, confidence and cooperation, and prevent feelings of marginalisation or resentment.

International and domestic terrorism have reconfigured the dangers and security priorities for much of the world, and Australia is no exception. The government is continually monitoring the threat to assess whether any further legislation or other action is required. These new challenges require us to be responsive. I believe that a strongly preventative approach, underscored by robust but fair laws, is the best way forward for Australia and her interests.

Notes

1 See, for example, Parliament of Australia, *Parliamentary Debates*, House of Representatives, 19 June 1923, 117 (John Latham, Attorney-General); *Australian Communist Party v Commonwealth* (1951) 83 CLR 1, 141.

2 *Chu Kheng Lim v Minister for Immigration* (1992) 176 CLR 1, 28 (Brennan, Deane and Dawson JJ).

3 *Lloyd v Wallach* (1915) 20 CLR 299; *Ex p Walsh* [1941] ALR 359. McHugh J made mention of these cases in his Honour's reasons for judgment in *Al-Kateb v Godwin* (2004) 219 CLR 562, 588-9.

4 *Fardon v Attorney-General (Qld)* (2004) 223 CLR 575.

5 *Kable v Director of Public Prosecutions (NSW)* (1996) 189 CLR 51.

6 *Thomas v Mowbray* [2007] HCA 33.

7 *Criminal Code* (Cth) Divs 104-5.

8 *Australian Security Intelligence Organisation 1979* (Cth) Pt II, Div 3.

9 *Criminal Code* (Cth) Divs 101-2.

10 *Thomas v Mowbray* [2007] HCA 33, [17].

11 AV Dicey, *Introduction to the Study of the Law of the Constitution* (10th ed, 1959) 171. See also William Gummow, *Change and Continuity: Statute, Equity and Federalism* (1999) 72; and Murray Gleeson, 'Courts and the Rule of Law' in Cheryl Saunders and Katherine Le Roy (eds), *The Rule of Law* (2003) 181.

12 Evidence to Senate Standing Committee on Legal and Constitutional Affairs, Parliament of Australia, Canberra, 23 May 2007, 129 (Paul O'Sullivan).

2

Legality and Emergency – The Judiciary in a Time of Terror

*David Dyzenhaus and Rayner Thwaites**

The title of this chapter, and indeed this entire book, is deeply, even dangerously, misleading. Western legal orders are not living in a time of emergency or terror, despite the best efforts of our leaders to convince us otherwise. Additionally, the idea that the way to deal with the challenges to the West sharpened by the events of 9/11 is by waging a 'war on terror' was from the beginning, and is ever more, preposterous. There are, of course, many people in the world who face a daily situation of wartime emergency in which their lives are wrecked by fear of real terror. But it is important to keep in mind that among them are the peoples of Iraq and Afghanistan, whose present situation is directly attributable to the fact that foreign policy in much of the West since 9/11 has been based on this preposterous idea.

However, our topic is still useful. The judiciary does have an important role to play in countering the hyperbolic terms of the debates about the rule of law since 9/11, indeed, in imposing the rule of law on executive and legislative responses to 9/11. This argument is not an easy one to make. The history of the judiciary in times of emergency and alleged emergency is a dismal one of judges deferring to executive claims. It is true that in many of the infamous wartime cases such as *Halliday*, *Liversidge* and *Korematsu*,[1] there were ringing dissents. It is also true that in the aftermath of the wars the majority judgments were regarded as badges of shame. Hence, the dissents were taken to represent the future path for judges faced with similar problems. But it also seemed that judges reverted to deference when national security concerns were alleged by the executive, even outside of the context of wartime emergency. One honourable exception is the Australian High Court's decision in the *Communist Party Case*.[2] But generally the record of the judiciary in 'a time of terror' is a dismal one.

There are two ways of understanding this phenomenon. Either judges cannot be counted on in a time of terror – they simply lack the spine to stand up for the rule of law – or they are in fact doing the right thing by deferring to the executive. In the second case, the dismal record speaks not to the judges' unwillingness to stand up for the rule of law but to the inappropriateness of their doing so. Indeed, there is another way of putting this point which complicates things: when judges defer they are in fact upholding the rule of law, on the best understanding of what the rule of law requires in such situations.

Thus in the US, prominent constitutional scholars now argue that the majority in *Korematsu* – the case in which the majority of the Supreme Court upheld the validity of the military order to detain Japanese-Americans – not only got things right in the sense that the court made the only decision it could, but that it also made the best decision from the perspective of the rule of law. Their position is that preventive detention is consistent with the rule of law as long as there is a legislative authorisation for the detention and as long as the decision to detain is subject to some amount of due process. But they endorse the fact that the courts read the authority to detain into general legislative authorisations that make no mention of such an authority and they regard very minimal due process as appropriate.[3]

Our argument takes its cue from the dissents in the infamous cases. It insists that the long-term interests of the rule of law require judges to uphold a robust set of principles during an emergency – principles which do not allow for judicial abdication of responsibility. This view seems to have some support in the recent judicial record, in United States Supreme Court decisions such as *Hamdan*, in the *Belmarsh* decision of the House of Lords and in the Canadian Supreme Court's decision in *Charkaoui*.[4] It also is, albeit implicitly, the theory of the rule of law that underpins the majority's judgments in the Australian High Court's 1951 *Communist Party Case*. There seems to be something like a judicial 'coalition of the willing' forming – judges prepared to uphold the rule of law in the face of executive claims about national security. These courts seem to disprove the claim that judges always defer to the executive and the legislature when national security is allegedly at stake.

However, it is much too early for optimism. All of the institutional actors involved, the legislatures, the executive and the judiciary, demonstrate what we call the compulsion of legality: the compulsion to justify all acts of state as having a legal warrant – the authority of law. However, the compulsion of legality can set in motion two very different cycles of legality. In one cycle, the institutions of legal order cooperate in devising controls on public actors which ensure that their decisions comply with the principle of legality, understood as a substantive conception of the rule of law. In the other cycle, the content of legality is understood in a more formal or empty manner, resulting in the mere appearance or even the pretence of legality. With the second cycle, the compulsion of legality results in the subversion of constitutionalism – the project of achieving government in accordance with the rule of law. Arbitrariness is covered by what an English judge referred to recently as a 'thin veneer of legality'.[5] Noteworthy here is that the legal regime on which he was commenting is the system of control orders substituted for the indefinite detention of aliens by the UK government in response to the *Belmarsh* decision.

The central question in the topic of the judicial role in a time of alleged war on terror is thus not whether judges will play a role in policing the legality of legislative and executive responses to terror. Rather, it is whether judges can avoid participating in the second cycle of legality – the one that results in the mere appearance, even the pretence of legality.

We seek to answer this question through an analysis of the recent decision of the Australian High Court on control orders, *Thomas v Mowbray*.[6] *Thomas*, taken by itself, does not give a clear indication of whether the High Court is going to form part of the judicial coalition of the willing, in part because there is as yet no clear answer to where that coalition should fall on the kind of question that confronted the court. However, in the Australian context the decision might be considered grounds for pessimism rather than optimism and so we will start by setting out what we take to be that context.

A positivistic High Court?

The portents were not good for the High Court joining the coalition of the willing, given its majority decision in *Al-Kateb v Godwin*. Although that case did not concern national security, it justified indefinite administrative detention, partly on grounds of community protection. It also fits within a trend of increased judicial deference to the executive that has accelerated since 9/11, and one of the majority judgments and two of the dissents spoke to the relevance of the *Communist Party Case* to the case before them, and thus to their understanding of the high water mark of the Australian judiciary when it comes to upholding the rule of law.[7] In addition, two of the judges, one in the majority and one dissenting, considered the implications of their reasoning for the issue of indefinite detention during wartime.[8]

Ahmed Al-Kateb was detained under the *Migration Act 1958* (Cth), which requires the compulsory administrative detention of unlawful non-citizens. Under s 198 of the Act, such non-citizens are supposed to be removed 'as soon as reasonably practicable'. But Al-Kateb was stateless and diplomatic channels had failed to find another state willing to accept him. The question thus arose whether the legislation required his indefinite detention given the absence of any evidence that his removal would ever be 'reasonably practicable'. The High Court split 4-3 on this question.

The judges in the majority (McHugh, Hayne, Callinan and Heydon JJ), regarded the statute as capable of being interpreted in only one way: to require detention of unlawful non-citizens until it became possible to remove them. As long as removal was a possibility, no matter how remote, the executive was merely carrying out its statutory duty by keeping such non-citizens in detention. Thus, the only possible basis for a challenge to the statute would be a constitutional one – that the statute infringed on the separation of powers, given the protection of judicial power in Chapter III of the Australian Constitution.

The majority reasoned that Chapter III protection is trenched on only if detention is a matter over which the courts and not the executive have jurisdiction, so that the legislature is incapable of delegating detention powers to the executive. But since non-citizens have no right to be in Australia, and since constitutionally the legislature has authority to determine the terms on which they may be permitted entry to or excluded from Australia, detention for the purpose of deportation is constitutionally authorised. Only detention for specific other purposes, notably the purpose of punishment, could be said to fall within Chapter III and detention in this case was for the purpose of deportation.

In addition, three of the majority judgments – those of McHugh, Hayne and Heydon JJ – endorsed a purpose of detention independent of processing and removal, that of segregation from the Australian community.[9] These judges seem committed to the position that lifelong imprisonment is a matter fit for executive determination on the basis of its position on what protecting the community requires. One commentator has suggested that such protective detention would be justifiable in relation to aliens considered to be a danger to the community because it might be very expensive to require that the state keep such people under surveillance when they cannot be deported. That is, the state should not be required to use the methods deployed against lawful Australian residents who are similarly dangerous and who cannot legally be detained.[10]

But this is to make the mistake of inferring from the fact that non-citizens suffer from a disability which citizens do not – vulnerability to deportation – that they are generally second class legal subjects. A legal order that is committed to an idea of the legal subject as a bearer of human rights is also committed to absorbing the cost of maintaining those rights. This protective purpose brings the Australian legal order uncomfortably close to authoritarian understandings of the role of law in protecting the 'community'.[11]

None of the dissenting judges in *Al-Kateb* – Gleeson CJ and Gummow[12] and Kirby JJ – saw the need to treat the question as one in which the options were either letting the statute stand with the meaning attributed to it by the majority or finding it invalid because it contravened explicit constitutional guarantees of the separation of powers. Rather, they saw the question as an interpretative one – one about how to understand the statute given the commitment of their legal order to the rule of law or the principle of legality. This is particularly true of Gleeson CJ's judgment, in part because he did not rely on the *Communist Party Case*.

Gleeson CJ reasoned that because the government's claim was that the legislation conferred on the executive a 'power of administrative detention that is indefinite in duration, and that may be permanent, there comes into play a principle of legality, which governs both Parliament and the courts'. He went on:

> In exercising their judicial function, courts seek to give effect to the will of Parliament by declaring the meaning of what Parliament has enacted. Courts do not impute to the legislature an intention to abrogate or curtail certain human rights or freedoms (of which personal liberty is the most basic) unless such an intention is clearly manifested by unambiguous language, which indicates that the legislature has directed its attention to the rights or freedoms in question, and has consciously decided upon abrogation or curtailment.[13]

While Gleeson CJ treated the matter as an exercise in statutory interpretation, Gummow and Kirby JJ undertook a constitutional analysis. They held that the constitutional separation of powers places purposive limits on immigration detention, and that the location of the limits legality sets for executive action cannot be determined by the executive. Just as the executive cannot finally determine the meaning of statutory terms, so parliament cannot finally determine the meaning of constitutional terms. In this regard, Gummow J said:

> The continued viability of the purpose of deportation or expulsion cannot be treated by the legislature as a matter purely for the opinion of the executive government. The reason is that it cannot be for the executive government to determine the placing from time to time of that boundary line which marks off a category of deprivation of liberty from the reach of Ch III. The location of that boundary line itself is a question arising under the Constitution or involving its interpretation, hence the present significance of the *Communist Party Case*.[14]

Kirby J shared this view, saying:

> [T]he *Communist Party Case* is of substantial assistance to Mr Al-Kateb. It is inconsistent with a basic proposition of Australian constitutional doctrine, at least since 1951, that the validity of a law or of an act of the Executive should depend on the conclusive assertion or opinion of the Parliament (eg, expressed in recitals to an Act) or the assertion or opinion of an officer of the Executive (eg that the preconditions for the exercise of power

> have been satisfied). This is why the *Communist Party Case* is such an important statement of the rule of law as it operates in Australia. It remains for the judiciary in each contested case to interpret the applicable law. As in the *Communist Party Case*, this requirement has proved an important, even vital, protection for individual liberty … [15]

He thus asserted that 'indefinite detention at the will of the Executive, and according to its opinions, actions and judgments, is alien to Australia's constitutional arrangements'.[16]

But while Gummow and Kirby JJ are articulating the same basic principle as Gleeson CJ, their manner of articulating it risks turning it into a doctrine of positivistically construed constitutional facts. That is, the question of whether a fact precedent to the exercise of a power by the executive exists (in this case, that detention is for the purpose of deportation) cannot collapse into the executive's claim that it has that purpose. If it does, then the executive becomes a law unto itself, able to set the limits of its authority.

It is significant that McHugh J did not dispute the constitutional fact doctrine. He said that a detention law which was otherwise constitutionally valid would 'infringe Ch III if it prevents the Ch III courts from determining some matter that is a condition precedent to authorising detention'.[17] He had in mind that the court has to be able to check on whether in fact an individual is an 'unlawful non-citizen'. Because the law did not, in his view, have the effect of depriving the court of this role, he reasoned that the *Communist Party Case* had no relevance to *Al-Kateb*.[18]

Strictly speaking, McHugh J was right. The majority in the *Communist Party Case* confined themselves to a rather positivistic, text-based constitutional argument. In their view, the federal legislature was not permitted to enact the statute banning the Communist Party because as a matter of constitutional fact only the state legislatures had authority to regulate voluntary associations. The only time at which one of their number strayed from this kind of constitutional positivism was in Dixon J's famous dictum that 'the rule of law forms an assumption'[19] of the Constitution, that is, the Constitution is evidence of, rather than the basis for, the legal order's commitment to the rule of law.

As a result, the majority in the *Communist Party Case* committed themselves to the proposition that the state legislatures would be perfectly entitled to enact equivalent legislation. And despite the fact that the majority was clearly uneasy with the thought that the executive might wield arbitrary power over important individual interests, they also committed themselves to the proposition that a plenary legislature is entitled to delegate such power to the executive. Moreover, they seemed to think that such a delegation is appropriate in a situation of wartime emergency.

It is no surprise then that, some three years before his judgment in the *Communist Party Case*, Dixon J had held, in *Little v Commonwealth*, that a detention order made under wartime regulations was not reviewable except on the ground of bad faith. He came to this conclusion despite the fact that he acknowledged that Little was likely right that there was no real ground for suspecting Little's loyalty and thus for his detention.[20] Moreover, this decision followed High Court decisions during the first and second world wars which, like the House of Lords in *Halliday*, held that an authority for the executive to make a detention regulation is necessarily implied in a general statutory grant of authority to deal with the emergency.[21]

In *Al-Kateb*, McHugh J endorsed these decisions, because they fell under the defence power, and thus rejected Kirby J's claim that indefinite detention is 'alien to Australia's constitutional arrangements'.[22] In response, Kirby J said these cases 'hardly amount to a proud moment in Australian law. Nor are they ones that should be propounded as a precedent and statement of contemporary legal authority'. Indeed he likened the cases to *Korematsu*, saying that just as such cases 'are now viewed with embarrassment in the United States and generally regarded as incorrect … [w]e should be no less embarrassed by the local equivalents'.[23] However, McHugh J is closer than Kirby J to the letter if not the spirit of the majority's judgments in the *Communist Party Case*, and only Gleeson CJ appropriately expresses the spirit of the case, though he does so without any reference to it.

As Professor George Winterton argues, in what remains the classic treatment of the *Communist Party Case*, the 'fundamental constitutional flaw of the legislation [banning the Party] proved to be its nature as an Act of Pains and Penalties (or 'Bill of Attainder' in its generic sense)'.[24] But the majority expressly denied this, with the result that the sole judge who took seriously a bill of attainder argument, only to reject it, was Latham CJ in dissent. Thus when Winterton hails the case as a significant victory for the rule of law and constitutionalism, he also cautions against reading too much into the decision. He even suggests that the case 'fits squarely within [a] tradition of judicial self-preservation'. It was not 'primarily about civil liberties, but about the limits of legislative and executive power and supremacy of the judiciary in deciding such questions'.[25] And if that is what the case is about, then it might seem that the majority in *Al-Kateb* is part of the same tradition, for McHugh J and the other judges in the majority do wish to preserve a constitutional role for judges.

Recall in this regard McHugh J's remark that a detention law which was otherwise constitutionally valid would 'infringe Ch III if it prevents the Ch III courts from determining some matter that is a condition precedent to authorising detention'.[26] However, at least in the case of detention on national security grounds, that role is an empty one, since, as McHugh J's endorsement of Dixon J's judgment in *Little* shows, if judges follow this path they end up as rubber stamps for the executive. Judges claim that they will review for bad faith in situations in which it is next to impossible to prove bad faith. In doing so, they give the stamp of legitimacy to the executive by permitting a thin veneer of legality to substitute for the substantive protection of the rule of law. Indeed, matters are even worse, since this kind of empty review follows hard on the heels of the failure to require that regulations that permit the executive to deprive someone of liberty must be based on altogether explicit statutory authorisation.

In our view, the insistence on a clear statement rule makes sense only if it is followed by meaningful review of the executive decisions once properly authorised. Moreover, such insistence also makes possible such review, because it forces the executive to bring its activity within the scope of a deliberately and democratically designed statutory regime, one which has at least the potential of providing rule of law teeth. At least, the insistence has that effect as long as judges are not content with a thin veneer of procedural legality.

It is important at this stage to emphasise the democratic aspect of our argument because the kind of constitutional positivism evidenced by the majority in *Al-Kateb* is usually given a democratic justification. A constitutional positivist holds that judges must defer to clear legislative intention on a plain fact understanding of intention,[27] that is, one uncontaminated by any judicial sense of fundamental principles of legality that have no source in a written constitutional document. And they must so defer because it is their role to implement the intentions of those elected to make decisions, not to substitute their views as to what is appropriate. Thus in his judgment, Hayne J quoted with approval from a dissent by Judge Learned Hand:

> Think what one may of a statute … when passed by a society which professed to put its faith in [freedom], a court has no warrant for refusing to enforce it. If that society chooses to flinch when its principles are put to the test, courts are not set up to give it derring-do.[28]

However, in this context such a democratic justification is a little disingenuous, because the society is not given the opportunity to decide whether to flinch or not. The legislation did not after all expressly provide for indefinite detention. Society would only have the opportunity to flinch if the government and the legislature were faced with the prospect of having to override explicitly a fundamental principle of legality in order to give to the executive the authority to detain non-citizens indefinitely and that requires judges to put the other institutions to the test, as they did in the *Communist Party Case*. And here one should not forget that following that decision the Australian government sought to procure a constitutional amendment to achieve the result it wanted, but was rebuffed in a referendum.

One can make a similar point about McHugh J's claim that if parliament were unable to provide for potentially indefinite detention through the Migration Act, it could create a criminal offence of being a prohibited immigrant in Australia, which would have exactly the same result, the only difference being that the detention would be the result of a judicial order upon a finding that the person was a prohibited immigrant. This, he said, would allow 'form [to] triumph over substance'.[29] But any reasonable conception of democratic politics must ascribe value to the fact that a provision which trenches on human rights is introduced and debated in the legislature and scrutinised by the media and public. McHugh J thus overlooks the value in demanding that the legislature be explicit about its ends. Moreover, it is hardly insignificant that it would be a court that would decide whether someone were guilty of the crime, rather than detention occurring because an executive official reasonably suspects that a person is an unlawful non-citizen, and presumably the sentence would be a determinate one, not the torment of indefinite detention.

Here it is worth recalling Lord Bingham's riposte in *Belmarsh* to the Attorney-General's argument for constitutional positivism. Lord Bingham said that while parliament, the executive and the judges have 'different functions', 'the function of independent judges charged to interpret and apply the law is universally recognised as a cardinal feature of the modern democratic state, a cornerstone of the rule of law itself'. It was thus wrong to 'stigmatise judicial decision-making as in some way undemocratic'.[30] It is significant that Lord Bingham did not find his ultimate ground in the United Kingdom's *Human Rights Act 1998*, but in the constitutional nature of the democratic state with its inherent commitment to the rule of law. Put differently, his understanding of the judicial role does not look to any particular statute, not even the Human Rights Act itself, as the basis for the judicial authority to review legislation and executive decisions for their compliance with human rights and the rule of law, since the legal order is assumed to be a constitutional one, and thus premised on judges having such authority.[31]

Risk, evidence and the rule of law

Counter-terrorism laws enacted after the attacks of 11 September 2001 have placed an increasing emphasis on anticipatory risk assessments.[32] In *Thomas* the High Court engages with this dynamic. The potentially horrific outcomes of terrorist action are seen to mandate a pre-emptive or preventative response reflective of 'a new and urgent emphasis upon the need for security, the containment of danger, the identification and management of any kind of risk'.[33] This emphasis on prevention is legally manifested in 'control' measures directed towards acts in the future rather than events in the past, such as the control orders introduced into Division 104 of the *Criminal Code* (Cth) and applied to Jack Thomas.

In line with our argument about the rule of law, our position is informed by the belief that the courts' institutional expertise in testing evidence should play a role in the national security context. This belief runs counter to the general view that the national security context puts constraints on the disclosure of information such that there can be no meaningful review of decisions made on grounds of national security. The upshot of our view is that it is a necessary condition for the conformity of such control orders to the rule of law for them to be subject to appropriately intense review by an independent official. We do not, it should be noted, make the further claim that such subjection is sufficient to make the orders conform. It might, that is, be the case that such preventive measures can never sufficiently conform to the rule of law to make them a legitimate measure for a constitutional state to adopt.

In *Thomas*, five judges of the High Court held that the part of Division 104 relating to interim control orders was valid. In dissent, Kirby and Hayne JJ found that the whole of the Division invalid. Under s 104.4(1), the Division authorises an issuing court to make an interim control order where, amongst other matters:

> (c) the court is satisfied on the balance of probabilities:
>
> (i) that making the order would substantially assist in preventing a terrorist act; or
>
> (ii) that the person has provided training to, or received training from, a listed terrorist organisation; and
>
> (d) the court is satisfied on the balance of probabilities that each of the obligations, prohibitions and restrictions to be imposed on the person by the order is reasonably necessary, and reasonably appropriate and adapted, for the purpose of protecting the public from a terrorist act.

Under s 104.12A(3), the Division also provides for non-disclosure of evidence 'likely … to prejudice national security', but the majority deferred the question of the constitutionality of the rest of Division 104, including the non-disclosure provision, until a future case raised these issues.

In this chapter we focus on the first question stated for the court: 'Is Division 104 of the Criminal Code invalid because it confers on a federal court non-judicial power contrary to Chapter III of the Commonwealth Constitution?' In the majority, Gleeson CJ and Gummow and Crennan JJ in their joint judgment emphasise that it is open to the judiciary to regulate and discipline the broad conferral of power in accordance with judicial methods and standards. They give a broad purposive reading to the grant of power, reading it as subject to the requirement that it be exercised in accordance with such standards and methods.[34]

To the objection that the criteria are simply too broad for the exercise of judicial power, Gleeson CJ responds with reference to judicial and legislative usage of the concept of reasonable necessity, contained in s 104.4(1)(d), in diverse private and public law contexts. He concludes that 'it cannot plausibly be suggested that the standard of reasonably necessary and reasonably appropriate and adapted for the purpose of protecting the public is inherently too vague for use in judicial decision making'.[35]

The joint judgment endorses this view and also takes the step of aligning judicial consideration of broadly expressed standards with modern legislative developments, emphasising the proliferation of legislative regimes regulating and modifying contractual rights and obligations by reference to broadly expressed criteria to be implemented by the courts, and the need for the court's separation of powers jurisprudence to accommodate these developments.[36]

The argument that the Division confers non-judicial power on a court is also expressed as an objection to the issuing court being involved in the assessment of risk to the public.[37] But Gleeson CJ rejects the contention that the prediction of dangers to the public is incapable of judicial evaluation.[38] He draws on risk assessments in other areas of law that have received legal sanction, stating that he is:

> unable to accept that there is a qualitative difference between deciding whether an angry person poses an unacceptable risk to his or her family, or to the community or some section of the community, or whether a sexually dysfunctional man poses an unacceptable risk to women, and deciding whether someone who has been trained as a terrorist poses an unacceptable risk to the public.[39]

Both the dissenters hold that the power conferred on the federal courts by Division 104 is non-judicial in nature. And they reject the possibility that the powers could be saved by transferring them to an executive official.[40] Hayne J suggests that this is because the defence power does not suffice in a time of 'ostensible peace' absent extraordinary circumstances that are not present.[41] Kirby J finds against the government on all the questions stated for the court. None of the sources of legislative power nominated by the Commonwealth support the validity of the Division, and if the power conferred on the issuing court by Division 104 *is* judicial, the exercise of that power is contrary to the requirements of Chapter III.[42]

Underlying the reasoning of Gleeson CJ and the joint judgment is the view, to quote the Chief Justice, that 'the exercise of powers, independently, impartially and judicially, especially when those powers affect the liberty of the individual, would ordinarily be regarded as a good thing, not something to be avoided'.[43] At its simplest, the difference between these members of the majority and the dissenting judgments is contained in Kirby J's response that the exercise by a judge of serious powers affecting individual liberty 'becomes a bad thing if the powers are granted in vague and inappropriate terms'.[44]

Hayne J responds to the majority's proposition that there is nothing to preclude the courts from developing standards to regulate the criteria in s 104.4 that this 'assumes rather than demonstrates that there is a basis to be found *in the impugned provisions* for the development of those criteria'.[45] However, one can accept that standards developed judicially to regulate a statutory regime need to be *consistent* with the legislation, without insisting that they derive from it. But, the dissenters seem to regard such development as involving a court in applying 'its own idiosyncratic notion as to what is just'.[46]

Hayne J's position on this issue is consistent with his reasoning in *Al-Kateb* on legal authority to impose conditions on release from immigration detention. There, he held that there was no legal basis for a court to impose conditions on release from immigration detention, if authority to detain had ceased.[47] In the same decision, Gleeson CJ and Gummow J held that while the Migration Act itself did not authorise the imposition of restraints when a person was not detained, the statutory powers of the Federal Court did provide a sufficient legal basis for the imposition of such conditions.[48] These competing views of the courts' legal authority align with the contrast in *Thomas* between Hayne J's rejection of the courts' ability to supply legal standards to regulate the power, and the reliance of Gleeson J and Gummow and Crennan JJ on such judicial developments.

A second strand of opposition to the more sanguine view of judicial capability held by Gleeson CJ and the joint judgment is the dissenters' aversion to the courts becoming involved in exercises of anticipatory risk assessment. Both Hayne and Kirby JJ object to the courts being saddled with the decision as to 'whether and how a particular order against a named person will achieve or tend to achieve a future consequence'.[49] Again, there are resonances between Hayne J's judgment here and his judgment in *Al-Kateb*. In both, an operative assumption is that the courts cannot engage with conditions of uncertainty. In *Al-Kateb*, Hayne J argued that the prospects for removal were inextricably entangled with the vicissitudes of international diplomacy, and that this rendered any judicial determination of the prospects for deportation not only manifestly inappropriate but impossible.[50] He used this claim about lack of institutional competence as a basis for his conclusion that the courts should simply vacate the field, only supervising detention pending deportation both to determine that the individual was an unlawful non-citizen and that the government continued to pursue removal in good faith.

In *Thomas*, the dissenters' opposition to judicial involvement in anticipatory risk assessment is linked to their view that the courts are institutionally incapable of dealing with the sort of material relied upon by the police and intelligence communities in counter-terrorism. This thesis of institutional incapability in the national security area is most fully developed by Hayne J. His objection is not simply to problems arising from secrecy, but that:

> intelligence material will often require evaluative judgments to be made about the weight to be given to diffuse, fragmentary and even conflicting pieces of intelligence. Those are judgments of a kind very different from those ordinarily made by courts.[51]

While we take Hayne J's comments on the distance between intelligence and evidence seriously, we think that he concedes too much on the basis of too little. He assumes that courts cannot adequately examine government intelligence or test government expertise. And he does so without mentioning the substantial efforts and numerous proposals made to accommodate intelligence in the evidence-based legal process.[52] The institutional creativity and resources devoted to the problem cannot simply be ignored. In this respect we note that prominent examples of proposals designed to test government intelligence originated with the reviewing bodies themselves.[53]

Finally, Kirby J focuses on the legal significance of the consequence that a determination on the basis of apprehended conduct has in this context for liberty.[54] On the issue of involuntary detention, Kirby J and the joint judgment hold some common ground. The joint judgment seeks to 'adhere' to the proposition that, 'exceptional cases' aside, 'the involuntary detention of a citizen in custody by the State is permissible only as a consequential step in the adjudication of criminal guilt of that citizen for past acts'.[55] The joint judgment, however, holds that this proposition is inapplicable to the present case because '[d]etention in the custody of the State differs significantly in degree and quality from what may be entailed by observance of an interim control order'.[56]

There are two sets of issues here. First, there is the question of where the line lies. One can foresee the Australian government pressing for conditions whose cumulative effect comes perilously close to, or equates with, detention. Here, the dissents are pessimistic as to the ability and inclination of the courts to call the government's bluff. However, the courts are not in fact confronted with an all or nothing decision. Section 104.14 of the Code leaves them the option of varying the conditions in addition to confirming, voiding or revoking them.

Secondly, there is the issue of whether restrictions on liberty that do not contravene the constitutional prohibition on involuntary detention are legal when they are imposed on the basis of apprehended conduct, either on the part of the individual subject to the order or third parties. The debate between the judges on this point proceeds by assessing historical and contemporary legal devices offered as analogies to the control orders, including 'binding over' orders, bail orders and restraining orders under family law. These instances are assessed to determine whether the control orders mark a qualitative departure from what has gone before, such that they go beyond what can be asked of the judicial function.[57]

Kirby J is more careful in his assessment of the analogies offered, making the case that the control orders constitute a new departure, particularly in their allowance for a deprivation of liberty to be based on the conduct of third parties.[58] The joint judgment and Gleeson CJ conclude that the control orders do not constitute a qualitative leap from protective measures already accommodated within the law, and thus do not go beyond the judicial function.[59] Gleeson CJ clearly expresses his concern that, should the courts not take up the challenge, the government will find other ways of acting on intelligence that bypass judicial scrutiny. The result, he says, 'would not constitute an advance in the protection of human rights'.[60]

The legacy of the Communist Party Case

We have focused exclusively on separation of powers issues raised in *Thomas*, more particularly on the question of whether the power conferred on the federal courts is non-judicial. In closing we want to take up one aspect of the debate whether the provisions are supported by the defence power. This aspect raised directly the question of the legacy of the *Communist Party Case*. The most publicised aspect of *Thomas* has been Kirby J's concluding criticisms of his colleagues, particularly Callinan J because of his attempt to vindicate Latham CJ's dissent in the *Communist Party Case*.[61]

Callinan J's reasoning is indeed troubling. It evinces a reflex where national security is concerned, consistent with a tradition of uncritical judicial deference. One can agree with him that the *Communist Party Case* should not be 'uniquely immune to critical examination and analysis',[62] but he seems to endorse a prudential, executive minded approach that makes a mockery of the rule of law.

The basis for Callinan J's re-evaluation of the *Communist Party Case* is the benefit of hindsight which allows him, in his view, to take judicial notice of the horrors perpetrated by communist regimes and the 'designs of the communist state upon the rest of the world'.[63] In taking such notice, Callinan J did not seek in any way to place the *Communist Party Case* in its context, nor to deal with the draconian nature of the government's attempt to silence political opposition by statute. But even more disturbing is his conviction that with the benefit of hindsight we should see that the distinctions made in the *Communist Party Case* between the operation of the defence power in peacetime and under a formal declaration of war, and between internal and external threats, are 'questionable'.[64] We should, he thinks, conclude that the majority in the *Communist Party Case* were naïve and that Latham CJ's supposed realism is appealing.[65] Applied to the present time, the moral is that where the government establishes that catastrophic events are a possibility,[66] judges should not focus on the niceties of distinctions between declared war and 'ostensible peace' or between internal and external threats.

Callinan J's longest quote from Latham CJ extends to two paragraphs.[67] The first paragraph mocks concerns about 'dangers likely to arise from within the institutions to be protected', most famously expressed by Dixon J in the *Communist Party Case* when he said that '[h]istory and not only ancient history, shows that in countries where democratic institutions have been unconstitutionally superseded, it has been done not seldom by those holding the executive power'.[68] Callinan J does not seem much bothered by such concerns.[69] The danger here is that the low priority he gives to the protection of the liberty interests of the individual, when coupled with the disposition to accept uncritically the executive's assessment of risk to security, leads almost inevitably to the corrosion of constitutionalism in the name of national security.

Similarly, in *Al-Kateb* Callinan J adopted extended quotes from the minority judgments in the US Supreme Court's decision in *Zadvydas v Davis* on the basis that they were 'more orthodox expressions of constitutional principle and practical reality'. That appreciation of practical reality counseled against judicial review of the prospects for deportation in the context of immigration detention on the grounds that it would place 'foreign relations … into judicially supervised receivership'.[70] The countervailing practical reality of indefinite immigration detention did not get a look in.

From the second quoted paragraph, Callinan J reasons from the informational asymmetry between government and the courts to hold that if the government and parliament think there is a threat that justifies banning the Communist Party, it is entitled to press ahead under the defence power and '[i]t is immaterial whether the courts agree with Parliament or not'. It is hard to see how the views expressed by Latham CJ, quoted approvingly by Callinan J, are consistent with the principle that the courts should have the final say on whether legislation is within constitutional power or not, a principle Callinan J purports to endorse.[71]

It is not clear how much weight one should put on Callinan J's remarks in predicting future trends in the High Court. They could be viewed as the maverick stance of a lone judge, but they complement McHugh J's endorsement in *Al-Kateb* of executive-minded decisions on indefinite detention in wartime, and there is the fact that Kirby J thought that the joint judgment in *Thomas* contributed to revisionism about the *Communist Party Case* by emphasising the application of the defence power to threats arising from within Australia.[72]

Any assessment of *Thomas* has to take into account that the judgments of the Chief Justice and Gummow and Crennan JJ manifest an attitude to the administrative state which is not only appropriate for a modern constitutional democracy but necessary if judges are going to play a meaningful role in ensuring that the so-called 'war on terror' is conducted in accordance with the rule of law. If intelligence is not going to substitute for evidence[73] in decisions which make grave inroads into the liberty interests of the individual, judges might have to rethink their role when it comes to evaluation of claims of national security. As those majority judges make clear, that rethinking does not involve reinventing the wheel, since much work has already been done by common law judges in coming to terms with the administrative state. To the extent that Kirby and Hayne JJ distance themselves from this position, they might be considered both to exhibit an anachronistic attitude towards the administrative state and to give up on the hope of having the rule of law control the war on terror.

These competing considerations leave us with a serious question about whether the dissent of Kirby J will be regarded in the future as in the lineage of the dissents in *Halliday*, *Liversidge* and *Korematsu*, and thus as upholding the rule of law. On the one hand, there is our nagging concern that Kirby J might well be correct that regimes like the control order regime have no place in the constitutional state because they cannot be made consistent with the rule of law. If so, his dissent will stand on a par with the great dissents of the past, since he may be taken as predicting that control order regimes can be brought within the law only by placing a thin veneer of legality over what is in substance arbitrary power.[74]

On the other hand, it is important to keep in mind that in an era of real fear and anxiety about terrorism, governments will address the perceived threat through some legal regime. And if judges declare a regime illegal, governments will devise new preventive regimes or will resort to existing legal procedures, notably, those already in place for dealing with immigration.[75] There are distinct benefits to new regimes, including that if they apply to citizens as well as the alien other, governments have more of an inducement to make the regimes comply with the rule of law.[76] But for the regimes to comply, there has to be independent scrutiny of the basis of the decisions, and that makes it inevitable that judges will have to take a significant role, whether as the first instance decision-makers or in the process of review. There might, that is, be no option for judges but to engage in the experiment of trying to devise preventive regimes that live up to the aspirations of the rule of law.

Notes

* This chapter develops the central themes of the paper presented by David Dyzenhaus at the Symposium on Law and Liberty in the War on Terror, Gilbert + Tobin Centre of Public Law, University of New South Wales, Sydney, 6 July 2007. That paper, published as 'Cycles of legality in emergency times' (2007) 18 *Public Law Review* 165, does not consider the central focus of this chapter, the High Court's recent decision on control orders.

1 *R v Halliday* [1917] AC 260; *Liversidge v Anderson* [1942] AC 206; *Korematsu v United States* 323 US 214 (1944).

2 *Australian Communist Party v Commonwealth* (1951) 83 CLR 1.

3 See, for example, Cass Sunstein, 'Minimalism at War' (2004) *Supreme Court Review* 47.

4 *Hamdan v Rumsfeld* 126 SCt 2749 (2006); *A v Secretary of State for the Home Department* [2005] 2 AC 68; *Re Charkaoui* 2007 SCC 9.

5 *Re MB* [2006] EWHC 1000 (Admin), [103] (Sullivan J).

6 *Thomas v Mowbray* [2007] HCA 33.

7 *Al-Kateb v Godwin* (2004) 219 CLR 562, 586 (McHugh J); 599, 613 (Gummow J); 616, 618 (Kirby J).

8 Above, 588-89 (McHugh J); 620-22 (Kirby J).

9 See, for example, above, 648 (Hayne J).

10 Dennis Rose, 'The High Court decisions in *Al Kateb* and *Al Khafaji* – A Different Perspective' (2005) 8(3) *Constitutional Law and Policy Review* 58, 62-63.

11 See *Re Woolley; ex p Applicants M276/2003* (2004) 225 CLR 1, 52 (Gummow J).

12 In *The Constitution of Law* (2006) 92, note 56, Dyzenhaus misrepresented Gummow J's position by claiming that he put his dissent on a 'purely textual basis'. His position, properly represented, is problematic for a different reason, one which equally affects Kirby J's position.

13 *Al-Kateb v Godwin* (2004) 219 CLR 562, 577.

14 Above, 613.

15 Above, 618.

16 Above, 615.

17 Above, 584.

18 Above, 585-86.

19 *Australian Communist Party v Commonwealth* (1951) 83 CLR 1, 193.

20 *Little v Commonwealth* (1947) 75 CLR 94, 102-3, relying on *Liversidge v Anderson* [1942] AC 206, 104. This case involved an action for false imprisonment during the war.

21 See *Lloyd v Wallach* (1915) 20 CLR 299; *Ex p Walsh* [1942] ALR 359.

22 *Al-Kateb v Godwin* (2004) 219 CLR 562, 588-89.

23 Above, 620-22.

24 George Winterton, 'The Communist Party Case' in HP Lee and George Winterton (eds), *Australian Constitutional Landmarks* (2003) 108, 127.

25 Above, 133, quoting from Brian Galligan, *Politics of the High Court* (1987) 203.

26 *Al-Kateb v Godwin* (2004) 219 CLR 562, 584.

27 See David Dyzenhaus, *Hard Cases in Wicked Legal Systems: South African Law in the Perspective of Legal Philosophy* (1991) 57-58.

28 *Shaughnessy v Mezei* 345 US 206 (1953), quoted in *Al-Kateb v Godwin* (2004) 219 CLR 562, 651.

29 *Al-Kateb v Godwin* (2004) 219 CLR 562, 585.

30 *A v Secretary of State for the Home Department* [2005] 2 AC 68, 110.

31 Above, Lord Rodger, at 155, elaborated the implications of this point.

32 See Clive Walker, 'Keeping Control of Terrorists without Losing Control of Constitutionalism' (2007) 59 *Stanford Law Review* 1395.

33 David Garland, *The Culture of Control: Crime and Social Order in Contemporary Society* (2001) 12, quoted in above, 1396.

34 A similar approach was adopted in by a majority of the Supreme Court of Canada in regard to investigative hearing provisions introduced under counter-terrorism legislation: *Re Application under s 83.28 of the Criminal Code* [2004] 2 SCR 248.

35 *Thomas v Mowbray* [2007] HCA 33, [27]. See more generally [20]-[27].

36 Above, [71]-[77]. See also [88] and [100]-[103].

37 Above, [110] (Gummow and Crennan JJ).

38 Above, [28]. See also [19].

39 Above, [28]. See also [78]-[79] and [109] (Gummow and Crennan JJ).

40 Above, [349] (Kirby J); [506] (Hayne J).

41 Above, [506].

42 Above, [516].

43 Above, [17]. He holds that there is no reason to regard judicial involvement otherwise here. Heydon J also endorses this view by reference, [651], and Callinan J expresses agreement with it, [595]-[600]. However, Callinan J's agreement on this point falls within the context of a strongly and explicitly deferential approach in matters of national security, discussed below.

44 Above, [370].

45 Above, [498].

46 Above, [516] (Hayne J). This phrase is expressly adopted by Kirby J, [322].

47 *Al-Kateb v Godwin* (2004) 219 CLR 562, 643-44.

48 Above, 578-80 (Gleeson CJ) and 643-44 (Gummow J). Gleeson CJ also emphasises the broad and flexible nature of the remedy of habeas corpus. Section 22 of the *Federal Court of Australia Act 1976* (Cth) enjoins the Court to grant the appropriate remedies 'either absolutely or on such terms and conditions as the Court thinks just'.

49 *Thomas v Mowbray* [2007] HCA 33, [476] (Hayne J).

50 *Al-Kateb v Godwin* (2004) 219 CLR 562, 639-40.

51 *Thomas v Mowbray* [2007] HCA 33, [510].

52 Walker, above n 32, provides a recent and careful review of such measures.

53 The use of security-cleared counsel in the Commission of Inquiry into the Actions of Canadian Officials in relation to Maher Arar is one such example.

54 *Thomas v Mowbray* [2007] HCA 33, [351]-[359].

55 This proposition was expressed by Gummow J in *Fardon v Attorney-General (Qld)* (2004) 223 CLR 575, 612, quoted in the joint judgment in above, [114].

56 *Thomas v Mowbray* [2007] HCA 33, [116].

57 For a discussion of different approaches to defining judicial power in the Australian context see Simon Evans, 'The Meaning of Constitutional Terms: Essential Features, Family Resemblance and Theory-Based Approaches' (2006) 29 *University of New South Wales Law Journal* 207, 227-230.

58 *Thomas v Mowbray* [2007] HCA 33, [331]-[338]. See also [354]-[357].

59 See above, [28] (Gleeson CJ); [121] (Gummow and Crennan JJ); [17] (Gleeson CJ).

60 Above, [17].

61 Above, [386].

62 Above, [584].

63 Above, [533].

64 Above, [589].

65 Above, [532]-[533], [583]-[589].

66 Above, [544].

67 From the *Australian Communist Party v Commonwealth* (1951) 83 CLR 1, 155-56, quoted in Callinan J's judgment in *Thomas v Mowbray* [2007] HCA 33, [589].

68 *Australian Communist Party v Commonwealth* (1951) 83 CLR 1, 187-88.

69 *Thomas v Mowbray* [2007] HCA 33, [590].

70 *Zadvydas v Davis* 533 US 678 (2001), 703-705, 705-12 quoted in *Al-Kateb v Godwin* (2004) 219 CLR 562, 654-57.

71 *Thomas v Mowbray* [2007] HCA 33, [584].

72 The relevant passage from the joint judgment is found, above, [139]-[140].

73 The phrase is that of the President of the International Commission of Jurists, Arthur Chaskalson.

74 *Re MB* [2006] EWHC Admin 1000, [103] (Sullivan J).

75 The cancellation of Dr Mohamed Haneef's visa following a decision to grant bail, discussed in Chapter 20 of this book, is a good example of this.

76 See Neal Katyal, 'Equality in the War on Terror' (2007) 59 *Stanford Law Review* 1365.

3

The Curious Element of Motive in Definitions of Terrorism: Essential Ingredient or Criminalising Thought?

Ben Saul

Motive is anathema to criminal lawyers, who are schooled in the overriding importance of the intention behind conduct and the irrelevance of the motivations underlying it. As a result, some traditional criminal lawyers have been alarmed by the creeping emphasis on motive in new terrorism offences in various jurisdictions. Typical is the motive element in the Australian criminal law definition of 'terrorist act', which is also reflected in similar definitions in Britain, Canada, New Zealand and South Africa. Australian law defines terrorism as certain violent criminal acts done 'with the intention of advancing a political, religious or ideological cause', coupled with the intention of (i) 'coercing, or influencing by intimidation' a government, or (ii) 'intimidating the public' or a section of it.[1]

Although described in the Australian definition as an 'intention', and in the comparable definitions as a 'purpose' requirement, the element of a political, religious or ideological cause in these definitions is commonly understood as a motive requirement; that is, as the emotion or belief prompting the prohibited physical conduct which also forms part of most terrorism definitions. The distinction between intention and motive, and different types of each, has been much discussed in criminal law. While more could be said about the jurisprudential issues, this chapter focuses on the common identification of politics, religion or ideology as elements central to the criminal law concept of terrorism. In passing, a number of courts have approached these definitional elements as motive requirements.[2]

For proponents of such definitions, requiring proof of a political, religious or ideological motive allows the criminal law to more finely target, stigmatise and deter what is considered by society to be especially wrongful about terrorism. For opponents of such definitions, a focus on such motives is an invitation to racial, religious and political profiling by law enforcement and intelligence agencies, which encourages discrimination and suspicion, politicises investigations and criminal trials, and chills democratic freedoms of expression, association and religion.

There are, however, no bright lines in the debate between human rights advocates on one side and national security types on the other. Rather, both camps are divided about the proper role of motive in terrorism definitions. Set against the inclusion of motive are the Canadian *Khawaja* decision, which found that a motive element unjustifiably infringed constitutional rights; the UN Human Rights Committee; a UK human rights parliamentary committee; the Australian Attorney-General's Department and prosecutor's office; former Australian High Court Chief Justice Sir Gerard Brennan; a former Canadian Prime Minister; and some legal scholars on terrorism, such as Professor Kent Roach, author of the following chapter.

In favour of a motive element are Australia's Human Rights and Equal Opportunity Commission; Canadian and Australian security parliamentary committees; the independent reviewer of the British anti-terrorism laws; the independent Australian Security Legislation Review Committee; and other legal scholars. This chapter carefully considers the arguments on both sides, before concluding that, on balance, the interests of human rights are better served by including motive in the definition rather than by omitting it.

Why motive matters in terrorism definitions

A compelling reason for including a motive element in an international or domestic definition of terrorist offences is that it helps to differentiate terrorism from other kinds of serious violence which may also generate fear (such as common assault, armed robbery, rape, or murder), while also according with commonplace public understanding of what constitutes terrorism. The core premise is that political violence or violence done for some other public-oriented reason (such as religion, ideology, or race/ethnicity) is conceptually and morally different to violence perpetrated for private ends (such as profit, greed, jealousy, animosity, hatred, revenge, personal or family disputes and so on).

As such, the criminal law should recognise this distinction in defining terrorism, so as to more accurately express what is considered by the international and national communities to be distinctively wrongful about terrorism. This distinction does not necessarily imply that terrorism is always morally worse than organised crime (a mafia hit may cause as much fear as a terrorist act), but it does suggest that it is morally different, not least because it aims to disrupt and coerce peaceful political processes through violence.

Inevitably, this view reflects judgments of policy, politics and ethics, which may not be shared by all; but it is the critical impulse underlying arguments for including motive in definitions of terrorism.

Until recently, the international community's legal response to terrorism has not focused on motive. Since the early 1960s, thirteen sectoral anti-terrorism treaties have avoided any general definition of terrorism, including reference to motive. Instead, most of the treaties require states to prohibit and punish in domestic law certain physical or objective acts – such as hijacking, hostage taking, and misuse of nuclear material or bombings – regardless of whether such acts are motivated by private or political ends. Proof of the motive or motives behind the act is not required as an element of the offences.

At best, some of the treaties define their offences by including special intent requirements, which fall short of requiring a political or other motive as such. For instance, art 2 of the 1999 *Terrorist Financing Convention* prohibits the financing of certain acts where their purpose 'is to intimidate a population or to compel a government … to do or abstain from doing any act'. While this definition partly signals a focus on repressing public-oriented violence – by targeting acts directed at the community or a government – it still does not accurately capture what is most objectionable about terrorism. For it is still possible to intimidate a population or compel a government for a host of private, non-political reasons, including simple extortion.

As a result of their failure to include motive elements, many of the existing anti-terrorism treaties reach considerably beyond common understandings of terrorism, since violence for public and private motives alike is equally criminalised. The lack of differentiation arguably fails to capture what it distinctively wrongful about terrorism, which is not inherent in a physical act of violence alone.

Overreach undermines the offences' moral and political force, and dilutes the special character of terrorism as a crime against non-violent politics and social life. Prosecuting an individual for politically motivated terrorism, rather than for common crimes like murder or sectoral offences like hijacking, may help satisfy public indignation at terrorist acts, better express community condemnation, and placate popular (but reasonable) demands for justice.

In international practice, there is increasing support for the view that terrorism is political or other publicly motivated violence, which can and should be distinguished from private violence. In its influential and widely supported 1994 *Declaration on Measures to Eliminate International Terrorism*, the UN General Assembly distinguished terrorism from other violence because of its motivation 'for political purposes'. In the European Union's 2002 *Framework Decision on Combating Terrorism*, terrorism is considered a distinctive form of violence precisely because 'the motivation of the offender is different' than in ordinary crimes.[3]

The definitions of terrorism in Britain, Canada, Australia, New Zealand and South Africa similarly reflect a political judgment by those democratic communities that the motives of terrorists set them apart from other criminals. According to the Australian Parliamentary Joint Committee on Intelligence and Security, 'terrorism is qualitatively different from other types of serious crime' and is perceived as so distinct by the public.[4] Australia's independent Security Legislation Review Committee agreed that the motive element 'appropriately emphasises a publicly understood quality of terrorism'.[5] For Australia's Human Rights and Equal Opportunity Commission, the aim of terrorists to undermine the political system and institutions 'makes the differentiation between "terrorist" and "non-terrorist" offences meaningful'.[6] As the Canadian government suggests, removing the motive element would thus make terrorism offences indistinguishable from ordinary crimes.[7] In a review of British terrorism laws, Lord Lloyd of Berwick observed that labelling what would otherwise be ordinary crime as terrorism reflects that terrorism attacks society and democratic institutions.[8]

At the same time, the international community has equally recognised the distinctiveness of non-political crime. For instance, the oldest international crime, piracy, is defined as violence on the high seas for private ends. More recently, arts 2 and 5 of the 2000 UN *Convention against Transnational Organized Crime* define transnational organised crime as serious crime that is motivated by 'financial or other material benefit'.

Motive and the classical criminal law

The first objection to including motive in definitions of terrorism is a jurisprudential one. In most domestic legal systems (and in international criminal law), motive is normally irrelevant to criminal responsibility. Proof of motive is not typically required as an element of an offence, although it may be relevant in other ways, such as in evidence of fact, or in the exercise of judicial discretion in sentencing (especially in mitigation or aggravation). Instead, it is normally an offender's intention to commit a prohibited act that is essential to criminal responsibility.

That the criminal law has not historically embraced motive is not of itself a sufficient objection, unless compelling policy reasons underlie that traditional approach. Traditional disregard for motive appears to reflect the policy judgment identified by the US courts in the *Dynar* case:

> It does not matter to society, in its efforts to secure social peace and order, what an accused's motive was, but only what the accused intended to do. It

> is no consolation to one whose car has been stolen that the thief stole the car intending to sell it to purchase food for a food bank.[9]

There are numerous difficulties with this traditional approach. First, ignoring motive may well entrench substantive inequality before the law, as the example given in *Dynar* demonstrates. The assertion that it does not matter to society that private property interests are privileged over the avoidance of potential starvation (or homelessness, or other grave social ills) says much about the role of criminal law in society. Secondly, while the elaboration of motive may not console the victim, it may well be important to society as a whole, and the criminal law has never been solely oriented towards the interests of victims at the expense of the community.

Sometimes it clearly does matter to society *why* a crime is committed. Some jurisdictions, for instance, have enacted crimes of racial violence, in which racial hatred or motivation is not merely an aggravating factor in sentencing, but an element of the definition of a distinct crime embodying a political or social recognition that racial violence is conceptually and morally different – perhaps more insidious – than privately motivated ordinary crime. That motive elements are comparatively rare in the criminal law is no reason not to include such elements where there are compelling public interests for doing so. In a sophisticated criminal justice system, motive elements can promote a more finely calibrated legal response to specific types of socially unacceptable behaviour. Where society decides that certain social, ethical or political values are worth protecting, a motive requirement can more accurately target reprehensible infringements of those values. There may be a powerful symbolic or moral value in condemning the motive behind an act, quite separate from condemning the intentional physical act itself.

The traditional aversion to motive has been forcefully directed against new terrorism definitions. A former Chief Justice of the Australian High Court, Sir Gerard Brennan, has argued that a crime is no less reprehensible if committed to advance organised crime, industrial espionage, or to stifle dissent (as in the bombing of the *Rainbow Warrior*) and that 'motive adds nothing to the criminality of the acts constituting terrorism'.[10] A former Canadian Attorney-General, Irwin Cotler, similarly suggests that the identification of motive is not necessary in securing social peace and order.[11] Further, in *Khawaja*, a judge of the Ontario Superior Court of Justice argued that:

> The average person would be hard pressed … to recount much about the motives of the perpetrators of some if not all of these notorious crimes. Just what political, religious or ideological objectives or causes the perpetrators felt they were supporting with their actions is largely lost on the populations affected. And for good reason. It really doesn't matter. Such terrorist acts cannot be appreciated by the imputation of rational principles to the perpetrators anyway.[12]

Here it is rather surprising to learn that although a democratically elected Canadian Parliament decided – by specifically including a motive element – that the reasons for terrorist violence *do* matter to society, a single judge is willing to overrule that judgment by declaring that motives are irrelevant to society. No empirical evidence whatsoever was cited in support of that contention, which really amounts to a political or policy position. Yet, in the case of statutory crimes, it is surely the prerogative of parliament to identify and define social harms worthy of criminalisation, and not to be second-guessed by judges on criminological policy.

Moreover, the suggestion that 'rational principles' or motives may elude the perpetrators of terrorism misses the point, since political, religious or ideological motives need not be rational in order to be imputable to a person. There are plenty of utterly irrational political, religious and ideological views, which are no less political, religious or ideological on account of their irrationality.

Finally, to suggest that the motives for the seven high profile incidents of terrorism listed in *Khawaja* are 'lost' on the affected populations comes across as a paternalistic view, which casts the population as politically unaware. Three of those incidents are well-known Al-Qa'ida attacks (the 9/11 attacks, the 2004 Madrid bombings and the 2005 London bombings), carrying with them widely known political and religious claims as announced by Al-Qa'ida. The 1995 Tokyo sarin gas subway poisoning was widely known to be the work of a Japanese religious cult. The 1995 Oklahoma City bombing was perpetrated by Timothy McVeigh out of political antipathy towards his federal government. The 1985 Air India bombing was allegedly the work of a political/religious Sikh separatist group pressing for an independent Khalistan in the Punjab. The 2006 Mumbai train bombings in India were allegedly committed by radical Islamic groups including Lashkar-e-Taiba, possibly assisted by Pakistani intelligence agents. Educated publics in democracies with free media are often far more politically conscious than judges give them credit for.

Pragmatic considerations: evidentiary difficulties

The key practical disadvantage of requiring motive as a mental element of a criminal offence is that it may be genuinely difficult to prove and is an additional barrier to a successful prosecution. An early Australian review of security powers emphasised the evidentiary difficulties involved in proving an 'ulterior intention or motive' (such as 'political ends') in terrorism offences.[13] Australia's Attorney-General's Department and Director of Public Prosecutions also support removing motive, partly in response to the *Mallah* case, which involved a reckless threat to bomb a government building where it was unclear if the motive was personal frustration or political grievance.[14]

Plainly, requiring proof of motive necessarily makes prosecutions more difficult, since an additional element of the crime must be proved beyond intention. In some cases, there may also be difficulty in determining whether a cause falls within the concepts of 'political', 'ideological' or 'religious', although often those categories will be clear enough. Indeed, in many cases, it is precisely the aim of terrorists to amplify their political or religious claims through violence and their actions are often accompanied by explanation, justification or demands.

Where motives are difficult to discern – for example, when no-one claims responsibility and suspects are silent on motives – it may still be possible to prove motive by other means. The International Criminal Tribunal for the former Yugoslavia has found that intention 'is a mental factor which is difficult, even impossible, to determine' and consequently 'intent can be inferred from a certain number of presumptions of fact'.[15] Motive too might be inferred from the context and circumstances in appropriate cases, drawing careful inferences from the evidence.

Where the political or religious motives of suspects are not known for lack of evidence, violent attacks can always still be prosecuted as ordinary crime, which precludes impunity while ensuring that terrorism is a label reserved for those crimes that are conceptually and morally distinguishable because they involve political or religious coercion of the public or government. In such cases, nothing is lost by requiring a political motive to establish terrorism, since the community has not been harmed by knowledge of the political, religious or ideological coercion that justifies distinguishing terrorism from other violence.

Human rights considerations: risks of profiling, prejudice and chilling speech

The core objection to including motive elements in terrorism definitions is not so much that it is alien to the traditional criminal law but rather, as Kent Roach argues in the following chapter, the detrimental impact that such inclusion is thought to have on basic human rights. In *Khawaja*, it was found that the motive requirement in the Canadian definition was an unjustifiable infringement on constitutionally protected freedoms of conscience, religion, thought, belief, expression and association. The judge identified a cluster of human rights concerns including that investigative and prosecutorial scrutiny would inevitably focus on political, religious and ideological beliefs, opinions and expressions; freedoms and consequently democratic life would be chilled; and suspicion and anger would fall on anyone belonging to a religious, political or ideological group that is connected with terrorist acts.[16]

The court drew support from a variety of academic writings, including by Irwin Cotler, who further warned against politicising the investigative and trial processes. The UN Human Rights Committee recommended in 2006 that Canada 'adopt a more precise definition of terrorist offences, so as to ensure that individuals will not be targeted on political, religious or ideological grounds'.[17] The British Parliamentary Joint Committee on Human Rights similarly found that the motive element in the British definition gave rise to a 'high risk' of incompatibility with freedom of expression and related rights under the *European Convention on Human Rights*.[18] In Australia, the former Chief Justice Gerard Brennan warned that the focus on motive 'may easily be misunderstood as targeting the entire group who wish to advance the religious cause of Islam'.[19] Some civil society groups have supported omitting motive so as to avoid discrimination and the chilling of democratic dissent and expression.[20]

Are these concerns well founded? It is clear that by highlighting the political, religious or ideological reasons behind terrorism, a motive element necessarily draws more attention to those beliefs. But it must be emphasised that such attention is only triggered where such beliefs are connected with acts of, or threats or plans to commit, unlawful physical violence as enumerated in terrorism definitions, and which are already within the sights of the police. Peaceful politics, religions or ideologies are not at risk; and indeed efforts to focus on peaceful beliefs or expression would not be authorised by the law.

Law enforcement officials themselves have observed that racial and religious profiling is 'not useful for effective investigations and intelligence assessments'.[21] Given the scarcity of law enforcement resources, the natural focus is foremost on acts or threats of violence, and only secondarily on motives once the existence of (already criminal) violence has been established. In this sense, there is arguably little difference from ordinary law enforcement, since motive only becomes relevant at a later stage of the investigative process. To the extent that there remain concerns about racial or religious profiling, the solution is not to abandon the normatively important motive element but to ensure that the implementation and enforcement of the law is properly carried out, including through improved training and supervision of policing and intelligence, and better safeguards during the investigative process.

Many concerns about risks of profiling, prejudice or the chilling of expression are precisely risk assessments, rather than empirically evidenced or quantifiable phenomena. In *Khawaja*, for instance, these risks were highlighted primarily by academic writings, with little objective evidence to support them. This is inevitable to a point, since the chilling of speech is partly an intangible risk which must be evaluated based on policy judgments and a degree of intuition. But that does not erase the need for some hard evidence, and some of the risks identified in *Khawaja* seem more like speculative or predictive assertions not underpinned by empirical evidence to suggest that those risks will actually materialise.

There is also tendency to ascribe risks to the law when such risks may originate elsewhere. If there are real concerns about suspicion falling on those who hold particular political, religious or ideological beliefs, the root of those concerns may well be extra-legal – stemming from social and community prejudices, amplified no doubt by some politicians and sections of the media. This is not to deny that the law may entrench or formalise patterns of discrimination that exist outside of it, but it can equally dampen or restructure those patterns in a benevolent fashion. By focusing narrowly only on the politics or religion of particular individuals where it is connected with serious violence, a motive-based terrorism definition can help lift the veil of suspicion which others in the community may cast on all members of such political or religious movements.

As various inquiries have rightly emphasised, the inclusion of a motive element ultimately serves to protect, rather than diminish, basic human rights. In Australia, the independent Security Legislation Review Committee pointed out that the motive requirement is a 'narrowing provision' that tightens the ambit of terrorist offences, particularly in the Australian federal context where the States only agreed to refer their constitutional powers (over the criminal law) to the federal parliament on the understanding that terrorism would be tightly defined and capture only acts that the States would readily agree constitute terrorism, such as the 'high end' political/religious terrorist bombings in Bali in 2002, which killed almost 90 Australians.[22] The stigmatising 'terrorist' label is thus reserved for serious violent political or religious criminals if a motive element is retained, excluding private violence, which does not challenge democratic politics in the same way.

The Canadian Parliamentary Committee on Public Safety and National Security has noted the irony flowing from *Khawaja* that 'the Crown now has one less element of the criminal offence which it has to prove', making it easier to prosecute the defendant who had pleaded the unconstitutionality of motive. The committee observed that while a motive element is unusual, here it 'constitutes a safeguard' that 'limits the ability of enforcement agencies to go after certain people'.[23] For this reason, if the motive element were deleted, Australia's Human Rights and Equal Opportunity Commission has expressed its 'real concerns that the resultant breadth of the definition would render [the definition] a disproportionate limitation on the rights guaranteed by the ICCPR, in particular articles 19 and 22' (concerning freedoms of opinion, expression and association).[24]

Drawing on the 2003 Council of Europe *Convention on the Prevention of Terrorism* and 2004 UN Security Council Resolution 1566, Britain's independent reviewer of terrorism laws takes the human rights analysis a step further, by arguing that the motive element should be expanded to also include racial or ethnic cause.[25] Racially motivated violence that also intimidates the public or coerces a government could thus be prosecuted as the serious crime of terrorism, sending a strong deterrent message to those who propagate racial hatred or ethnic cleansing. The firmer suppression of extremist violence committed by neo-Nazis, skinheads or Balkan paramilitaries is something which advances human rights – far from undermining it. Motive-based terrorism definitions need not generate prejudice or discrimination, but can be harnessed to confront and quell those who would terrorise others in the pursuit of racial supremacy or eugenic fantasies.

Conclusion: The dubious martyr effect of political crime

A final policy objection to including a motive element is a long held view that marking out offenders as political (or religious or ideological) criminals would legitimise them or transform them into *cause célèbres*, lightning rods for dissent or martyrs for the cause. On this view, requiring proof of a political motive would expose fringe political claims to the judicial process, inevitably requiring the law to take such views seriously and bringing them greater public scrutiny. It is thus thought preferable to focus on the physical harm resulting from terrorist acts and accordingly to treat offenders as ordinary criminals.

The strength of these objections is doubtful. The political demands of terrorists will usually become prominent regardless of their ventilation in a courtroom, whether through the media or the internet. While the elucidation of political motives in court may amplify them, it equally allows erroneous, misconceived or poisonous ideas to be confronted and dissipated in the ensuing public debate.

The expressive function of the criminal law cannot be overstated; a conviction for political or religious violence sends a symbolic message that certain kinds of violence cannot be tolerated in plural, secular democracies, which are duty bound to ensure the safety of their peoples and to suppress those who wish to influence politics and interfere in the autonomy of others by resorting to violence. Here the criminal law has a role in reinforcing the ethical values of democratic political communities, which are constructed on a shared commitment to peaceful deliberation and participatory dialogue, rather than using the unilateral force of arms against one's fellow citizens or their democratic institutions.

Notes

1 *Criminal Code* (Cth) s 100.1. Other jurisdictions' definitions are found in the *Terrorism Act 2000* (UK) s 1(1)(c); *Criminal Code 1985* (Canada) s 83.1(1); *Terrorism Suppression Act 2002* (NZ) s 5; *Protection of Constitutional Democracy Against Terrorist and Related Activities Act 2004* (South Africa) s 1(1)(xxv).

2 *R v Khawaja* [2006] OJ 4245, [45]-[80]; *Thomas v Mowbray* [2007] HCA 33, [161], [280] (Kirby J), [442] (Hayne J).

3 *Proposal for a Council Framework Decision on Combating Terrorism*, EC, COM(2001) 521 Final, CNS/2001/0217 (2001) 6, 7.

4 Parliamentary Joint Committee on Intelligence and Security, Parliament of Australia, *Review of Security and Counter Terrorism Legislation* (2006) 57.

5 Security Legislation Review Committee (Sheller Committee), *Review of Security and Counter-Terrorism Legislation* (2006) 57.

6 Human Rights and Equal Opportunity Commission, Supplementary Submission to the Security Legislation Review Committee (2006) 8.

7 Cited in *R v Khawaja* [2006] OJ 4245, [66].

8 Lord Lloyd, *Inquiry into Legislation Against Terrorism* (1996) xi.

9 *United States of America v Dynar* [1997] 2 SCR 462, 497.

10 Gerard Brennan, 'Liberty's threat from executive power', *Sydney Morning Herald*, 6 July 2007, 11.

11 Irwin Cotler, quoted in *R v Khawaja* [2006] OJ 4245, [62].

12 *R v Khawaja* [2006] OJ 4245, [79].

13 *Thomas v Mowbray* [2007] HCA 33, [161] (Kirby J), citing Hope, *Protective Security Review: Report*, Parliamentary Paper No 397/1979 (1979) 291, quoting Sir Victor Windeyer.

14 Attorney-General's Department, Submission to the Security Legislation Review Committee, February 2006, 12; Commonwealth Director of Public Prosecutions, Submission to the Security Legislation Review Committee, February 2006, 9; *R v Mallah* [2005] NSWSC 358.

15 *Akayesu (Judgment)* ICTR-96-4-T (2 Sept 1998), [523].

16 *R v Khawaja* [2006] OJ 4245, [58] and [73].

17 *Concluding observations of the Human Rights Committee*, UN HRC, 85th sess, 2330th mtg, UN Doc CCPR/C/CAN/Co/5 (2006); quoted in *R v Khawaja* [2006] OJ 4245, [72].

18 Parliamentary Joint Committee on Human Rights, UK Parliament, *Counter-Terrorism Policy and Human Rights: Terrorism Bill and Related Matters* (2005).

19 Brennan, above n 10.

20 See, for example, Amnesty International, B'nai Brith Canada, Canadian Arab Federation, Canadian Council or Islamic-American Relations, Canadian Muslim Lawyers Association in *R v Khawaja* [2006] OJ 4245; submissions to the Canadian House of Commons, Final Report of the Standing Committee on Public Safety and National Security (2007), 8; and submissions to the Security Legislation Review Committee, above n 5.

21 Canadian House of Commons, above n 20, 7-9.

22 Security Legislation Review Committee, above n 5, 55 and 57; Parliamentary Joint Committee on Intelligence and Security above n 4, 53.

23 Canadian House of Commons, above n 20, 9.

24 Human Rights and Equal Opportunity Commission, above n 6, 8.

25 Lord Carlile, *The Definition of Terrorism* (2007) 37.

4

The Case for Defining Terrorism With Restraint and Without Reference to Political or Religious Motive

Kent Roach

People have been debating the definition of terrorism for a long time. Continued disagreement about a proper definition explains why terrorism is not yet a crime subject to the jurisdiction of the International Criminal Court and why the United Nations has not agreed on a comprehensive convention on terrorism. Some think that it is impossible to define terrorism. I do not. Nevertheless I argue that terrorism should be defined with restraint with a focus on intentional violence to civilians. The political, religious or other motives of the perpetrators should not excuse terrorism; conversely they should also not constitute part of the crime of terrorism.

Is the ordinary criminal law adequate?

I approach the issue of defining terrorism from a perspective that is rooted in the criminal law. Although many officials in Australia and Canada have repeatedly justified new anti-terrorism laws on the basis that the existing criminal law is inadequate to prevent acts of terrorism, we should not lightly assume that the existing criminal law is not up to the task. It is simply wrong to argue that the ordinary criminal law only applies after an act of terrorist violence has occurred. For example, Zaccarias Moussaoui, the so-called 20th hijacker, pleaded guilty to conspiracy to commit murder. Jack Roche was convicted of conspiring to bomb the Israeli embassy in Canberra. Richard Reid, the shoe bomber who was foiled on a transatlantic flight, was convicted of attempted murder. The ordinary criminal law can even apply to speech acts. Abu Hamza received a stiff penalty for inciting or counselling murder in relation to his calls for violence at the Finsbury Park Mosque.

The ordinary criminal law, including offences of conspiracy, incitement and attempt that apply long before actual acts of terrorist violence, can be applied to apprehended acts of terrorist violence. It can result in serious criminal convictions that carry with them significant stigma and punishment. The attractiveness of being able to condemn acts of terrorism on the basis that murder is murder and nothing excuses the commission of murder should not be underestimated.

I am not, however, dogmatic about whether the criminal law is an adequate response to terrorism. In some countries such as Indonesia the existing criminal law was inadequate to respond to apprehended acts of terrorism. There were no general laws prohibiting conspiracies or agreements to commit criminal acts in Indonesia. Attempted crimes were defined restrictively to require the accused effectively to have commenced the ultimate criminal act such as a bombing before that person would be guilty of an attempt. In Indonesia, the criminal law either had to be expanded or else a new terrorism law enacted. But that was not necessarily the case in Australia or Canada.

Post 9/11 terrorism laws: The flaws of British-inspired definitions of terrorism

In any event, many countries have enacted new anti-terrorism laws since 9/11. Australia and Canada based their definition of terrorist activities on that found in the British *Terrorism Act 2000*. In my view, definitions of terrorism inspired by the British definition are flawed for two reasons. The first is that they go well beyond what the Supreme Court of Canada recognised in 2002 was the essence of terrorism, namely the intentional murder and maiming of innocent civilians.[1] Instead the British-inspired definitions include various forms of property damage and interference with electronic and other essential services. To be sure, these are real harms that should be subject to the criminal law, but a more restrained and precise definition of terrorism that focuses on intentional acts of violence could respond to many concerns that anti-terrorism efforts will infringe human rights. A precise definition of terrorism that focuses on the murder and maiming of civilians could provide the firmest foundation for any expansion of police powers or investigative practices that could be justified as necessary to respond to the harms of terrorist violence. It would certainly capture the type of terrorism seen on 9/11 and afterwards in Bali, Madrid, London and elsewhere.

The second flaw with British-inspired definitions of terrorism is that they require proof that a terrorist acted for a political or religious motive. To be sure, terrorism laws must have a means to distinguish terrorism from ordinary crime, but relying on political and religious motive is not necessary. The proper focus should be on whether the terrorist is pursuing a purpose of intimidating a population or compelling governments or international organisations to act. This requirement avoids an official inquiry into the terrorist's political and religious beliefs that may promote the false impression that a democratic state is responding to the accused's politics or religion as opposed to his or her plans to commit acts of violence. It is also more consistent with the traditional criminal law principle that motive is not generally an essential element of crime. If no motive can excuse crime, as was recently affirmed when some accused attempted to challenge the application of British anti-terrorism laws to actions against a repressive regime in Libya,[2] then it is only consistent that motive should not be a constituent part of crime.

Two differing approaches to the definition of terrorism

My approach to the definition of terrorism differs from that of Dr Ben Saul who is the author of the preceding chapter and has written an important and learned book on the definition of terrorism in international law.[3] In his book, Dr Saul starts through the lens of international law and on that subject I agree completely with him that we need a definition of terrorism. Failure to agree on a definition of terrorism is a luxury that can no longer be afforded in the present context of increased anti-terrorism laws and activities. As Dr Saul argues, a legal definition of terrorism could help provide a restrained alternative to the use of war and extra legal measures. The absence of a precise and restrained definition of terrorism has allowed many states to define terrorism in an overly broad manner that raises concerns that protest and civil disobedience will be caught within the definition of terrorism. Although dissent may be able to survive an overbroad definition of terrorism in Australia, Britain or Canada, it may have more drastic consequences in China, Egypt or Saudi Arabia.

Dr Saul and I disagree on the breadth of a definition of terrorism and on the question of political and religious motive. He argues that a definition of terrorism should include all acts that endanger life, including acts against property, and that acts of terrorism should be defined to ensure that they are committed for a political, ideological, religious or ethnic purpose. Saul's views are supported by Lord Carlile, the Independent Reviewer of the UK's terrorism legislation, who has recently completed an extensive report that after a comparative study concludes that the British definition of terrorism is in almost all respects sound.[4] They are also supported by the Sheller and parliamentary committee reviews in Australia.[5] My position, however, I hope is not entirely hopeless. As will be seen in what follows, it has support in international and criminal law practice and the Canadian constitutional jurisprudence which has recently struck the political and religious motive requirement from Canadian anti-terrorism law.

The United Nations and the definition of terrorism

In the wake of 9/11, the United Nations in Resolution 1373 called on all states to ensure that terrorism was treated as a serious crime, without bothering to define what constitutes terrorism. Many states acted and relied on the broad definition of terrorism found in the British law. It is unfortunate that the Security Council did not provide guidance on the definition sooner. When it finally addressed the question in Resolution 1566 issued in 2004 it defined terrorism in a more restrained manner than found in Australian and Canadian law or proposed by Dr Saul.

Resolution 1566 singles out:

> [C]riminal acts, including against civilians, committed with the intent to cause death or serious bodily injury, or taking of hostages, with the purpose to provoke a state of terror in the general public or in a group of persons or particular persons, intimidate a population or compel a government or an international organisation to do or to abstain from doing any act.

This definition focuses on intentional causing of death or serious bodily injury or taking of hostages. It does not include property damage or the disruption of electronic systems or essential services as do Australian and Canadian law. It does not require proof of religious or political motive. Instead, it distinguishes terrorism from other crimes by the notion that the latter is committed to intimidate a population or compel governments to act. Resolution 1566 also provides that intentional acts of violence and hostage taking 'are under no circumstances justifiable by considerations of a political, philosophical, ideological, racial, ethnic, religious or other similar nature'. This follows the traditional criminal law principle that no motive can excuse an intentional crime.

Retaining the basics of a criminal law approach

In cases in which the existing criminal law is not sufficient to deal with apprehended acts of terrorism and in cases where countries have introduced new terrorism offences, it is important to retain as many of the virtues of the criminal law as possible. These virtues include the general requirement in criminal law for proof of fault, including requirements that the accused intend or have knowledge in relation to the prohibited act, at least for the most serious offences. Another virtue of the criminal law is its requirement that a specific culpable act be established. The requirement of some intentional act is essential to ensure that the innocent are not punished on the basis of their associations or status or thoughts. The requirements of evidence of a specific culpable act and a specific intent are bedrock principles of individual responsibility in the criminal law. They help distinguish criminal law from collective punishment or the common practices of intelligence agencies in identifying security risks on the basis of a person's associations or beliefs.

It is important to preserve as much of the traditional criminal law as possible in order to maximise its denunciatory effects in condemning and punishing terrorism. One of the great dangers of terrorism is that it will goad and scare liberal democracies into changing their fundamental defining rules. As much as possible we should retain our traditional principles and rules in the face of terrorism. It is particularly important to maintain the traditional approach that motive does not constitute an essential element of a criminal offence, if we are to rely on our equally as traditional rule that no motive excuses crime. If motive cannot be a shield for the accused, it should also not be a sword for the state.

The focus in terrorism prosecutions should be on violence and preparations to commit violence. Such conclusions are supported by both normative and practical concerns. There are normative arguments that the political and religious motive requirement should be removed in order to protect the accused and others from discrimination on the basis that they are members of an unpopular religious group or that they express unpopular religious or political views. The idea that terrorism trials will inevitably be political or religious trials may have some force from a historical, political science or sociological perspective, but it is contrary to the logic of the criminal law which suggests that motive neither excuses nor constitutes intentional crime.

There are also powerful practical objections to the political and religious motive requirement. A focus on the accused's religion and politics can prolong and distract trials. There should not be any need to call competing experts on the meaning of Islam or any other religion in a criminal trial, as sometimes has occurred when evidence about motive is admitted. It could also create harmful and counterproductive impressions that the accused are being prosecuted for their political or religious beliefs. The motive requirement could also provide an accused with a possible platform to politicise the trial process by offering extensive evidence about the true meaning of often ambiguous religious and political beliefs.

The bombing and killing of civilian targets should not be exempted from the label of terrorism in cases where we do not know what motivated the accused or in cases where the motive cannot easily be described as political, religious or ideological. From the perspective of public safety, it should not matter why someone explodes a bomb. It is an open question whether nihilistic or ethnic motivations are covered by the reference to political, religious or ideological motivations.[6] It should not be an open question. It should not matter why a person plans acts of intentional violence of such a magnitude that they are designed to intimidate populations or compel governments to act.

In order to avoid any impression that anti-terrorism efforts are directed against Islam or any other religion, it is best to focus not on the offender's motive, but whether they intentionally committed a culpable act. Focusing on motive may contribute to the dangerous process in which the distinction between intelligence that identifies risks of political or religious violence is blurred with evidence relating to culpable acts by identified individuals to plan or prepare to commit such acts.

The differences between crime and intelligence based approaches

Justice Dennis O'Connor's conclusions in his 2006 report on the activities of Canadian officials in relation to Canadian citizen Maher Arar underline the importance even at the investigative stage of focusing on criminality as opposed to the security risks that capture the attention of intelligence agencies. Justice O'Connor found that Canadian officials passed on unfair and inaccurate information branding Arar 'an Islamic extremist with connections to al Qaeda' to American officials and that this information likely played a role in the decisions of American officials to detain Arar and remove him to Syria where he was tortured, as well as detained for almost a year before being released. The information was based not on the actions of Mr Arar, but rather on the basis of his associations with others who were the target of a national security investigation and his religion.

One of the dangers of overbroad anti-terrorism laws is that they may blur important distinctions between law enforcement and security intelligence and between admissible evidence about planned wrongdoing and intelligence about a person's associations and expressive activities. Both the act and fault requirements of the criminal law help ensure that anti-terrorism law focuses on criminal wrongdoing. The act and fault requirement justify punishment of the offender and send a denunciatory message to society about the particular crime. The requirement for a culpable act and fault can protect the innocent.

The origins of a political and religious motive requirement

Anti-terrorism laws in Australia and Canada followed the British *Terrorism Act 2000* by defining terrorist activities in part on the basis of the intent to advance a political, religious or ideological cause. The origins of Britain's political or religious motive requirement are interesting. Lord Lloyd in his 1996 review of British anti-terrorism legislation expressed concerns that the existing definition might not catch some forms of terrorism and expressed approval for the following working definition of terrorism used by the Federal Bureau of Investigation (FBI) in the United States:

> The use of serious violence against persons or property, or the threat to use such violence, to intimidate or coerce a government, the public or any section of the public, in order to promote political, social or ideological objectives.[7]

As Professor Clive Walker notes, however, the FBI's definition of terrorism was used 'for jurisdictional, budgetary and other administrative purposes' and not 'as a legal term of art on which liberty depends'.[8] Because the United States has no domestic security intelligence agency, the FBI collects security intelligence as well as evidence. The codification of the FBI's definition of terrorism into the British law creates a danger of blurring the distinction between law enforcement and security intelligence. In any event, the definition of terrorism in American law both before and after 9/11 was less vague than the FBI's working definition and it makes no reference to political or religious motives, factors likely to attract critical scrutiny under the First Amendment of the American Bill of Rights.

Political and religious motive and the expansion of the criminal law

The development of Australian and British anti-terrorism law suggests that a focus on the political and religious motives of terrorism may lead to expansion of anti-terrorism law. In 2005, Australia expanded its anti-terrorism laws to include various forms of sedition and to allow groups to be proscribed as terrorist groups because they advocate terrorism. Britain played a leading role that same year in the formation of UN Security Council Resolution 1624 which calls for the enactment of laws against incitement of terrorism. The British *Terrorism Act 2006* included laws against the indirect advocacy of terrorism through the glorification of terrorism. Once policy-makers focus on the extremist politics and religion that motivate terrorism they may want to use the criminal law to respond directly to such politics and religion. One problem with such an approach is that it may blur the anti-hate and anti-terrorism rationales for criminalising speech. Although democracies can use the criminal sanction to prohibit the expression of racial and religious hatred, these crimes are usually treated as much less serious than terrorism offences.

New laws against speech associated with terrorism also blur distinctions between crime and intelligence based approaches. Security intelligence agencies may have a legitimate interest in keeping track of fiery religious and political radicals and their followers; it is another question entirely whether such people should be prosecuted for their speech. Democracies may want to fight those who do not believe in democracy but they should be reluctant to use the heavy hand of the criminal law lest they betray their own ideals and open themselves to criticisms that there are discriminatory double standards when it comes to democratic freedoms.

Canada's *Khawaja* case

In *R v Khawaja*, a trial judge in Canada held that the requirement for proof of political or religious motive with respect to crimes of terrorism constituted an unjustified violation of freedom of expression, religion and association. Rutherford J concluded that:

> [T]he focus on the essential ingredient of political, religious or ideological motive will chill freedom protected speech, religion, thought, belief, expression and association, and therefore, democratic life; and will promote fear and suspicion of targeted political or religious groups, and will result in racial or ethnic profiling by governmental authorities at many levels.[9]

Once he concluded that the political and religious motive requirement violated fundamental freedoms, Rutherford J then found that the government had failed to justify the limitation as a reasonable limit on those rights. He noted that the United Nations, the United States and a number of European countries have defined terrorism without a political or religious motive requirement. He also noted that the Supreme Court of Canada in *Suresh*[10] read a definition of terrorism taken from international law in to an otherwise undefined reference to terrorism in immigration law. Like Resolution 1566, that international law definition makes no reference to religious or political motive. He concluded that that the limit that the political or religious motive requirement placed on fundamental freedoms was not proportionate and had not been justified.

Although Rutherford J made no reference to the findings of the Arar commission in his judgment, the Arar report constituted part of the social backdrop of the decision. Justice O'Connor in the first Arar report commented:

> Although this may change in the future, anti-terrorism investigations at present focus largely on members of the Muslim and Arab communities. There is therefore an increased risk of racial, religious or ethnic profiling, in the sense that the race, religion or ethnicity of individuals may expose them to investigation. Profiling in this sense would be at odds with the need for equal application of the law without discrimination and with Canada's embrace of multiculturalism.[11]

In his second report, Justice O'Connor discussed the political and religious motive requirement as one of the factors that merited increased review of the national security activities of the RCMP, Canada's national police force.

Although designed to place an extra burden of proof on the state, the political or religious motive requirement could also contribute to a process in which investigators may 'lean towards increased inquiry and investigation based on religious and political beliefs. This could raise concerns about profiling in addition to the concerns about privacy and freedom of religion and expression'.[12] The political and religious motive provision required police to collect evidence about a terrorist suspect's religion and politics. The Arar report illustrates how the police could use this information to make inaccurate and unfair assumptions. The removal of the political and religious motive requirement is, of course, no guarantee that profiling or unfairness will not occur, but it is a step in the right direction.

The striking down of the political or religious motive requirement could also benefit those accused of terrorism offences and perhaps reduce the risk of miscarriages of justice in terrorism trials. If there is no requirement for proof of political or religious motive, the trial judge will no longer be required as a matter of law to admit evidence about the accused's religious and political views into the trial. Evidence of political and religious motive can distract and prolong a trial: turning it quite literally into a religious or political trial. The forced admissibility of political or religious motive evidence could also cause a jury to be exposed to prejudicial and inflammatory evidence about the accused's religious or political beliefs that may have little to do with whether the accused is guilty. Even if the correct result is reached, the process may be tainted by the admission of what should be irrelevant evidence.

Conclusion

Ben Saul argues that the inclusion of political and religious motive is necessary to distinguish private from public violence and to respond to the phenomena of terrorism which is in fact often driven by political and religious motives and extremism. In my view, it is possible to distinguish terrorism from other crimes without reliance on a political or religious motive requirement. Many definitions of terrorism require that the accused act with the intent to intimidate the public or compel governments or international organisations to act. This allows most crimes committed for financial gain to be distinguished from those designed to change governmental policy or scare the public at large.

Some might argue that requirements of intimidation of the public or compulsion of governments themselves constitute motive requirements. The differences between intent and motive can be slim. Nevertheless, intimidation and compulsion requirements differ in important respects from political and religious motive requirements. An accused's political or religious beliefs, the prayers that he or she says and the holy texts that he or she reads, lie at the core of the freedom of expression and freedom of religion. In contrast, beliefs that relate to the attempt to intimidate the public or compel governments to act exist more on the periphery of protected freedoms. A religious and political motive requirement authorises state inquiries into the deepest convictions and beliefs of the accused.

The closer that the definition of terrorism is to the basics of laws against murder and intentional injury that are accepted throughout the world, the less controversial anti-terrorism laws should be and the more consensus there should be on international definitions of terrorism. Overbroad definitions of terrorism are deficient not only from the perspective of protecting human rights, but also from the perspective of condemning terrorism. Overbroad terrorism laws that target the destruction of property or the disruption of essential services create an impression in civil society that those targeted as terrorists could include those involved in protest or civil disobedience. Overbroad terrorism laws that include religious and motive requirements play into dangerous ideas that the war against terrorism is a war against Islam as opposed to an effort to stop horrific violence against innocent civilians. The events of 9/11 and events in Bali, Madrid and London suggest that today's acts of terrorism do not involve activities that are on the margins of possible definitions of terrorism. Rather acts of terrorism involve the intentional murder and maiming of civilians that is intended to intimidate populations or compel governments to act. This should be the essence of any definition of terrorism.

Notes

1. *Suresh v Canada* [2002] 1 SCR 3, [98].
2. In *R v F*, the Court of Appeal rejected an argument that the *European Convention on Human Rights* was violated when British anti-terrorism laws were applied to acts of preparation for terrorism against the government of Libya and Colonel Gaddafi. It relied on the traditional idea that '[t]errorism is terrorism, whatever the motives of the perpetrators': [2007] 3 WLR 164, 172.
3. Ben Saul, *Defining Terrorism in International Law* (2006).
4. Lord Carlile, *The Definition of Terrorism* (2007).
5. Security Legislation Review Committee (Sheller Committee), *Review of Security and Counter-Terrorism Legislation* (2006); Parliamentary Joint Committee on Intelligence and Security, Parliament of Australia, *Review of Security and Counter Terrorism Legislation* (2006).
6. South African anti-terrorism law has added philosophical motive because of concerns that an anarchist or nihilistic terrorism might not be captured by British reference to political, religious and ideological causes: *Protection of Constitutional Democracy Against Terrorist and Related Activities Act 2004* s 1.
7. Lord Lloyd, *Inquiry into Legislation Against Terrorism* (1996) para 5.22.
8. Clive Walker, *Blackstone's Guide to the Anti-Terrorism Legislation* (2002) 21.
9. *R v Khawaja* [2006] OJ 4245, [73].
10. *Suresh v Canada* [2002] 1 SCR 3.
11. Commission of Inquiry into the Actions of Canadian Officials in Relation to Maher Arar, *Report of the Events Relating to Maher Arar Analysis and Recommendations* (2006) 356.
12. Commission of Inquiry into the Actions of Canadian Officials in Relation to Maher Arar, *A New Review Mechanism for the RCMP's National Security Activities* (2006) 438. The author served on the research advisory committee with respect to this report.

PART II

Criminalising Terrorism – How Far Should the Law Go?

5

The Effectiveness of Criminal Laws on Terrorism

Robert Cornall AO

A few days after the terrorist attacks in New York and Washington in September 2001, I was asked to chair a whole of government review of Australia's counter-terrorism arrangements. It was patently clear to everyone on that interdepartmental committee that our current arrangements were grossly inadequate. We recognised they were conceptually grounded in the past. They were designed to counter out-of- date terrorist threats, like plane hijacking and hostage taking. Put simply, we had to propose a new approach towards 21st century terrorism.

We handed our report to the National Security Committee of Cabinet by the end of October. Essentially, we made four groups of recommendations. They were to:

- increase resources to existing counter-terrorism agencies;
- consolidate some administrative functions to achieve a more cohesive outcome;
- make a wide range of security improvements (including in particular additional security at airports and the border); and
- introduce new laws to deal with this new type of terrorist threat.

It might be useful to define what I mean by 'new terrorism'. To me, its key features are that it has only a vague purpose, not a clear political objective; it deliberately attacks innocent citizens and non-military targets at random; and, as at least some of its perpetrators are willing to die for their cause, the prospect of punishment for a crime will have limited or no deterrent effect.

While on this question of definition, it is worth reflecting on the possible causes underpinning this lethal extremism. What is it that links disparate, disaffected groups across the world and inspires them to work with or emulate the terrorist acts of Al-Qa'ida and its affiliates?

I should state emphatically straightaway that none of the Australian government's policies are an attack on Islam. None of them are an attack on our Muslim citizens or neighbours. Australia's policies are a response to extremism that has hidden behind a perversion of what the Prime Minister has rightly described as one of the great religions of the world.

One analysis of the contributing causes is that, within the diversity of Islam, current radical strands share four broad features:

- a desire to return to an earlier, pure Islam, purged of outside influences;
- the aim to create Islamic states, and ultimately a pan-Islamic caliphate, ruled by strict Islamic law;
- a willingness to use violence; and
- a virulent anti-Westernism in reaction to grievances ranging from Muslim economic dispossession to what is seen as the contaminating influence of Western culture.

Radical Islam competes with other forms of Islamic belief. It provides not only a theology but also an explanation of Muslim disadvantage and how to address it. This perceived disadvantage includes concerns about cultural and economic globalisation and the power of the United States.

Western countries know they have to respond to both the consequences and the causes of these radical and misguided beliefs to discredit the ill-founded ideology that sustains them. But this will not be easy because this is, in essence – in the words of the former British Prime Minister – a battle of values and beliefs. In his address to the Australian parliament, Tony Blair said:

> It is a struggle about values and about modernity – whether to be at ease with it or in rage at it. To win this struggle we have to win the battle of values as much as arms. We have to show that these are not Western – still less American or Anglo-Saxon – values, but values in the common ownership of humanity, universal values that should be the right of the global citizen.[1]

The creation of new criminal laws and increased powers for intelligence and law enforcement agencies over the past five and a half years has provoked considerable controversy. It has called into question the proper scope and function of the criminal law. It has prompted concern about whether the new laws have gone too far in putting national security ahead of individual freedoms. It has called into question the effectiveness of the criminal law as a response to terrorism. I will attempt to reply to those issues in this chapter.

Purpose of the criminal law

A great deal has been written about crime and punishment. Surprisingly, it is not easy to define 'crime' despite the importance of the criminal law in our society. One simple definition offered by Peter Gillies is that: 'Crime is … conduct which is recognised by the law (as made by the courts and legislatures) as being criminal'.[2] However, he acknowledges, as do a number of other authors, that this definition is rather circular.

Other commentators prefer to define criminal acts by reference to their consequences, which leads on to a consideration of the purposes of criminal sanctions. In broad terms, those purposes include retribution, general and specific deterrence, rehabilitation, preservation of morality and incapacitation or prevention of harm to others.

The parliament has made terrorist acts and related conduct a criminal offence based squarely on those principles. The rationale for doing so includes all of those nominated justifications for punishment for criminal actions but in particular deterrence and incapacitation.

This basis for these offences has been accepted by the judges who have heard terrorism trials in Australia over the past few years. During the *Thomas* trial, Cummins J noted: 'In the matter of terrorism offences the principle of general deterrence is of pre-eminent importance'.[3] And in the *Roche* case McKechnie J quoted this observation from Lord Bingham: 'In passing sentence for the most serious terrorism offences the object of the Court will be to punish, deter and incapacitate; rehabilitation is likely to play a minor (if any) part'.[4]

Adequacy of existing laws

The next issue is whether the laws that existed in Australia on 10 September 2001 were adequate to respond to terrorism as it has manifested itself in the 21st century. The unambiguous answer from the government and from the parliament is that they were not. Australia had some counter-terrorism legislation before 2001, but it was very limited and directed to specific behaviour. That legislation had its origins mainly in international treaties dealing with particular types of threats like plane hijacking.

This is understandable. Australia was a very safe country, protected by geography and social cohesion from the disputes that lead to conflict, insurgency and terrorism in other, less fortunate, parts of the world. We did not need sophisticated anti-terrorism offences. We could rely – if necessary – on traditional State offences such as murder and causing grievous bodily harm.

But those offences are primarily directed at punishing an offender after the event. They are based on the assumption that, in most cases, the threat of conviction and punishment is an effective deterrent. In my view, they suffer from an almost fatal flaw when related to terrorism. They largely depend on the completion of an act – such as murder – before the offence is committed. How would the threat of imprisonment deter a suicide bomber?

The judges who have heard recent terrorism cases understand this new legislation is directed to making certain conduct a criminal offence before a terrorist attack occurs. In the *Thomas* trial, Cummins J said: 'such offences need to be prevented before they occur; not simply punished after the event'.[5] And in *R v Lodhi,* Whealy J expressed this similar view: 'The very purpose of the legislation is to interrupt the preparatory stages leading to the engagement in a terrorist act so as to frustrate its ultimate commission'.[6]

New legislation

The first batch of new counter-terrorism laws – following on from the October 2001 review – was passed by parliament in June 2002. Those laws make it a crime, among other things, to commit a terrorist act, to prepare to commit a terrorist act, to be a member of a listed terrorist organisation, to train with a terrorist organisation or to fund a terrorist organisation.

A 'terrorist act' is defined in the *Criminal Code* (Cth) as an action or threat which is made with the intention of advancing a political, religious or ideological cause with the intent of coercing or intimidating a government or the public and with consequences including loss of life or serious damage to property. However, a terrorist act does not include advocacy, protest, dissent or industrial action. A 'terrorist organisation' is an organisation which has been proscribed by the Attorney-General on the advice of the Australian Security and Intelligence Organisation (ASIO) or is found by a court to be a terrorist organisation.

The aim of the legislation is to create clear and specific offences relating to modern terrorism and to give intelligence and law enforcement agencies the capacity to intervene earlier than they could under the conventional criminal law. The focus on preparatory conduct is intentional and essential. Conventional offences (including murder and other serious harm offences, conspiracy and attempt) may still be relevant in some circumstances. But any analysis of the offences alleged in recent or current terrorism cases will show that much of the conduct alleged against the accused would not have constituted a criminal offence under our pre-2001 laws.

The steady stream of new terrorism laws since 2001 to better protect Australians from terrorism since the dreadful events of 9/11 culminated in the passage of two significant Anti-Terrorism Acts in late 2005. That legislation included provisions relating to control orders and preventative detention. A control order allows a court to impose restrictions on a person's movements or activities for the purpose of protecting the public from a terrorist act without that person having been convicted of any offence. Preventative detention allows a judge, magistrate or senior member of the Administrative Appeals Tribunal, acting in a personal capacity, to order a person to be detained for the same reason for up to 14 days (under a combination of Commonwealth and State laws), subject to compliance with a number of strict safeguards, once again without having committed a criminal offence.

Taken together, all of these anti-terrorism Acts represent the evolution of a whole new area of criminal law and law enforcement procedure.

Do these laws go too far?

This process has, of course, not been free from criticism. Many commentators see these laws as eroding established civil liberties and legal protections. They argue that they give intelligence and law enforcement agencies unacceptably intrusive and unjustified additional powers. However, many of the critics do not offer any constructive options or counter-proposals. Most of the time they simply argue, either directly or by implication, for the retention of the status quo.

This approach doesn't wash with *The Australian*, which has characterised some of the criticism as 'a polemical campaign by the legal and civil liberties lobby to delegitimise and strike down the recent provisions of the *Criminal Code*, a campaign enthusiastically embraced by sections of a gullible media'.[7]

The Australian government does not accept these criticisms either. It sees the new laws differently. It sees them as balancing civil liberties with its most basic responsibility to keep the whole community safe and secure. It recognises that the relationship between individual rights and community safety has altered since 9/11 but believes that it has achieved the right balance in the changed security environment.

In doing so, the Attorney-General has pointed out that these laws are consistent with the *Universal Declaration of Human Rights*, which states in art 3 that 'Every person has the right to life, liberty and security of person'.[8] The government's approach has been that individual rights have to sit comfortably with this overriding human right to which everyone in our community is entitled.

Other Western countries have taken a similar view. This point was made very eloquently by former Canadian Attorney-General Irwin Cotler, a leading civil rights lawyer who acted in the past for Nelson Mandela. Mr Cotler said:

> Indeed, as the United Nations put it, terrorism constitutes a fundamental assault on human rights – a threat to international peace and security – while counter-terrorism law involves the protection of the most fundamental of rights – the right to life, liberty and the security of the person – and the collective right to peace.[9]

And on 12 September 2006, the Hon John von Doussa QC, the President of the Human Rights and Equal Opportunity Commission, delivered an address at James Cook University in which he said:

> It is self-evident that terrorism is a gross violation of fundamental human rights. Only the misguided or the bad would suggest otherwise. The threat of terrorism is patently legitimate. The Government has both a right and duty to take action to protect its citizens.

This point is worth stressing. Governments have a duty to take action to protect their citizens.

In addition to this argument, I make four further points in response to these criticisms. The first is that there is nothing unusual about evolving or adapting the criminal law – like any other area of law – to meet changing circumstances. That happens all the time. Apart from counter-terrorism, some other notable areas of development of Australian criminal law over the past few years include legislation outlawing cybercrime, people trafficking, money laundering and child sex tourism.

The second observation is that changes were plainly necessary. Our existing laws had been drafted to meet different threats. They had become inadequate for the task. Journalist Paul Kelly put it this way: 'One sign of a mature democracy is its ability to change its security laws in response to an unprecedented threat to its society. What else would a mature nation do? Denial is not an option'.[10]

The third observation is that many other countries have also changed their laws to deal more effectively with the threat of modern terrorism.

The fourth, and most important, observation is that the changes to our counter-terrorism laws were the subject of intense public debate and parliamentary scrutiny. Anyone who has carefully followed the development of these new laws will know that there have been a number of parliamentary inquiries into the major pieces of counter-terrorism legislation over the past five years. The draft laws, as originally put forward, were amended by the government in the light of the parliamentary committee reports. They were also amended as a result of internal party consideration and negotiation with the opposition parties. In other words, the legislation was negotiated through a complex process that meant there was a considerable level of support for the final form of the new laws.

Let's look, for example, at the major package of counter-terrorism legislation passed by the Senate on 27 June 2002. The four bills passed at that time recorded 51 ayes, 12 noes – a majority of 39. Three years later, on 7 December 2005, the House of Representatives accepted Senate amendments to the Anti-Terrorism Bill (No 2) 2005 and, as there were only three no votes, the Deputy Speaker declared the question resolved in the affirmative. These statistics illustrate the support this legislation eventually had in the Australian parliament.

In the second reading debate on the Anti-Terrorism Bill, the then Shadow Attorney-General, Nicola Roxon said: 'Labor are convinced that the terrorist threat does require tough new laws, but we demand that their use be circumscribed carefully'. Later on, talking about amendments to the process for obtaining a control order, Ms Roxon said: 'These are very important improvements. They protect our basic freedoms without in any way compromising the effectiveness of the regime to fight terrorists'.[11]

These quotes from Ms Roxon's speech demonstrate that the changes made to the Bill resulted in it receiving Opposition support. The current Shadow Attorney-General, Senator Joe Ludwig, confirmed this position when I spoke with him at the Australian Legal Convention in March this year. When I told him I was speaking about control orders, he said I could say that 'the Opposition supports them'.

In addition, much of the legislation is underpinned by a referral of constitutional power from the States and some of it is reinforced by complementary Acts of the parliaments of the States and Territories. In short, these new laws are a very clear example of democracy in action. They have involved all Australian governments and parliaments in an extraordinary display of national cooperation.

Judicial consideration

Of course, passing new laws is only the first step in a process. Oversight by the courts is an essential element in determining their constitutionality, scope and proper application.

The judges who conducted the *Lodhi* and *Thomas* trials made a number of useful observations about the new counter-terrorism laws. Whealy J said in *Lodhi*:

> the obligation of the Court is to denounce terrorism and voice its stern disapproval of activities such as those contemplated by the offender here. … The community is owed this protection even if the obstinacy and madness of extreme views may mean that the protection is a fragile or uncertain one.[12]

Cummins J said in *Thomas*:

> Australia has a deep duty to protect its citizens from terrorism and so far as in its power to protect humanity from terrorism. That is why the Commonwealth Parliament enacted the laws against terrorism … and why the States of the Commonwealth likewise have enacted laws. The most fundamental right is the right to life. The law must protect that right. Australians are entitled to security. However, security is a necessary but not sufficient condition for a just society. Security is not enough. There must also be justice – for all citizens, including the weak, the marginalised, the unpopular and the alienated.[13]

Proper roles of the parliament, the executive and the courts

Some critics of the anti-terrorism legislation propose as an alternative to the present arrangements that the courts – rather than the executive – should exercise some powers, such as the proscription of a terrorist organisation. To my mind, those proposals blur the proper roles of the parliament, the executive and the courts.

Parliament has passed our anti-terrorism laws after very careful debate and consideration. It retains the right to monitor and, if it so decides, to amend or revoke them. In relation to proscribing terrorist organisations, the parliament supervises executive decisions taken by the Attorney-General through its power to disallow the proscribing regulations.

The executive implements the laws, taking decisions that are properly executive or administrative decisions. They include a timely assessment of the sufficiency of the information supporting a proposal to proscribe a terrorist organisation through direct dealings with ASIO and the Australian Public Service. In my view, these administrative decisions are properly made by the executive, not the courts.

It is also impractical to suggest they should be made by the courts after notice to all affected parties, on the basis of unrealistic criteria that are to be established beyond reasonable doubt and subject to possibly lengthy appeals. The proper role of the courts is to fairly and impartially interpret and apply the law and to correct or overrule any unauthorised action by the executive. This role sits comfortably with the positivist proposition set out by academics Simon Bronitt and Bernadette McSherry: 'Questions of what the criminal law is are primarily technical legal matters for the courts. Questions of what the law should be are political matters for the legislature'.[14]

Conclusion

Governments have to make decisions about difficult problems. They can't sit on the fence or be paralysed into inaction. These laws are an effective response to modern terrorism because they are working in practice. In fact, they are essential to provide an adequate legal basis to deal with this unprecedented terrorist threat.

New offences and criminal penalties are only part of a comprehensive governmental response to this complex crime. They must be accompanied by other measures directed at removing the root causes of modern terrorism and not just its terrible consequences.

Notes

1 Commonwealth, *Parliamentary Debates*, House of Representatives, 27 March 2006, 4 (Tony Blair, Prime Minister of the United Kingdom).

2 Peter Gillies, *Criminal Law* (4th ed, 1997), 5.

3 *DPP v Thomas* [2006] VSC 120, [14].

4 *R v Martin* (1999) 1 Cr App R (S) 477, 480 quoted in *R v Roche* (2005) 188 FLR 336, 358.

5 *DPP v Thomas* [2006] VSC 120, [14].

6 *R v Lodhi* (2006) 199 FLR 364, 373.

7 Paul Kelly, 'Clearly Crying out for Control', *The Australian,* 2 September 2006, 18.

8 For example, Commonwealth, *Parliamentary Debates*, House of Representatives, 24 June 2004, 31,701 (Philip Ruddock, Attorney-General).

9 Irwin Cotler, 'Thinking Outside the Box: Foundational Principles for a Counter-Terrorism Law and Policy' in Ronald J Daniels, Patrick Macklem & Kent Roach (eds), *The Security of Freedom: Essays on Canada's Anti-Terrorism Bill* (2001) 111,112-13.

10 Kelly, above n 7.

11 Commonwealth, *Parliamentary Debates*, House of Representatives, 10 November 2005, 80, 83.

12 *R v Lodhi* (2006) 199 FLR 364, 381.

13 *DPP v Thomas* [2006] VSC 120, [10].

14 Simon Bronitt and Bernadette McSherry, *Principles of Criminal Law* (2005) 16.

6

Preparation for Terrorism: Catastrophic Risk and Precautionary Criminal Law

Andrew Goldsmith

We live in anxious times. Consciousness of risk to our personal safety from a variety of sources, human and natural, permeates the media and public debates. Climate change and terrorism compete for media attention. What is to be done? Politicians and policy-makers look frequently to the law to provide reassurance in the face of public anxieties. The criminal law, however, has mainly focused on past wrongdoings – punishing offenders for what they have already done. Jihadist terrorism, in which the terrorists are prepared to die for their cause, seems unlikely to be deterred by the prospect of criminal punishment. Prevention, not punishment, is more likely to be reassuring for a concerned public. In the popular 2002 film, *Minority Report,* the audience witnesses events within a Department of Pre-Crime, a law enforcement unit dedicated to anticipating and pre-empting cases of imminent murder. The film's theme captures the idea that with respect to crime and terrorism, as well as matters such as public health, there is a clear policy preference for 'prevention' over 'cure'.

This chapter considers how capable the criminal law is in preventing terrorism. In particular, it focuses on activities that can be considered preparatory to the execution of terrorist acts. Arguably, acts that directly or indirectly contribute causally to a potential major terrorist attack should be considered for criminalisation. If such acts are the target of criminal offences themselves, police can arrest and prosecute people for these offences, rather than waiting for the commission of a major terrorist attack. Collecting materials for making a bomb is a pretty clear example of a preparatory act that most would agree should be criminalised if it is not already an offence. Providing a SIM card to a relative who is engaged in planning a terrorist attack, as the *Haneef* case recently showed, would seem far less clear cut in terms of constituting conduct worthy of criminalisation. Determining what is preparatory in this sense implies a capacity to predict what may eventuate if not prevented. It also implies taking a position on what degree of risk we are prepared to accept in balancing the desire for prevention (security) against the consequences for those deemed risky by whatever risk prediction tools may be at our disposal (liberty). Greater awareness of the risks of a major terrorist attack has prompted calls for a more preventive approach to counter-terrorism, yet prediction is an uncertain process here. By whom, when and how the next major attack will occur is very difficult to predict. Prevention therefore is linked to precaution – how do we act to prevent something when its very occurrence and nature is uncertain? A precautionary criminal law focused upon terrorism is one that, at least in part, tries to identify and criminalise acts that can be considered preparatory to terrorist attacks.

Two basic concerns arise regarding the use of the criminal law for preventive purposes. One is efficacy (can the criminal law indeed prevent terrorism?) and the other is fairness (is it just to use the criminal law for prevention?). While the criminal law has long played a part in preventing crime, as the centuries-long history of vagrancy, consorting and possession offences attests, its efficacy is not well understood by scholars and policy-makers alike. Yet this aspect has become more relevant amid calls for improved preventive capacity against terrorism. Concerns about fairness in preventive criminal law largely relate to the 'false positive' problem. In a precautionary climate, we are more likely to over-predict potential terrorists, causing hardship to those wrongly identified as posing a risk. Those opposed to expanding the criminal law to avert future dangers point to a recent shift from a culture of control to a culture of suspicion. The consequences of such a shift are themselves viewed by some as catastrophic. Criminologist Professor Richard Ericson, for example, takes the view that the impact of precautionary logic on the criminal law has rendered it 'a lost cause', adding that '[w]e are witnessing the end of criminal law'.[1] Other critics who do not go as far still express serious reservations about the implications of recent changes.[2] There are certainly sound reasons to be sceptical about these changes. Prevention, as noted earlier, raises questions about our capacity to predict future danger. Here, the record of past achievements by Western criminal justice and health systems is modest at best.[3] Within the criminal law itself, there has been an absence of sustained doctrinal or scholarly analysis in relation to preparatory offences generally, and specifically with respect to terrorism.

In this chapter I suggest that, while changed conditions in the security environment have supported a recalibration of the criminal law, Ericson's conclusion is somewhat overdrawn. I rely on recent criminological and social science understandings of contemporary jihadist terrorism in making my assessment. In looking at preparation for terrorism, my principal focus is on the changes to the Commonwealth *Criminal Code*, in particular the addition of specific terrorism offences in Divisions 100 to 102. There are a range of offences in those Divisions that focus on preparatory acts for terrorist attacks. There is not space here to look, for instance, at control and preventative detention orders, or terrorist financing legislation, which might also be broadly considered as preventative criminal law.

In the next section, I look at the concept of the precautionary principle in the context of catastrophic terrorism. Then, in some detail, I examine some key reforms to the *Criminal Code* that deal specifically with terrorism. My fundamental question is: Are these provisions justified given current threats? Here, counter-productive outcomes from expanded criminal liability must form part of any reckoning. In concluding, I enter some caveats in terms of how these substantive laws should be monitored and reviewed.

Preparing for uncertainty: Catastrophic terrorism

Counter-terrorist policies inevitably make assumptions about the nature and magnitude of the terrorist threat. Security agencies in Australia and elsewhere in the West inform us that, at the very least, Australia in mid-2007 continues to face the 'possibility' of a major terrorist attack from jihadist type groups, and that the authorities cannot guarantee that they will be able to detect and prevent such an attack.[4] The uncertainty surrounding what could happen – and thus the difficulty of assigning probabilities to various outcomes, and weighing of costs and benefits of particular counter-terrorist measures – profoundly challenges the policy-making process. As US national security analyst Anthony Cordesman has noted, 'there is no "standard distribution curve" of past events that can be used to predict the future' of a terrorist attack.[5]

Uncertainty here stems from a number of sources. The secretive nature of the activity is one. Terrorist groups and cells are very difficult to penetrate via human sources, and the ability of our law enforcement and security agencies to effectively monitor their various communications remains uncertain in itself, though significant steps to improve on the pre-9/11 position have been taken. Another major source is the force-multiplier effect available to small groups or even committed individuals through access to destructive technologies, including readily assembled highly lethal bombs, chemical and biological weapons and even, potentially, nuclear materials. One does not need an army or to conduct conventional warfare to exact major physical and psychological damage to a population. Hence, knowing how, when and who will launch such an attack lies at the heart of the challenge for counter-terrorist agencies.

Uncertainty regarding potential environmental disasters as well as catastrophic terrorist attacks has given rise among some scholars to the discussion of a 'precautionary principle' – the notion that if 'there is a potential for harm from an activity and there is uncertainty about the magnitude of impacts or causality, then anticipatory action should be taken to avoid harm'.[6] Its significance lies as a guide to decision-makers facing uncertainty about potential serious or even catastrophic harm. Because we don't know when something bad will happen, it tells us, we should take action of a preventive or pre-emptive kind. When harm is not just serious in scale but also thought to be irreversible, the case for adopting some form of this principle in setting policy becomes stronger. In terms of the burgeoning literature on risk relating to possible grave harms, we have arrived theoretically at the point of developing a 'Catastrophic Harm Precautionary Principle'.[7]

Applying such notions to counter-terrorist policy is hardly straightforward, and is likely to be controversial. As noted, concerns about false positives loom large, and the related danger that over-predicting particular populations as posing risk could create counter-productive outcomes (for example, group alienation and hostility to mainstream society) must be acknowledged. The choice of policy responses is always partly normative as considerations of justice and fairness, as well as of safety and prevention, are at stake. Figuring out a proportionate response to an uncertain risk is practically impossible. The consequences and benefits of any action may not be clear until much later or perhaps never, but policy decisions will have immediate costs and consequences for societies, communities and individuals, including for personal liberty and individual freedoms. On moral as well as pragmatic grounds, such consequences of anticipatory action cannot be ignored in any calculation of the case for such action.

Opposition to a more precautionary approach to counter-terrorism is sometimes grounded in comparisons of likely harm. For example, some suggest that a person is more likely to be hit by an asteroid than to die in a terrorist attack. Others point to the fact that terrorists in the past have rarely, if ever, unseated legitimate, liberal-democratic governments. The Cold War, others say, posed the risk of mutually assured destruction on a massive scale unimaginable by comparison with the harm demonstrated to date by transnational jihadists. In Australia and elsewhere, many believe politicians are exploiting public fears on this topic. Those largely convinced by these arguments are inclined to find traditional criminal law offences adequate to current challenges from jihadist terrorism.

Another perspective on the current uncertainty surrounding terrorism gives more credence to public concerns about further potential major terrorist attacks. It posits that the current situation is distinguishable from earlier terrorist activity and that the risks faced are different: in particular, the capability for terrorism is far more widely dispersed among small groups, whom are mainly unknown to security agencies, rather than large formal militaries, and therefore their potential threat is more immediate and likely to be more lethal than in the past. While more than 3000 people died in Irish terrorism over a 30-year period, a similar number died in around 30 minutes on 11 September 2001. 'Sleeper-cell' terrorism, largely a figment of the anti-Communist hysteria of the 1950s, has become a reality of 21st century jihadism. It has been accompanied by 'home-grown terrorism' in a number of Western countries in the past three years or so, since Madrid in 2004. Large quantities of materials used for making bombs have been discovered in the UK (Operation Crevice – 600 kgs of ammonium nitrate) and Canada (the 'Toronto 18' – 3 tonnes of ammonium nitrate), as have the uncovering of plans to attack infrastructure in Australia (for example, Faheem Khalid Lodhi). The alleged involvement of 13 men in Melbourne and nine in Sydney in planning terrorist attacks in Australia (Operation Pendennis) suggests that Australia's threat environment has changed, or at least that the grave dangers are now more apparent, even since the conviction of Jack Roche on a conspiracy to endanger lives charge in 2004.

Further support for a more precautionary approach arises from consideration of the subjective dimension of populations facing terrorism. This perspective accords the precautionary approach more weight than those who limit their analysis to relative physical harm or death counts, or those who see public fear as largely exaggerated. Cass Sunstein, an American professor of jurisprudence, has suggested that the 'effect of a catastrophe greatly outruns a simple multiplication of a certain number of lives lost'. He discusses the 'Buffalo Creek Syndrome', a set of psychological and sociological impacts on human communities in the aftermath of a disaster. These 'secondary social losses', as he refers to them, are an expression of the 'social amplification of risk', a phenomenon that is only beginning to be the subject of extensive study and research. Studies about the significant psychiatric and related stress problems in the aftermath of 9/11 are now emerging. As awareness of these effects is better understood, the case for 'catastrophe aversion' can hardly be dismissed as an unwarranted or clearly irrational ingredient of counter-terrorist policy in a democratic setting.[8]

An expanded role for criminal law in reducing the threat from terrorist attacks also finds support by comparison to other policy options, in particular the military option. An important argument for the use of criminal law is that it is measured, accountable and targeted, especially relative to the bluntness of military action and the covert (and hence less accountable) nature of many intelligence actions. Use of criminal law against suspected terrorists also serves to delegitimate the political validity of those resorting to terrorism, by treating them as criminals rather than 'freedom fighters'. Finally, another obvious reason for a more precautionary approach is the potentially catastrophic and irreversible nature of the threat: most would accept that the potentially extreme nature of the harm occasioned (say through a small nuclear bomb being exploded in a heavily populated area) and the difficulty of reversing such harm justify a more precautionary approach.

The next section examines recent changes to the *Criminal Code* directed at preparation for terrorism. Adopting a criminological approach, drawing particularly upon social network theory, my assessment attempts to match our understanding of the threat from violent jihadist terrorism with the preparatory offences in the Code.

The law enforcement response: Lessons from criminology?

Unfortunately, while there are fruitful analogies to be drawn with studies of organised crime groups and gangs, there is little if any empirical research specifically on jihadist groups within criminology. Studies of social movements and networks, particularly from political science and sociology, provide additional, much needed insights regarding the nature of the threat. The transnational character of the phenomenon is one reason for its relative neglect; empirical work on this topic is also difficult and dangerous for pretty obvious reasons. It is therefore useful to look beyond criminology and also consider recent journalistic investigations of jihadist groups and terrorism by persons of similar cultural and linguistic background.

I am less interested in the roots of terrorism or its underlying causes and more interested, from a law enforcement and criminalisation perspective, in identifying the sources of particular danger within contemporary terrorism as well as the structural vulnerabilities of these activities to law enforcement. Here, the empirical evidence pushes us towards consideration of not just actual or imminent threats, which are already well covered by the criminal law, but also of emergent threats. A commitment to prevention challenges the criminal law to look to those threats that are emergent, yet real in terms of the potential danger they pose. Such a focus is much broader in nature, raising real difficulties of classification and hence of determining the appropriate limits of criminal liability.

Another difficulty is that the organisational forms within which terrorist activities are encouraged, planned and executed differ in many cases from traditional organisational forms. We need to look beyond a 'Mafia Model' approach – that of a relatively stable, hierarchically organised body headed by an individual or small cadre providing critical direction and control of the organisation's illicit activities – to a more decentralised or 'networked' model. Today, analysts widely employ social network analysis, recognising the diffuse, changeable and often 'leaderless' nature of jihadist and similar networked groups.[9] Even a network analysis may have its limits, as terrorism becomes 'amateurised' and seen by some analysts to resemble spontaneous, viral activity.[10]

The following two propositions emerge from recent social science understandings of jihadist terrorism as well as from recent experience of this activity in several jurisdictions (including Australia), briefly discussed already. Each has implications for law enforcement and the scope of current *Criminal Code* offences.

Proposition 1

The first proposition is that terrorist networks have a core, a periphery and a context, each of which has implications for preventive law enforcement and broader counter-terrorism policy.

Criminalising the core

In network terms, terrorist groups will have 'critical nodes', ones that 'generally [have] a high level of importance and a low level of redundancy'.[11] These particular nodes (or 'hubs') will often reflect key leadership or direction roles, or possess unique skills within the network on which much of the success of the network's activities depends (for example, bomb-making). Attacking critical nodes makes sense because of the disruptive effect on lesser nodes that depend on them for resources and direction. Of course the transnational character of these networks means that international police cooperation and harmonisation of domestic laws are often necessary if these critical nodes are to be effectively targeted.

Here it is noteworthy that in the recent 'Melbourne 13' case, three charges appear to have been laid under s 102.2 (directing activities) of the *Criminal Code.* To date in Australia no other charges have yet been laid under this provision.

Criminalising participants

In addition to hubs, the *Criminal Code* directly targets the smaller nodes within terrorist organisations. Division 102 directly deals with the threat posed by terrorist organisations. Section 102.3 establishes the offence of intentionally or knowingly being a member of a terrorist organisation. This offence has been used recently against all defendants in the Melbourne 13 case, as well as against two people connected to the Tamil Tigers movement. A member can include informal members and people who have taken steps to join an organisation. Membership can be to an organisation 'directly or indirectly engaged in, preparing, planning, assisting in or fostering the doing of a terrorist act (whether or not a terrorist act has occurred or will occur)', or an organisation specified by regulation. A specified organisation may include one that 'advocates the doing of a terrorist act' ('whether or not an act has occurred or will occur'). 'Advocates' is defined extensively in the Act to include counselling or urging, providing instruction on, and directly praising, the doing of a terrorist act. The scope of advocacy is an issue that has generated much discussion. Yet, as discussed below, the role of advocacy is a key one in terms of the ideological determinants of terrorism.

How the courts interpret the membership offence remains to be seen, pending the resolution of the Melbourne 13 and Tamil Tigers cases. Parliament, undoubtedly on advice from the Australian Federal Police and other security agencies, has recognised that informal groups are significant agents in promoting terrorism and therefore need to be targeted, a conclusion that is consistent with informed understandings of the variety and nature of these groups. The legislation does not limit offences targeting membership to formally proscribed organisations, as is the case in the United Kingdom.[12] Traditional criminal law principles, however, have difficulty with status offences of this kind; on this basis, Canada has chosen not to criminalise membership. In Australia, the Parliamentary Joint Committee on Intelligence and Security (PJCIS) was sympathetic to this view, preferring the New Zealand offence of 'participation in a terrorist organisation' in place of the membership offence. It went further and queried whether participation in any revised offence should be linked to the purpose of 'furthering the terrorist aims of the organisation'.[13]

However, a participation offence may be too narrow to capture public personal endorsements of terrorist organisations through disclosure of membership. The symbolic significance of a well-known identity professing membership of a group may well be considerable within certain communities, in effect endorsing the activities of the group. The UK membership offence includes 'professing' to belong to a terrorist organisation, which would seem to capture such a disclosure. An offence of professing membership of a terrorist organisation (whether specified or not) combined with a further offence of participation (along the New Zealand lines) may well go to the 'mischief' behind such provisions without the breadth, or affront to general criminal law principles, of a purely 'status' membership offence, as is currently provided under the *Criminal Code*.

A key provision in terms of addressing the activities of persons engaged in terrorism-related activities is s 101.6 (other acts done in preparation, planning). This section has been used against Zeky Mallah, Faheem Khalid Lodhi, the Melbourne 13 (2 counts) and the 'Sydney 9' (conspiracy to commit). Despite concerns expressed to the Sheller Committee – an independent statutory committee – about the offence's apparent vagueness and breadth, it was satisfied that this offence was specified with sufficient certainty, a view not challenged by the PJCIS.[14] The Sheller Committee did recommend that 'threat of action' be excluded from the definition of 'terrorist act' so as to reduce the risk of acts 'simply preparatory to making a threat' being targeted. This provision clearly has the potential to sweep up a range of activities not otherwise covered by other provisions in the Act. The notion of 'preparation', more than the act of planning, is likely to engender a lot of discussion in particular cases about the connection between the relevant act and the advancement of terrorist objectives. How the courts approach this seems likely to evolve as more is learnt about the activities and methods of terrorist groups and individuals engaged in these activities. Traditional criminal law notions of 'proximity' and 'imminent danger', derived from the inchoate offences area of criminal law, are likely to be sorely tested as more is learned about the sophistication and potential to do significant harm of these groups, raising the prospects for further tackling emergent threats.

The 'the' to 'a' change

Another issue going to scope of activities covered by these provisions is the so-called 'the' to 'a' change, introduced by the Anti-Terrorism Acts of 2005. As the Sheller Committee noted, the amendments were prompted by 'concern that the preparatory acts could only be prosecuted, under the offences as originally drafted, if they pointed to some specifically planned terrorist attack'.[15] This change means that preparatory acts towards a terrorist attack not clearly determined in terms of time or place can nonetheless be criminalised.

From a preventive perspective, this makes considerable sense. A danger can have emerged, and even be imminent, without clear evidence of a particular target. The amendment was urgently sought and obtained in late 2005, and shortly followed by the arrests of the Melbourne 13 and the Sydney 9 in respect of what the media has called 'Australia's largest alleged terrorist conspiracy'.[16] This change affected, among others, the membership and preparation offences, both of which have been used against these two groups. The Sheller Committee concluded that, since the cases were pending at the time it reported (and remain pending at the time of writing) and the changes had been fully debated in parliament, it would be premature to comment on provisions affected by this change.

Criminalising the periphery

Next, while identifying the boundaries of networks (and hence criminalisation) is often difficult, attacking the boundaries makes sense in terms of limiting access into and out of that network. Finding ways to effectively restrain such activities as recruitment, training, provisioning and formation of more powerful constellations, or 'networks of networks', denies networks the capacity to sustain and grow their activities. Certain boundary types are relevant to this kind of analysis. In network theory terms, one can point to both 'extenders' – those whose role is to strengthen the network through recruitment and building relations with other networks and organisations, including governments (through corruption of individuals) – and 'cross-overs' – '[p]eople who have been recruited into a criminal network but who continue to operate in legal institutions, whether governmental, financial, or commercial'.[17]

Those at the periphery who act as experts and service providers in areas such as recruitment have been called 'human bridges'.[18] They frequently play a crucial role in introducing radicalised young Islamist cliques to terrorist networks, leading to training for, and sometimes engagement in, terrorist activities including suicide bomb attacks. Because these figures are peripheral in network terms, they may be hard to identify in some cases and not obviously covered by membership offences. According to terrorism researcher Dr Marc Sageman, 'they are probably where the members of the clique found them, namely around the mosques that traditionally send potential candidates to Afghan training camps'.[19] Recent evidence suggests that other meeting places, as well as mosques, often provide the setting for recruitment and other preparatory activities.[20] In the Australian context, one can consider the role the Ayub brothers played in the case of Jack Roche by socialising with and ultimately recruiting him for terrorist training in Afghanistan.[21] Such 'bridges' may on occasions prove useful as informants; however, preventing bridges and recruiting such people as informants would seem to require the ability to criminalise these activities.

The terrorism offences in the *Criminal Code* target these activities quite directly. Recruitment is covered by s 102.4, though no charges have yet been laid under this provision. The low visibility of such activities may be a factor here. The small in-group nature of latent jihadist groups and the wide range of their casual acquaintances within particular ethnic and religious communities make it hard to identify recruiters, especially given the lack of traceable formalities. Training, funding and providing support are also directly criminalised. The support offence (s 102.7) has generated considerable discussion regarding its breadth. The importance of such an offence from a law enforcement perspective is underlined by the fact that it appears to have been used relatively extensively by Australian law enforcement agencies – not less than 16 counts in the period 2002-07. The recent *Haneef* case, however, has drawn attention to the fact that mounting a case of 'support' can be difficult, especially when a suspect has, for some time before an attack, been located in another part of the world from those alleged to have carried it out.

What constitutes 'support' is not defined in the Act. The two inquiries in 2006 both expressed concern about its scope, in particular that it might cover words and not just material support, and therefore impinge on freedom of expression, including discussions in news media. The PJCIS recommended that the offence be amended to 'material support'.[22] 'Human bridge' activity such as providing specialist services (legal, financial, logistical, etc) would seem to avoid this concern by being sufficiently material. Specific training and financing provisions in Divisions 102 and 103 target some particular forms of material support, whereas s 102.7 would seem to play a complementary role. The importance of dealing with verbal encouragement and support for jihadist violence is considered further below.

Another specific 'periphery' offence is s 102.8 – the offence of associating with terrorist organisations. Like the membership offence but even to a greater degree, this offence has significant 'category-expanding' implications in terms of rendering potentially large groups of people suspect under the criminal law. Under this complex provision, an offence may be committed where a person 'on 2 or more occasions' intentionally and knowingly associates with a member of a terrorist organisation, the 'association provides support to the organisation', and that person 'intends that the support assist the organisation to expand or to continue to exist'. It is no surprise then that it received considerable attention from the Sheller Committee and the PJCIS, in part driven by submissions received by them about its difficulty of definition and complexity of proof. The Sheller Committee recommended the repeal of s 102.8 for a variety of reasons, while the PJCIS largely endorsed the Sheller recommendations and recommended review of this section.

The Attorney-General's Department sought to justify retention of the provision in the following way:

> The offence is predicated on the need to address the deplorability of the organisation itself by making associating with the organisation in a manner which assists the continued existence or the expansion of the organisation illegal. For example, the preliminary stages of recruiting a person into a terrorist organisation, or the lending of public support to a terrorist organisation in an effort to lend credibility to that organisation. Although more remote, such conduct can play an important part in the life cycle and growth of terrorist organisations. In recognition of the fact that relevant conduct is more remote, lower penalties apply to the association offence.[23]

The nub of the issue faced here is that the difficulty of identifying and targeting particular associations by individuals, thereby impinging on their freedom of association, does not detract from the importance of addressing the risks that these associations can pose. It might be that part of the mischief here would be addressed by a separate offence of professing an association, similar to professing membership as discussed earlier, where the act of professing is intended to assist the organisation to expand or exist. So long as these associations can provide inspiration and moral support for the continuation of terrorist organisations, there will be a case for preventive monitoring and occasional disruption of them. Inevitably, imprecision between criminalised activity and threat is greatest at this point, ensuring that the scope of offences will remain subject to controversy and debate. Close monitoring of these and similar offences between, as well as within, jurisdictions is therefore important to informing discussion in this area.

Proposition 2

The second proposition is that the context in which jihadist groups emerge and undertake terrorist activities is heavily ideological rather than formally structured in organisational terms, pointing to the central importance of shared values, common socialisation, effective bonds and modern communication technologies.

In networked terrorist groups, often operating in cell-like structures insulated from each other, 'doctrine or common purpose is more important than hierarchical leadership'.[24] The ready availability of cyber cafes and the internet has played a force-multiplying effect in terms of the ability of disaffected Islamists to reach out to jihadist ideas and terrorist tactics, and to connect generally with like-minded people, without regard to limitations of geography, race or citizenship. These technologies pose difficulties for law enforcement in detection as well as by expanding the pool of potential suspects. In addition to sharing strategies and tactics, there is also a narrative level evident in networks of this kind, whereby a particular story is being told that gives shape and meaning to jihadist beliefs and actions. American academics John Arquilla and David Ronfeldt suggest that dealing with doctrinal leadership is necessary to counter terrorist or criminal 'netwars':

> [T]he individual or set of individuals who, far from acting as commander, is in charge of shaping the flow of communications, the 'story' expressing the netwar, and the doctrine guiding its strategy and tactics.[25]

Doctrinal leaders within a terrorist network clearly meet the standard of a critical node or hub mentioned earlier.

It is not clear that such doctrinal leaders would readily be covered by s 102.2, which criminalises directing the activities of a terrorist organisation. As 'narrators' of a story sympathetic to the goals of jihadist groups, they may nonetheless remain distanced from operational terrorist activities and planning. If their principal role appears to be as a religious or other legitimate leader, the protection of freedom of speech may provide a cover. Policing the limits of these narratives is no easy matter. There may also be two narratives: one for public consumption and another for the private meetings with those undergoing indoctrination. Clearly, incitements to violence and other criminal acts can constitute crimes in themselves, but here we encounter the limits of inchoate offences. In particular, the requirement of a specific offence as the subject of incitement, attempt or conspiracy limits the scope of these offences, making them less effective in cases where speech broadly exhorts acts of a criminal nature rather than a particular crime.

Ideological leadership or the promotion of a jihadist narrative may be depersonalised, or at least mediated, through resort to written and other published materials, including videos and even computer games. The exponential enhancement of access to such materials provided by the internet is widely conceded by experts on contemporary terrorism. Prevention strategies in part require attention in respect of current proposals to tighten the national classification legislation.[26] Yet if we concede the vital contribution these narrative figures play in encouraging or facilitating terrorism (as informed observation tells us we must), we need, from a policy perspective, to consider how to deal with them. More may be learnt about the scope of the directing offence once the pending charges in the Melbourne 13 case are heard and determined.

Whether the support offence has application here is not clear. The PJCIS recommendation that the term 'support' be qualified by 'material' is directed at preventing 'mere words' from being sufficient to commit the offence. However, the same committee acknowledges that 'active engagement in propaganda activities could fall within the offence' as currently defined.[27] While the definition of 'terrorist organisation' refers to 'fostering the doing of a terrorist act' – meaning promoting or encouraging the doing of such an act – there must still be a connection established to one of the Division 102 offences to found liability. Distinguishing 'mere words' from propaganda remains a real difficulty under this legislation. It is a challenge that is not obviously well met by any of the current offences in Divisions 101 and 102. It is a problem that the PJCIS has acknowledged but not provided any real solution.

How prevention is reconciled with free speech is likely to present an ongoing challenge. It seems clear, however, that traditional civil libertarians will need to reckon with new insights on this question. There is a body of opinion emerging within Western Muslim communities, as well as from academic researchers, that narratives promoting the waging of violent jihad and the virtues of martyrdom as an expression of being a good Muslim are causally relevant in the promotion of violent jihadism against Western and Middle-Eastern targets. For example, according to Ed Husain in his book *The Islamist*, 'if you read the literature [the radical Islamists] keep for their private meetings, its aim is to attack the West, destroy Israel and to kill non-Muslims and Muslims who oppose [them]'. A drawback of the defence of 'free speech' for such actions, says Husain, is that it denies more moderate Muslims incentives for taking action against the promotion of violent jihadism, including reporting such activities to the police. So long as such activity remains legal, Husain argues, 'there's no point in ordinary Muslims who can identify it trying to combat it because we can't do anything'.[28]

Conclusion

The case for a more preventive criminal law to deal with the threat from contemporary jihadist terrorism has become clearer in the past three years. Our geographical isolation and alleged lack of a 'terrorist human infrastructure'[29] no longer apply – if they ever did – as reasons for not adopting counter-terrorist approaches similar to those adopted in the United Kingdom and Canada. Recent arrests related to the Melbourne 13 and the Sydney 9, as well as convictions in a number of other terrorism-related cases, should have by now put us on notice that greater preventive activity is justified.

While too much precaution comes with its own risks, too little effort in response to serious threats does also. Governments have historically been slow to react to low-probability, high-risk events.[30] Here, lawyers, law reformers and civil liberties groups have also been deficient in their assessment of the adequacy of pre-existing criminal law:

> Despite significant questioning by the [Sheller Committee] of a number of organisations [submitting that] the general criminal law would accommodate, particularly on a national basis, all types of terrorist activity contained in the legislation under review – *importantly the prevention of such activity* – this has not been demonstrated [emphasis added].[31]

The general criminal law, including inchoate offences, will continue indefinitely to play a role in dealing with imminent threats. Defining the extent of its involvement in what can be considered preparatory matters is likely to fall to legislative action, as evidenced in the *Criminal Code* amendments discussed here. While public opinion and political opportunism will continue to influence the policy process on counter-terrorism, empirically based assessments as well as scholarly analyses of the preventive role of criminal law are urgently needed to inform deliberations and choices. In this way, what is criminalised as 'preparatory' to terrorism can be subjected to greater checks than otherwise has been or would be the case.

Last, more effective targeting of preparatory offences requires that there be a new level of scrutiny and oversight in their operation. Risks of over-regulation, and counter-productive law enforcement, through an overly expansive concept of emergent risk, must be guarded against. Existing parliamentary oversight mechanisms need to be evaluated and, where necessary, further strengthened. This might in part be by providing them with their own enhanced research capacity. Other mechanisms of review were considered by the Sheller Committee, including an Independent Reviewer, as established in the United Kingdom and a Public Interest Monitor. Strict review timeframes and sunset clauses should be established and observed. In short, if a more precautionary criminal law is justified, its expanded preventive capacity should also be accompanied by more effective, and comprehensive, mechanisms for review of these laws.

Notes

1 Richard Ericson, *Crime in an Insecure World* (2006) 213.

2 Jenny Hocking, *Terror Laws: ASIO, Counter-Terrorism and the Threat to Democracy* (2004); Bernadette McSherry, 'The Introduction of Terrorism-Related Offences in Australia: Comfort or Concern?' (2005) 12 *Psychiatry, Psychology and Law* 279; Christopher Michaelsen, 'Antiterrorism Legislation in Australia: A Proportionate Response to the Terrorist Threat' (2005) 28 *Studies in Conflict and Terrorism* 321.

3 Mark Moore, 'Public Health and Criminal Justice Approaches to Prevention' (1995) 19 *Crime and Justice* 237.

4 Paul O'Sullivan, 'Strategy and Geography in the Current Security Environment' (Speech delivered at the Australian Strategic Policy Institute, 20 June 2007).

5 Quoted in Melinda Cooper, 'Pre-empting Emergence: The Biological Turn in the War on Terror' (2006) 23 *Theory, Culture and Society* 113, 123.

6 Carolyn Raffensberger and Joe Tickner, *Protecting Public Health and the Environment: Implementing the Precautionary Principle* (1999) 1; cited in Stephen Gardiner, 'A Core Precautionary Principle' (2006) 14 *Journal of Political Philosophy* 33, 36.

7 See Cass Sunstein, 'The Catastrophic Harm Precautionary Principle' (2007) 10 *Issues in Legal Scholarship – Catastrophic Risks: Prevention, Compensation, and Recovery* Article 3.

8 Ibid, 6.

9 Marc Sageman, *Understanding Terror Networks* (2004); John Arquilla and David Ronfeldt (eds), *Networks and Netwars* (2001).

10 Karin Knorr Cetina, 'Complex Global Microstructures: The New Terrorist Societies Theory' (2005) 22 *Theory, Culture and Society* 213.

11 Phil Williams 'Transnational Criminal Networks' in Arquilla and Ronfeldt, above n 9, 61, 93.

12 *Terrorism Act 2000* (UK) s 11.

13 *Terrorism Suppression Act 2002* (NZ) s 13; Parliamentary Joint Committee on Intelligence and Security, Parliament of Australia *Review of Security and Counter Terrorism Legislation* (2006) 73-4.

14 Security Legislation Review Committee (Sheller Committee), *Review of Security and Counter-Terrorism Legislation* (2006) 59-60.

15 Ibid, 149.

16 Associated Press, '9 Terror Suspects Plead Not Guilty', 31 May 2007.

17 Williams, above n 11, 83.

18 Sageman, above n 9.

19 Ibid, 178.

20 Ed Husain, *The Islamist* (2007).

21 Sally Neighbour, *In the Shadow of Swords: On the Trail of Terrorism from Afghanistan to Australia* (2004).

22 Sheller Committee, above n 14, 78-9; Parliamentary Joint Committee on Intelligence and Security, above n 13, 122-3.

23 Attorney-General's Department, Supplementary Submission to the Security Legislation Review Committee, February 2006, 3.

24 John Sullivan, 'Gangs, Hooligans and Anarchists: The Vanguard of Netwar in the Streets' in Arquilla and Ronfeldt, above n 9, 99, 105.

25 John Arquilla and David Ronfeldt, 'What Next for Networks and Netwars?' in Arquilla and Ronfeldt, above n 9, 311, 324-7.

26 Classification (Publications, Films and Computer Games) Amendment (Terrorist Material) Bill 2007.

27 Parliamentary Joint Committee on Intelligence and Security, above n 13, 78.

28 Peter Wilson, 'The enemy within', *Weekend Australian*, 16 June 2007, Review, 8, 9.

29 Michaelsen, above n 2, 333.

30 John Ikenberry and Anne-Marie Slaughter, *Forging a World of Liberty Under Law*, Final Report of the Princeton Project on National Security (2006).

31 Sheller Committee, above n 14, 140.

7

Australia's Terrorism Offences – A Case Against

Patrick Emerton[*]

Many different arguments could be given against Australia's anti-terrorism laws. When one considers aspects of the preventative detention regime, for example, or the power of the Australian Security Intelligence Organisation (ASIO) to compulsorily question, and in some cases detain, non-suspects, or the period of time for which a person arrested for a terrorism offence may be held without being charged, it is tempting to offer a rule-of-law-based argument. And those who have argued against these laws from a human rights perspective have suggested criticism based on the concepts of necessity and proportionality. But this chapter will come at the matter from a slightly different angle. It is written not from the perspective of a policy maker or risk analyst, nor from that of a practicing lawyer. My perspective is that of an academic lawyer and political philosopher who, as a member of the Anti-Terrorism Laws Working Group of the Federation of Community Legal Centres, is also an activist; and the chapter's chief concern is with the consequences of these laws – particularly the offences established in Divisions 101 to 103 of the Commonwealth *Criminal Code* – on Australians' political freedoms.

The chapter begins with an anecdote, which I take to be illustrative of the potential consequences of these laws. That anecdote will then lead into a more legal and theoretical argument.

Talking to Australian Somalis about Australia's anti-terrorism laws

In May 2007 I spoke at a meeting organised by members of Melbourne's Somali community. The impetus for this meeting was the reported remark of a Somali community leader in Sydney, that 'young Somali refugees in Melbourne are being seduced by Muslim extremists'.[1] My job was to explain, in simple language, the range of conduct that is criminalised by Divisions 101 to 103 of the *Criminal Code*. Section 100.1 of the *Criminal Code* defines 'terrorist act' in very broad terms, as including any action or threat of action meeting the following four criteria:

- the action is done, or the threat made, with the intention of advancing a political, religious or ideological cause;
- the action is done, or the threat made, with the intention of coercing, or influencing by intimidation, any government, Australian or foreign, or any section of the public of any country anywhere in the world;
- the action does, or the threatened action would:
    - cause serious physical harm, or death, to a person;
    - endanger the life of a person other then the one taking the action;
    - create a serious risk to the health and safety of the public, or of a section of the public;
    - cause serious damage to property; or
    - destroy, or seriously interfere with or disrupt, an electronic system;
- the action is, or the threatened action would be:
    - action that is not advocacy, protest, dissent or industrial action;
    - intended to cause either serious physical harm, or death, to a person;
    - intended to endanger the life of a person other then the one taking the action; or
    - intended to create a serious risk to the health and safety of the public, or of a section of the public.

As I explained to those at the meeting, this definition includes a good deal, perhaps the bulk of, actual, attempted or threatened politically or religiously motivated violence.

Divisions 101 to 103 of the *Criminal Code* then go on to criminalise any engagement in such acts or threats, a wide range of ancillary and preparatory conduct, and membership of or other involvement with any organisation that is 'directly or indirectly engaged in, preparing, planning, assisting in or fostering the doing of' such acts or threats.[2] These offences are all serious ones. Each has a maximum penalty of at least 10 years imprisonment, and several have a maximum penalty of life imprisonment. And all can be committed anywhere in the world, with no nexus to Australia required.

Section 102.1 of the *Criminal Code* also confers on the Attorney-General the power to list an organisation as a 'terrorist organisation', by way of regulation, if satisfied on reasonable grounds that the organisation is:

- directly or indirectly engaged in, preparing, planning, assisting in or fostering the doing of a terrorist act (whether or not a terrorist act has occurred or will occur);
- directly or indirectly counsels or urges the doing of a terrorist act (whether or not a terrorist act has occurred or will occur);
- directly or indirectly provides instruction on the doing of a terrorist act (whether or not a terrorist act has occurred or will occur);
- directly praises the doing of a terrorist act in circumstances where there is a risk that such praise might have the effect of leading a person (regardless of his or her age or any mental impairment) to engage in a terrorist act (whether or not a terrorist act has occurred or will occur).

The last three of these grounds are, somewhat misleadingly, characterised as the 'advocacy' of terrorism.

Once an organisation is listed, the same offences of membership and involvement are triggered in respect of that organisation,[3] as is a further offence of supporting the organisation by meeting or communicating with a member, promoter or director of it. The listing of an organisation also acts as a possible trigger for the issuing of a control order,[4] and affects the scope of liability under s 6 of the *Crimes (Foreign Incursion and Recruitment) Act 1978* by removing a possible defence.

My Somali audience was quite surprised to learn of the breadth of these laws. In particular, they were shocked that the laws draw no distinction between conduct undertaken in, or directed at, Australia and conduct undertaken in other parts of the world; that the laws draw no distinction between conduct undertaken by governments and by private individuals, nor between that aimed at soldiers and that aimed at civilians; that the laws draw no distinction between conduct undertaken in support of or in opposition to democracy; and that the laws draw no distinction between conduct undertaken aggressively or in self-defence. In short, the laws provide no avenue for consideration of whether the conduct undertaken might be morally justified.

The failure to draw such distinctions is particularly significant for Somalis, because (as is well known) Somalia has been wracked by civil violence for many years. It is currently subject to foreign intervention by Ethiopia, and has also been targeted by the United States. Ethiopia has justified its intervention in part by claiming that it is acting in self-defence, in response to support it alleges the Somali Islamic Courts movement have provided to Somali secessionists within Ethiopia.[5] (Several members of the audience I spoke to explained that the acts of Somali secessionists within Ethiopia are a response to various acts of discrimination and violence carried out by Ethiopian soldiers and officials against Somalis living within Ethiopia.)

In this context, many Somali families and clans quite plausibly constitute organisations that are directly or indirectly engaged in, preparing, planning, assisting in or fostering acts and threats of politically or religiously motivated violence. A result of this is that any Australian Somali who travels to Somalia in order to provide humanitarian assistance runs the risk of committing offences under Australia's anti-terrorism laws, in particular offences of providing training or funds, which is defined in s 100.1 of the *Criminal Code* to include all tangible, intangible, movable and immovable assets, and all forms of legal documents or interests evidencing title or interests. At around the time that this implication became clear to the audience members it became necessary to advise them against telling any more personal stories, for fear that some of these might be incriminating. Senior Detective Simon Artz of the Victoria Police Security Intelligence Group, who was also present at the meeting, agreed that this was sensible advice.

How broad are Australia's anti-terrorism laws?

Are Australia's anti-terrorism laws really this broad? It is tempting to think that they might be read more narrowly than has been suggested, keeping in mind some sort of common-sense understanding of what terrorism is, and of the goal of preventing such activity at which the legislation is presumably aimed. Kirby J, for example, during the course of argument in *Thomas v Mowbray*, suggested such an interpretation:

> [W]ould you not read – it says:
>
> > coercing, or influencing by intimidation, the government of the Commonwealth –
>
> et cetera. You would read that, would you not, as taking colour from each of those expressions and as meaning something more than a big demonstration by workers in Melbourne Federation Square. …
>
> Also, the words 'terrorist act'. I mean, you are not going to read the definition without regard to the matter that is being defined.[6]

For a number of reasons, I doubt that this sort of interpretive exercise will significantly narrow the scope of the laws, so as to exempt from criminalisation (for example) a Somali Australian who offers humanitarian support or training to the members of a Somali clan that is engaged in resistance against elements of the Ethiopian army.

Consider, first, what constitutes an *organisation* for the purposes of the Division 102 offences. 'Organisation' is defined in s 100.1 to mean a body corporate or unincorporated body, including a part of a larger organisation. To date, Australian authorities have interpreted this definition broadly, as including not only organisations such as Al-Qa'ida that are constituted in a semi-formal manner,[7] but quite informal organisations such as that allegedly constituted by those who have been charged in Melbourne following Operation Pendennis. This suggests that the threshold at which a collection of individuals becomes an organisation is quite low.

Secondly, consider the steps taken in the legislative drafting to exclude any connection to Australia as an element of criminality under Divisions 101 to 103: there is the express use of Category D extended geographical jurisdiction in each of the Divisions, the express reference to organisations based outside Australia or made up of foreigners and the express inclusion, as potential targets of terrorist coercion, of foreign governments and publics. Three people – Jack Thomas, Aruran Vinayagamoorthy and Sivarajah Yathavan – have been charged under Australian anti-terrorism laws despite the police acknowledging that no evidence suggests any attacks in Australia were planned.[8] It therefore follows that the mere fact that a country or conflict is relatively obscure, from the point of view of mainstream Australian law or politics, does not take it outside the scope of these laws.

Thirdly, the laws draw no distinction between either the perpetrators or the targets of violence, in terms of combatant or non-combatant status: a distinction that has frequently been regarded as central to the concept of terrorism.[9] As to targets, the inclusion of combatants as well as non-combatants is suggested both by the fact that a terrorist act can be characterised by an intention to intimidate a government, or a public, and by the fact that ASIO, in adducing evidence that various organisations have engaged in terrorist acts, has pointed to attacks on military targets and personnel.[10] As to perpetrators, the inclusion of combatants as well as non-combatants is suggested by the fact that s 6 of the *Crimes (Foreign Incursions and Recruitment) Act 1978* (Cth), which generally allows as a defence to the crime of incursion that the accused was serving with the armed forces of a foreign state, excludes from that defence a person serving with an organisation that has been listed. This provision thus clearly contemplates that the armed forces of a state might be listed as a terrorist organisation, and this in turn generates a clear implication that terrorist acts, as conceived of by the *Criminal Code*, can be perpetrated by soldiers as well as civilians. This implication is strengthened by the fact that the provision was introduced by the *Anti-Terrorism Act 2004* (Cth), which was enacted when the sole ground for listing was satisfaction on reasonable grounds that the organisation be directly or indirectly engaged in, preparing, planning, assisting in or fostering the doing of a terrorist act.

Fourthly, the offences of training with, or getting funds to or from, an organisation do not require that the training or the funding be itself connected to the perpetration of any act of violence. A number of considerations make this clear. First, there is the contrast between the text of ss 102.5 and 102.6, and that of s 102.7: the latter, but not the former two, requires that the criminal support be such as to 'help the organisation [engage in, prepare, plan, assist in or foster the doing of a "terrorist act"]'. Secondly, as to training, there is the contrast between s 102.5, which criminalises training with a 'terrorist organisation', and s 101.2, which criminalises the receipt or provision of training connected with preparing for, engaging in or assisting a 'terrorist act'. Section 102.5 would be redundant if it did not extend to training that is not so connected.[11] Thirdly, as to funding, there is the contrast between s 102.6, which criminalises the receipt of funds from or the making of funds available to a 'terrorist organisation', and ss 103.1 and 103.2, which criminalise the provision or collection of funds while being reckless as to whether the funds will be used to facilitate or engage in a 'terrorist act'. This contrast generates a strong implication that the offence created by s 102.6 can be committed although the funds are not themselves linked to political violence. This conclusion is also supported by the fact that it appears to be necessary to explain the outcome in the trial of Jack Thomas, who was acquitted by a jury of two counts of providing support or resources under s 102.7, but was found guilty of receiving funds under s 102.6.[12] This outcome seems to indicate that liability under s 102.6 in any particular case does not depend on the presence of any terroristic intention.

I therefore conclude that Australia's anti-terrorism laws are as broad as the initial sketch of them suggested – members of the Somali community (and of many other Australian communities) are right to be concerned that these laws have the potential to criminalise what hitherto they have taken to be quite ordinary aspects of their ongoing relationships with families and communities outside Australia.

The role of official discretion

At this point it might be objected that, whatever the theoretical possibility that a number of Australians might be committing serious offences under Australian law, the practical reality is that they will never be charged: investigatory and prosecutorial discretion will be exercised in their favour.

The first response to this objection is that it can only get off the ground if the point about breadth is conceded, such that the exercise of discretion becomes crucial to the practical operation of these laws (in a way that it is not, for example, with respect to the law of murder – we expect every killing to be investigated and, where evidence of murder exists, to be prosecuted).[13] Russell Hogg has noted this centrality of discretion to the operation of these laws:

> [T]he laws are not so much designed to guide citizen conduct; to a significant extent they are incapable of doing that with vague, undefined terms such as 'support' or 'membership', including informal membership. They are essentially designed to empower officials, often enabling the threat of prosecution to be used to compel cooperation that escapes legal scrutiny.[14]

The second response to the objection is that, as a prediction about the future course of official activity it may be true, or it may not be: given that these laws have been in operation for only a short period of time, it is impossible to tell. Introduced in response to Al-Qa'ida's attacks on New York and the Pentagon, they have already swept up in their net Australia's Kurdish and Tamil communities.[15] These examples demonstrate that the operation of Australia's anti-terrorism laws, as mediated through exercises of official discretion, can have a profound impact on many Australians' political activities and expressions of communal identity.

More important for the argument in this chapter, however, is the consequence for political democracy of the existence of these discretions, and the implication that their exercise has for the enjoyment by many Australians of political and social freedoms that they have hitherto taken to be part and parcel of living in a pluralist democratic society. Because of the sorts of activity that these laws criminalise – political, religious and ideological, and particularly organised political, religious and ideological activity – it is crucial that they be applied in a way that does not undermine their own democratic legitimacy.

It goes without saying that even in the most democratic community freedom cannot be total. Violence, in particular, must be regulated and in many cases prohibited: this can be seen as a particularly trivial application of Mill's well-known 'harm principle'; that is, that 'the only purpose for which power can be rightfully exercised over any member of a civilised community, against his will, is to prevent harm to others'.[16] However, for several reasons an appeal to this basic principle is not sufficient to justify Australia's anti-terrorism laws.

First, these laws are not aimed simply at protecting Australia from violence. They could, therefore, be justified only by some globalised application of the harm principle, as has been suggested by some members of the Parliamentary Joint Committee on Intelligence and Security.[17] But the way in which official discretion has in fact been exercised rules out its justification by reference to a global harm principle. For in relation to a number of conflicts, it is only one of many harm-inflicting organisations that has been targeted by these laws. Thus, in relation to the conflict over the Palestinian Territories, both Palestinian Islamic Jihad and Hamas' Izz al-Din al-Qassam Brigades have been listed as terrorist organisations, but no agency of the Israeli state has been so listed. Likewise in relation to the conflict between Israel and Lebanon: Hizballah's External Security Organisation has been listed, but no agency of the Israeli or Lebanese state has been. The same is true in relation to the conflict in Sri Lanka. Following the arrest of two men for their alleged connections to the Liberation Tigers of Tamil Eelam a member of the Sri Lankan government predicted further such arrests in Australia.[18] There has been no suggestion from Australian officials that agencies of the government of Sri Lanka, responsible for a great deal of harm,[19] will also be looked at through the lens of the anti-terrorism laws, and the comments from the Sri Lankan government suggest that they do not anticipate any such change in perspective.

A second reason for concluding that the operation of these laws cannot be justified by appeal to the need to prevent violence is that, as we have noted in relation to the organisational training and funding offences, the laws impose liability in circumstances which may be far removed from any actual or threatened acts of violence. Indeed, given the breadth of the notion of 'indirectly fostering', it seems that *all* of the organisational offences might be committed in circumstances where there is only the remotest of connections between the organisation in question, and any actual or threatened act of violence.

It is, in any event, far from clear that the harm principle justifies the prohibition of all political violence. For if we put to one side a position of principled pacifism (which is certainly not one to which the Australian polity, with its long history of military and other official violence, can consistently appeal), not all violence can be regarded as inconsistent with democratic politics. In particular, violence is often an important means of *achieving* democratic government. Ted Honderich emphasises this point:

> It is remarkably easy, if one has always been a member of a group that attained freedom and power long ago, to think that groups who have not, and who struggle for autonomy, are in fact pursuing something not worth the shedding of blood. It is also remarkably easy, if one has always been a member of an autonomous group, to count the worth of autonomy for little as against the worth of … some material level of well-being, or peace. … There is a clear unreality about this. … [T]here is some kind of absurdity in trying to devalue [autonomy]. Something for which sane and admirable men have always been willing to risk and to accept death, torture, punishment … is something worth having if anything is.[20]

Certainly, we do not expect the French or American republics to repudiate the violent revolutions that are the foundations of their contemporary democracies. And, consistently with this, we cannot deny that other contemporary actors might have comparable grounds for violently pursuing their own self-determination.

But there is no connection between the exercise of official discretion pursuant to Australia's anti-terrorism laws, and the support of democratic struggles or the prevention of the suppression of democracy. This is shown by the approach taken towards the Kurdistan Workers' Party and the Tamil Tigers, which has not been responsive to the circumstances of the conflicts to which these organisations are party, and their claims, vindicated to some extent at least by the failure to crush them of the governments that they oppose, to be acting in pursuit of national self-determination. As Michael Walzer observes:

> A civil war is the sign of a divided society. As an extended insurrection indicates popular support for the rebels ... so an extended resistance to insurrection indicates popular support for the government.[21]

Given this, respect for democracy requires non-intervention by foreigners, who should defer to the political process (violent or otherwise) unfolding in the society in question. For foreigners to intervene would be for them to impose their own political history and culture on another people which is yet to determine its own fate in accordance with its own history and culture. Although Walzer has in mind primarily military intervention, similar considerations weigh against the use of criminal law to discriminate between parties to an ongoing civil conflict.

The failure of democratic considerations to support the exercise of official discretion pursuant to Australia's anti-terrorism laws is also shown, in a slightly different way, by the listing of Hamas' Izz al-Din al-Qassam Brigades and Hizballah's External Security Organisation as terrorist organisations. For both of these organisations enjoy a degree of democratic legitimacy, Hamas having been elected the government of the Palestinian Territories (and now enjoying largely uncontested control of Gaza) and Hizballah being a participant in the electoral process in Lebanon, and enjoying representation in that country's legislature and government.

I therefore conclude that the official discretion which determines, as a practical matter, the operation of Australia's anti-terrorism laws, is not guided by an application of the harm principle at either a domestic or a global level. Nor is it guided by a commitment to the defence or furtherance of democracy. Whatever political ideals are driving it, then, they would seem to be ones which any individual Australian could reasonably reject, while nevertheless remaining a fully-committed participant in Australia's own political democracy. Furthermore, those ideals are being determined and applied not as part of a public political debate, but to a great extent in secret, through the determinations of security and investigatory agencies as to which sorts of political activities will be subject to investigation (and, hence, to prosecution) and which will not. The role of ASIO, in particular, is of great concern: a democratic culture simply cannot thrive when a necessarily clandestine security agency is given a significant degree of power to determine which political outlooks are legitimate, and which are not, and are liable to lead to criminal prosecution.

It is this usurpation of the public political process by agencies of the state, acting by means of the discretions conferred on them by Australia's broad anti-terrorism laws, that constitutes a grave objection to these laws. Their operation, and this consequence of that operation, is not consistent with pluralist democracy. It undermines much of what is valuable in Australian political culture.

Conclusion

I conclude this chapter with some remarks from two supporters of Australia's anti-terrorism laws. I take these remarks to vindicate the case I have presented against those laws.

Recently, the Commonwealth Attorney-General discussed the extent to which Australians are travelling overseas to engage in 'extremist activity':

> There are a variety of motivations for that engagement (overseas). Some of it is because very vulnerable and susceptible people are influenced by certain types of preaching and the like.
>
> And that is in addition to what you might normally see ... where people haven't sufficiently disconnected from hostilities that exist with their own cultural or country of origin.[22]

In a pluralist democracy, however, there is no general reason for holding that people should disconnect from hostilities within their own culture or country of origin, at least where such connections do not threaten democracy either at home or abroad. Australian history is replete with examples where just such connections have been maintained: the Sudan, the Boer War and the two World Wars, for instance. And not all Australians are expected today to engage in such disconnection: when Australian Israeli Assaf Namer was killed in the 2006 conflict between Israel and Lebanon, no Australian official suggested that he had failed to properly sever his connections to hostilities in Israel. Indeed, the Minister for Foreign Affairs offered his condolences to the man's family.[23] The discriminatory exercise of official discretion that is reflected in the Attorney-General's remarks is precisely at odds with the values of pluralist democracy.

I recently put the argument, that in a liberal democracy political questions ought to be resolved through the public political process, and not by the operation of the criminal law as directed by the (frequently clandestine) exercise of official discretions, to the Parliamentary Joint Committee on Intelligence and Security, in the course of the committee's hearings in relation to the process of listing terrorist organisations. The following observation in response was made by Steven Ciobo, a government member of the House of Representatives:

> I feel that the executive, and government in the executive sense of the word as well, have taken a decision about what we believe is appropriate ideology and what is inappropriate ideology and that the legislation reflects the decision that we have taken.[24]

Let us put to one side the fact that the legislation is silent on these matters, and that it is the operation of official discretions that determines which ideologies are appropriate in Australia, and which are not. Having put that detail to one side, I have no reason to doubt that what Mr Ciobo said is true. I do not believe, however, that it refutes the argument made in this chapter.

Notes

* I would like to thank Pratheepan Balasubramaniam, Marika Dias, Kushanthi Harasgama, Jane Hearn, Jayani Nadarajalingam, Annie Pettitt, Vicki Sentas and Joo-Cheong Tham for many helpful discussions on the subject matter of this chapter.

1 The remark is attributed to Herse Hilole, 'a Sydney community leader and Islamic scholar' in Barney Zwartz, 'Local Somalis "terror recruits"', *The Age*, 13 April 2007, 1.

2 The quote is from para (a) of the definition of 'terrorist organisation': *Criminal Code* (Cth) s 102.1. The offences in Div 102 include being a member of such an organisation, directing its activities, recruiting for it, training with it, getting funds to or from it, or providing it with support or resources that would help it to directly or indirectly engage in, prepare, plan, assist in or foster the doing of a terrorist act. It does not matter whether or not the organisation is based outside Australia or consists of persons who are not Australian citizens: *Criminal Code* (Cth) s 100.1(1).

3 In the case of the training offence, if an organisation is listed as a terrorist organisation the offence takes on a quasi-reverse onus character, whereby the prosecution need not prove any fault on the part of the accused unless the latter is able to adduce evidence as to the absence of recklessness on his or her part: *Criminal Code* (Cth) s 102.5.

4 *Criminal Code* ss 104.2(2)(b), 104.4(1)(c)(ii).

5 Stephanie McCrummen, 'Ethiopia Steps up Attacks on Somalia; Planes Strike Airport; Refugees Flee to Kenya', *The Washington Post*, 26 December 2006, A01.

6 [2006] HCATrans 661 (6 December 2006). In his judgment in the case, Kirby J appears to accept the broad scope of the legislative definition of terrorist acts: *Thomas v Mowbray* [2007] HCA 33, [263]-[266].

7 ASIO describes Al-Qa'ida as 'a loose-knit grouping of individuals and organisations that espouses a violent Islamic extremist ideology … founded, and … led at all times, by Usama Bin Laden': cited in Parliamentary Joint Committee on ASIO, ASIS and DSD, Parliament of Australia, *Review of the Listing of Six Terrorist Organisations* (2005) 24.

8 Tom Allard, 'No Evidence on Thomas, Police Admit', *The Age*, 22 September 2006, 3; Australian Federal Police, 'Two men charged with terrorism offences' (Press Release, 1 May 2007).

9 For a discussion of this matter drawing on the traditions of just war theory, see CAJ Coady, 'The Morality of Terrorism' (1985) 60 *Philosophy* 47.

10 As reported by the Parliamentary Joint Committee on ASIO, ASIS and DSD; for example, above n 7, 40 (pertaining to the Armed Islamic Group), 45 (pertaining to Jamiat ul-Ansar), 49 (pertaining to the Salafist Group for Call and Combat).

11 This point is noted in *Thomas v Mowbray* [2007] HCA 33, [482] (Hayne J).

12 The conviction was later quashed on appeal and Thomas is facing a retrial on the basis of new evidence: *R v Thomas* (2006) 14 VR 475; *R v Thomas (No 3)* (2006) 14 VR 512.

13 Some marginal cases of euthanasia might provide an exception to this general expectation.

14 Evidence to the Parliamentary Joint Committee on Intelligence and Security, Parliament of Australia, Canberra, 4 April 2007, 16.

15 The Kurdish Workers' Party is a listed terrorist organisation and in May 2007 two men were arrested in Melbourne, charged with involvement with the Liberation Tigers of Tamil Eelam.

16 John Stuart Mill, *On Liberty* (1859, Everyman's Library edition with *Utilitarianism* and *Representative Government*, 1910) 73.

17 Transcript of Hearings of the Parliamentary Joint Committee on Intelligence and Security, Parliament of Australia, Canberra, 4 April 2007, 22, 44 (Senator Robert Ray), 45 (Duncan Kerr).

18 'Sri Lanka FM Tips More Arrests', *The Australian*, 2 May 2007 <http://theaustralian.news.com.au/story/0,20867,21657994-421,00.html> at 3 July 2007.

19 For recent reports of increased extra-judicial abductions and killings by agencies of the Sri Lankan government, see Mian Ridge, 'No middle way for Sri Lanka's militant monks', *The Age*, 16 June 2007; Dylan Welch, 'Dark Days in Paradise', *The Sydney Morning Herald*, 30 June 2007.

20 Ted Honderich, *Terrorism for Humanity: Inquiries in political philosophy* (2003) 191. John Rawls agrees that violence becomes permissible when other means of achieving justice will be ineffective: *A Theory of Justice* (1971) 366, 390-1.

21 Michael Walzer, 'The Moral Standing of States: A response to four critics' (1980) 9 *Philosophy and Public Affairs* 209, 221.

22 Nick McKenzie and Sarah Smiles, with Ed O'Loughlin 'Australians travel for terrorism, says Ruddock', *The Age*, 30 June 2007, 1. The phrase 'extremist activity' is used by the journalists, but not by the Attorney-General.

23 Emma Griffiths, 'Israel mulls wider offensive after soldiers' deaths', *ABC News Online*, 27 July 2006 <http://www.abc.net.au/news/newsitems/200607/s1698921.htm> at 3 July 2007.

24 Transcript of Hearings of the Parliamentary Joint Committee on Intelligence and Security, Parliament of Australia, Canberra, 4 April 2007, 36.

8

Reconciling Security and the Right to a Fair Trial: The National Security Information Act in Practice

Stephen Donaghue

It is easy to conceptualise the tension between fair trials and national security in grand terms; to imagine the courts being confronted with a clash between a serious threat to national security and a demand for information upon which the innocence of an accused depends.

In reality, the issues are rarely so stark. National security issues most frequently arise in practice when accused persons subpoena classified documents that they have not seen, but that they hope will assist their case. Very often that attempt will be successfully met with the objection that the accused is 'fishing' for a case, but if that objection fails the documents in question will be assembled by the agency that received the subpoena. At that point, it usually becomes clear that the documents will be of no assistance to the accused. At the same time, however, it also becomes clear that the accused cannot be shown the documents in their entirety, sometimes because of the sensitivity of the information in the documents themselves, but more often because of national security concerns relating to the source of the information or the prospect that it could be combined with other sensitive information in a way that would damage national security.

In the above situation, if the issue is litigated the court will uphold the claim that documents should not be produced for the simple reason that, once the national security information that is sought by the accused is identified, it is clear that it would not assist the defence. There can be no interference with a fair trial if a court refuses to order the production of documents that are irrelevant to the issues in the trial, or that are relevant but that actually tend to undermine the defence case.

That said, the accused cannot be expected to take the Commonwealth's word that documents he or she has sought pursuant to a subpoena will not assist the defence. Further, sometimes the documents sought will be relevant to the defence, and in some cases classified material may form part of the prosecution case. For those reasons, there is a process that must be followed in order to determine the way in which information that may prejudice national security may be used in court proceedings. In Australia, that process is now heavily influenced by the *National Security Information (Criminal and Civil Proceedings) Act 2004* (Cth) (NSI Act).

This chapter focuses on three issues that have assumed some significance in practice in relation to the operation of that Act. They are, first, the circumstances in which the Act should be invoked; secondly, the significant role of consent arrangements under that Act; and thirdly, the requirements that the Act imposes in relation to security clearances.

The circumstances in which the Act should be invoked

There is sometimes a tendency to assume that, now that the Commonwealth has enacted the NSI Act, it should be applied in every court proceeding that relates to national security. In this chapter I argue that that assumption is wrong, and that the NSI Act should be invoked only in cases in which either the prosecution or defence case depends on tendering classified material. In all other cases, the disadvantages of applying the Act outweigh the advantages. That argument has a number of steps.

The starting point is the definition of 'national security' upon which the Act is built. Section 8 defines that term very widely, in a way that picks up a number of other defined terms. By reason of s 9, the Act picks up, as one part of the definition of 'national security', the definition of 'security' in s 4 of the *Australian Security Intelligence Organisation Act 1979* (Cth). That definition includes, amongst other things, 'politically motivated violence', which in turn is defined to include 'terrorism offences'. It follows that anything that relates to a terrorism offence relates to national security for the purpose of the NSI Act.

The NSI Act does not apply of its own force simply because a proceeding involves the potential disclosure of national security information. Instead, s 6 makes it clear that the Act applies in a particular criminal proceeding only from the point at which the Director of Public Prosecutions (DPP) gives notice to the defendant and the court that the Act applies. That can be done either at the start of the proceeding, or later.

Anyone who has participated in a proceeding in which the NSI Act applies would accept that that Act has costs for the smooth functioning of the proceeding. Those costs arise principally from the possible operations of ss 24 and 25.

Section 24 is a notice provision that is directed primarily to circumstances that exist before the trial. It provides that a party must notify the Attorney-General if that party knows or believes that information that *relates to*, or the disclosure of which *may affect*, national security may be disclosed in the proceeding. Once such a notice is given, the proceeding must be adjourned until the Attorney-General responds to it.

Section 25 applies if, during the trial, the prosecutor or defendant knows or believes that a witness may give an answer that will disclose information that relates to or may affect national security. On forming that belief, the prosecutor or defendant must inform the court, which must then order that the court be closed. The witness is then instructed to provide a written answer to the question. That answer is shown only to the prosecutor. The prosecutor must then advise the court if the answer relates to or may affect national security. If so, the court must adjourn the proceeding to allow notice to be given to the Attorney-General, and to await the Attorney's response. That process must be followed each time a question is asked that relates to, or may affect, national security, subject to the discussion below concerning consent arrangements. Its potential for disruption is obvious.

The low notification thresholds contained in ss 24 and 25 (that is, 'relates to' or 'may affect' national security) were intended to cast the notification net widely, so that the Attorney-General would have an opportunity to consider all of the issues that may give rise to national security problems. In practice, however, the notice provisions have not functioned as was intended. One of the reasons for that is that the low thresholds at which the notification obligations arise, when combined with the width of the definition of 'national security', mean that notice is required in relation to an enormous range of matters. In a terrorism case, for example, virtually any evidence that is relevant to the trial (including all the evidence in the brief) would relate to national security, for the simple reason that it relates to a terrorism offence. Yet a s 24 notice that referred to the entire brief would not be useful in identifying the possible disclosures that require the Attorney's attention.

A further difficulty with the s 24 procedure is that it is very common for defence lawyers to issue notices under s 24 that are so general as to lack any utility, probably in order to avoid being compelled to reveal their defence in advance of the trial. There is little that can be done under the Act to require improved notification. In practice, therefore, the notice provisions provide little assistance in identifying the national security issues that will arise in a particular case.

It might be thought important to invoke the NSI Act in national security cases because the Act will assist the Commonwealth in preventing the disclosure of information that will damage national security. There is, however, real doubt as to whether the NSI Act provides significant advantages in that regard beyond those available under the common law.

Traditional public interest immunity claims are, in the vast majority of cases, just as effective as the NSI Act in preventing any disclosure of information that is likely to prejudice national security. The case law has for a long period made it clear that the public interest in national security will ordinarily prevail over competing public interests, and that in undertaking any balancing process the court will give great weight to the view of the executive as to what national security requires.[1] In recent years the courts have emphasised that point, observing that the 'interest[s] of national security and effective intelligence operations … , especially in an age of heightened terrorist activity, are plainly of great importance'.[2]

Not only is a traditional public interest immunity claim ordinarily just as effective as an NSI Act claim, it also has three practical advantages over such a claim. First, public interest immunity claims do not require the personal involvement of the Attorney-General, but can be made by a senior departmental official or by the head of the agency from whom a document is sought. They may therefore be able to be made more quickly than NSI Act claims. Secondly, public interest immunity claims can often be heard in public, whereas claims made under the NSI Act must be held in private (s 29). Thirdly, a public interest immunity claim does not require the adjournment of the entire proceeding while the claim is prepared, but it is arguable that ss 24 and 25 of the NSI Act do require such an adjournment.

The principal difference between the NSI Act procedure and a common law public interest immunity claim is that the NSI Act contains a statutory direction as to the weight that should be given to national security when the court comes to balance the competing public interests. That direction is found in s 31(8), which provides that 'the Court must give greatest weight' to the Attorney-General's certificate. It is not clear whether that provision involves a significant departure from the common law test, which already provides that claims by the executive as to the requirements of national security must be given great weight. If it does then, as former High Court Justice Michael McHugh has argued, that may imperil its validity under Chapter III of the Constitution.[3] That argument is among those to be argued before the NSW Court of Criminal Appeal as part of an appeal by Faheem Lodhi in November 2007.[4]

For present purposes, the important point is that in the large majority of cases national security can be adequately protected either through a public interest immunity claim *or* under the NSI Act, but that in many cases a public interest immunity claim will provide greater flexibility.

In my opinion, it follows that the main type of case that calls for the invocation of the NSI Act is a case where either the prosecution or the defence needs to rely, as a central part of their case, on information that, if disclosed, would damage national security. In cases of that type, if a public interest immunity claim was made and upheld the result would be that crucial evidence would not be available. Depending on which side needed that information, either the prosecution would fail, or it would be stayed because crucial information had been denied to the defence.[5]

It is in this situation that the NSI Act comes into its own, because it creates a mechanism by which classified material can be admitted into evidence after it is put in a form that ensures that sensitive information does not become public in a way that will prejudice national security. That can be done through the use of edited documents, summaries, or statements or facts of the kind contemplated in s 26. The accuracy and adequacy of any summary of statement of facts is subject to verification by the court in any proceeding relating to the certificate.

If, however, the case does not depend on evidence of that kind, then even if it involves national security the invocation of the NSI Act may simply impose burdens on the parties and create a risk of unnecessary mandatory adjournments, without affording adequate corresponding benefits.

The role of consent arrangements under the National Security Information Act

Section 22, which provides for the making of consent orders in relation to the disclosure of national security information, appears to be an innocuous provision, but in practice it is one of the most important provisions in the Act. It is important because it provides a way of dealing with the complications that can arise from ss 24 and 25, and with a range of other issues that frequently arise during national security cases.

Section 22 can play such a central role because the Commonwealth Attorney-General has successfully argued on several occasions that Division 1 (ss 21-23) and Division 2 (ss 24-28) of Part 3 constitute alternative 'tracks' for the management of national security information issues.[6] Accordingly, once a matter is dealt with under Division 1, there is no need to comply with the procedures specified in Division 2 in relation to that same matter.

Division 1 of Part 3 is a consensual track. It allows the parties to work out between themselves arrangements relating to the use and disclosure of national security information during the proceeding. If the parties reach agreement, and if the court accepts that agreement, then the agreement is embodied in a set of s 22 orders that in effect lay the ground rules for what can be done with national security information during the trial.

If the parties cannot reach agreement, or if the agreement reached is not acceptable to the court, then the mandatory provisions in Division 2 (including ss 24 and 25) will apply. In that event the parties must proceed to give the notices required by that Division, and mandatory adjournments will apply until the Attorney-General responds to those notices.

The result is that the almost invariable practice for parties in matters where the NSI Act applies is to attempt to negotiate detailed orders under s 22 as part of the pre-trial process. Such orders normally deal with topics including the circumstances in which classified documents may be used in evidence or submissions, the circumstances in which the court should be closed, the identities of the persons who may have access to classified information, the production of secure transcript of closed court hearings and, in some cases, the manner in which evidence will be given by officers from security agencies such as the Australian Security Intelligence Organisation. A recent example of such orders can be found annexed to Bongiorno J's ruling in *R v Benbrika*.[7]

While s 22 orders can formally be made only with the consent of the prosecution and defence, in practice such orders are usually negotiated between counsel for the Attorney-General and the defence. If no agreement is reached in relation to s 22 orders, the Attorney-General will often obtain many of the same kinds of orders pursuant to specific powers such as s 93.2 of the *Criminal Code* (Cth), which relates to closed hearings, or pursuant to the inherent power of the Supreme Court. That is what occurred in the *Lodhi* proceeding, after attempts to negotiate s 22 orders were unsuccessful.[8]

Security clearances

The requirements of the NSI Act in relation to security clearances are somewhat complex, and they are frequently misunderstood. In particular, and contrary to much of the commentary, the Act does not require all lawyers who act in terrorism matters to hold security clearances.

It is true that there are many situations in which the Commonwealth considers that people should not be given access to particular information unless they hold the necessary security clearance. That requirement is applied by the Commonwealth to its own employees, including to solicitors employed by the Australian Government Solicitor or the Commonwealth DPP. It is also applied to all external barristers briefed for either the DPP or the Attorney-General in national security matters.

Accordingly, when defence barristers or solicitors are asked to obtain security clearances, the Commonwealth is doing no more than seeking to apply to the defence lawyers the same requirement that it applies to everyone else before they can access classified information.

Nevertheless, defence lawyers now routinely refuse to seek security clearances. In the face of that refusal, a significant number of terrorism matters have now been conducted pursuant to the NSI Act in circumstances in which none of the barristers have held security clearances. In the current Operation Pendennis matter in Melbourne, for example, none of the approximately 15 defence barristers, and only a few of the defence solicitors, hold clearances. Similarly, defence counsel in the *Lodhi* matter did not hold security clearances.

The absence of clearances has been dealt with to some extent by the court making s 22 orders that require security classified documents to be handled and used only in the manner specified in the orders. Before the enactment of the NSI Act, undertakings were sought for a similar purpose. In most cases to date these arrangements have worked adequately, mainly because the classified material that has been relevant to the proceedings has not been of the highest levels of sensitivity. There are, however, cases, for example *R v Khazaal*,[9] where the national security material relevant to the proceeding has been of such sensitivity that the court has held that it should not be disclosed even to counsel of high standing who offered undertakings in relation to the preservation of the confidentiality of that material.

In cases concerning highly sensitive material the Commonwealth can be confronted with a difficult situation. The provision of the material to uncleared lawyers may carry the potential to cause real prejudice to national security or danger to the safety of particular officers, but on the other hand the prosecution may be unable to proceed unless the lawyers have access to the classified information.

The tools that are available to the Commonwealth in that situation are not as demanding as is often suggested. Section 39 empowers the Secretary of the Attorney-General's Department to give a written notice to a legal representative of a defendant that an issue is likely to arise in the proceeding relating to the disclosure of information that is likely to prejudice national security. A person who receives such a notice can apply for a security clearance, and is entitled to an adjournment of the proceeding while the application is processed. If the person decides not to apply for a clearance, however, the consequence is simply that the court is empowered to advise the defendant of the consequences of engaging a legal representative who is not cleared, and to recommend that the defendant engage a person who is cleared.

Under the NSI Act itself, the main consequence of a defendant not having a security cleared lawyer is that the uncleared lawyer *may* be excluded – not from the trial proper – but from the closed hearing to determine whether certificates issued by the Attorney-General to prevent the disclosure of particular information should be upheld. Even that power of exclusion arises only if the Court is satisfied that the presence of the uncleared lawyer is likely to prejudice national security. As far as I am aware, the power to exclude an uncleared lawyer from an NSI Act closed hearing has never been used, and it is unlikely to be used unless the information in question is extremely sensitive, or there is some reason to doubt the integrity of the specific lawyer who is acting in the proceeding. If it is used, there will be a question as to whether 'special counsel' can be appointed to act for the accused in the closed hearing.[10] Even if such an appointment can be made, however, it is clear, as Lord Bingham said in *R v H*, that 'Such an appointment will always be exceptional, never automatic; a course of last and never first resort'.[11]

Even if a lawyer who has refused to seek a security clearance is excluded from the closed hearing relating to an Attorney-General's certificate, that lawyer can continue to act in the trial. There are, therefore, limits on the direct legal significance of a notice under s 39.

In practice, however, if such a notice is issued it may have crucial significance, because it may result in the termination of legal aid funding. That follows because under *Commonwealth Legal Aid Funding Guidelines* which commenced on 4 July 2006, once a notice is issued under s 39, Commonwealth legal aid funding can be paid only to security cleared lawyers or to lawyers who have lodged an application for a security clearance and are awaiting the determination of that application. The consequence of this guideline is that, if the Secretary issues a notice under s 39 during a trial, that notice may result in the termination of funding in relation to that trial if the lawyer in question refuses to apply for a clearance. That will create a real practical pressure against the use of the s 39 procedure.

In practice, it seems probable that the provisions in s 39 will rarely be used. Instead, the Commonwealth will factor into its consideration of the content of the necessary s 22 orders or Attorney-General's certificates the fact that its information is to be produced to people who do not have security clearances. If the information is sufficiently sensitive, then it may conclude that the disclosure of the information to persons without a clearance would be likely to prejudice national security, and as a result the disclosure of the information will be resisted on public interest immunity grounds, or appropriate certificates will be issued under the NSI Act.

Conclusion

In summary, while the NSI Act can be difficult to negotiate in practice, there are some cases in which it provides important tools for preventing prejudice to national security. In those cases the Act is capable of operating effectively and without unfairness to the accused, particularly as a result of the capacity of the parties to displace the more onerous provisions of the Act by reaching agreement as to consent orders.

The experience of the operation of the Act in practice to date is that this mechanism has allowed the Act to function without causing undue disruption or prejudice to the accused.

Notes

1 *Leghaei v Director-General of Security* [2007] FCAFC 56, [56]-[60]; *Alister v* R (1984) 154 CLR 404, 435, 455; *A v Secretary of State for the Home Department* [2004] 2 AC 68, 128.

2 R *v Lodhi* (2006) 163 A Crim R 508, 520.

3 Michael McHugh, 'Terrorism Legislation and the Constitution' (2006) 28 *Australian Bar Review* 117.

4 Faheem Lodhi was convicted in 2006 of several terrorism offences relating to preparing for a terrorist act. A challenge to the validity of parts of the NSI Act was rejected by Whealy J in the pre-trial stages of the *Lodhi* matter, and no appeal was brought against that judgment: R *v Lodhi* (2006) 163 A Crim R 448.

5 See *R v* Lappas [2001] ACTSC 115, [30].

6 R *v Lodhi* (2006) 163 A Crim R 448, 464-65; R *v Benbrika* [2007] VSC 141.

7 R *v Benbrika* [2007] VSC 141.

8 R *v Lodhi* (2006) 163 A Crim R 568; affirmed on appeal *Lodhi v* R (2006) 65 NSWLR 573.

9 R *v Khazaal* [2006] NSWSC 1061.

10 R *v Lodhi* (2006) 163 A Crim R 475 (where Whealy J held that special counsel could be appointed despite s 29(2)); R *v H* [2004] 2 AC 134, 150-51; *M v Secretary of State* [2004] 2 All ER 863, 868.

11 R *v H* [2004] 2 AC 134, 150.

9

Preserving National Security in the Courtroom: A New Battleground

Phillip Boulten SC

In the wake of the atrocities in New York and Washington in September 2001, the Australian government firmly embraced the concept of a never-ending 'war on terror', part of which has turned out to be a very proactive approach to intervention in criminal cases involving allegations of terrorism-related offences. The Commonwealth has extended the battleground to the courtrooms of Australia. It has done this by:

- introducing the *National Security Information (Criminal and Civil Proceedings) Act 2004* (NSI Act);
- issuing certificates under the NSI Act and arguing for ancillary protective measures in these court cases;
- seemingly always adopting in court the position of the Australian Security Intelligence Organisation (ASIO);
- instructing lawyers to continuously monitor the trials – not just at the stages of the proceedings where the NSI Act provisions are debated;
- taking action to attempt to enforce the security clearance of defence lawyers; and
- taking action to have particular lawyers excluded from the proceedings.

When these developments are added to the environment of loathing and fear of terrorism that exists outside the courtroom, the Commonwealth's measures to safeguard national security can provide formidable impediments to the smooth running of criminal justice.

As well as having a central role in protecting national security in the courtroom, the Attorney-General simultaneously carries out political functions. In this respect the current Attorney-General Philip Ruddock has chosen to:

- make commentaries about investigations into terrorist-related issues;
- give press conferences to announce the fact of arrests, convictions and, on several occasions, to explain significant defeats for the government in court; and
- amend legislation whenever he deems it appropriate, including on occasions when the Commonwealth has received 'set backs' in court or to address perceived flaws in the Commonwealth's position in court (even once retrospectively).

It is now clear that the government is prepared to use its legislative armoury against terrorist suspects in a way that is exceptional. The combination of ASIO's coercive powers, the broad definition of terrorist offences, the extremely harsh conditions of custody in which terrorist suspects are held, and the running commentary of politicians and the media about the arrest, prosecution and detention of terrorist suspects are all combining to create very difficult conditions for the trials of these people. These cases are increasingly using provisions that enable evidence to be heard in a closed court, the use of pseudonyms, the suppression of evidence from publication and the use of witnesses held in overseas prisons, including some held without charge under severe security legislation and evidence extracted from suspects being held in conditions that would be regarded as illegal or tyrannical in Australia.

The National Security Information Act

The NSI Act is now likely to become a regular feature of terrorist-related criminal litigation. It was first triggered in New South Wales in the Faheem Lodhi trial which, consequently, was subject to a series of procedural hearings that slowed the progress of the trial down to a snail's pace. The NSI Act casts extraordinary burdens on the lawyers acting for the accused and the prosecution. If they know or believe that they, or that one of their intended witnesses (either in giving evidence or by his or her mere presence), will disclose information that relates to national security or that the disclosure may affect national security, the lawyer must, as soon as practicable, give the Attorney-General notice of that knowledge or belief and advise the court that the notice has been given. Failure to give the notice is a criminal offence punishable by up to two years in jail.[1]

Likewise, during the course of the trial, if a witness is asked a question and either the prosecution or the defendant knows or believes that the answer might reveal information relating to national security or that it may affect national security, he or she must advise the judge who must adjourn the proceedings. In a closed court, the witness must write down the answer to the question on a piece of paper and give it to the judge. The answer must then be shown to the prosecutor (not to the accused) who, if he or she knows or believes that the written answer relates to or affects national security, must then give notice to the court and the Attorney-General.[2]

If the Attorney-General is given notice of either of these matters, he or she must *personally* consider the evidence concerned and may issue a 'non-disclosure certificate'. The proceedings remain adjourned until the Attorney-General issues such a certificate or determines not to issue one. If such a certificate is issued, the court must convene in a special closed court session to consider whether or not to make orders that conform with the certificate or otherwise.[3]

These steps were all utilised in the Lodhi trial, which was adjourned from time to time to allow the procedure to take its course.

The real sting in the tail of the NSI Act is the effect it has on the way the trial judge must consider the exercise of his or her discretion in determining whether or not to make orders in conformity with the Attorney-General's certificate. In deciding what order to make, the court must consider various factors including whether, having regard to the Attorney-General's certificate, there would be a risk of prejudice to national security and whether any such order would have a substantial adverse effect on the defendant's right to receive a fair hearing. But the Act provides that, in making its decision, the court must give *greatest weight* to the Attorney-General's certificate.[4]

Largely because of this fettered discretion, during the pre-trial arguments in the Lodhi case, lawyers acting for media interests challenged the constitutional validity of the relevant part of the NSI Act. They argued that the Act:

- altered the nature of the Supreme Court by obliterating its power to discharge, without interference, its ability to determine guilt or innocence;
- conferred on the Supreme Court, in its exercise of the judicial power of the Commonwealth, a discretion which is incompatible with the exercise of that power; and
- is inconsistent with the implied freedom of speech in relation to the discussion of political matters which arises under the Australian Constitution.

Whealy J dismissed the constitutional challenge. A central reason in his judgment was the very narrow construction that he gave to the Act's operation: 'In my opinion, the function [of the Act] is a very limited one and is concerned only with the disclosure of information'.[5] His Honour held that:

> The mere fact that the legislation states that more weight, that is the greater weight, is to be given to one factor over another does not mean that the other factor is to be disregarded. … Read fairly, it seems to me that the

> legislation does no more than to give the Court guidance as to the comparative weight it is to give one factor when considering it alongside a number of others. Yet the discretion remains intact and … in a proper case the Court will order disclosure or a form of disclosure other than that preferred by the Attorney-General.[6]

Mr Lodhi's current appeal to the Court of Criminal Appeal involves a ground which repeats the constitutional challenge to the validity of the key provisions of the NSI Act.

In Lodhi's trial, Whealy J decided all issues relating to the closure of the court, non-publication orders and orders about the identity of witnesses in accordance with the established common law and the relevant statutory provisions. The NSI Act was held not to have any effect on these ancillary orders. Nevertheless, much of the evidence was heard in closed court. Some of the evidence was suppressed. But a system was implemented for releasing edited forms of the transcripts of the closed court sessions within days of the evidence being heard.

Ancillary orders designed to protect national security information can themselves impact on a jury's perception of the accused. The process of opening and closing the court, ASIO witnesses' giving evidence from remote locations on video link, suppression orders, the use of pseudonyms and the various security measures (such as subjecting members of the public and lawyers to metal detectors and the number of prison officers guarding the accused) all combine to cause a significant degree of prejudice to the accused. Even the number of lawyers arrayed against the accused, together with the attendant police officers and ASIO officials, make a forceful and theatrical statement about what the state thinks about the accused.

Special Counsel

One mechanism which may help even up the courtroom balance is the concept of 'Special Counsel'. In Lodhi's case, over the objection of counsel for the Commonwealth, the accused successfully argued that Special Counsel could be appointed if it became necessary to argue about the disclosure of particularly sensitive national security information.[7] Had Whealy J chosen to take this course it would have involved the appointment of a security-cleared counsel who could have viewed the subject material, obtained instructions from the accused about its importance to the defence case and then mounted informed arguments in favour of disclosure of the information to the accused. This concept has been developed in the United Kingdom in the background of terrorist-related issues in immigration cases and some criminal cases, and has been applied in a similar context in Hong Kong.[8] Ultimately, though, Whealy J determined that the appointment of Special Counsel was not necessary. His Honour inspected contested material with the assistance of confidential affidavits filed by the Commonwealth. Both the accused and the prosecution were forced to make submissions in a vacuum about why access should be granted to the documents. Then Whealy J upheld Commonwealth objections to the release of the documents.

The atmosphere in court

Participating as defence counsel in terrorist-related trials exposes one to a completely different dynamic. These trials are not just traditional battles between adversaries where the Director of Public Prosecution (DPP) prosecutes and the accused defends. There is another layer altogether. The bar table is also commonly occupied by a battery of lawyers representing the Attorney-General and ASIO. The state's security apparatus is an ever-present force.

It can be very intimidating. The Commonwealth's lawyers are there to maintain national security. Usually this is done through the operation of the NSI Act, which provides criminal punishments, including imprisonment, for lawyers who fail to properly anticipate the requirements of the Act. A loosely framed question or a decision to call a witness about a matter that will disclose information touching on national security could lead the lawyer to a criminal prosecution, disciplinary action and motions to exclude them from the case. The Commonwealth has shown itself as very willing to threaten defence lawyers with action and, in some cases, to take action against them for alleged breaches of security.

In the past two years defence lawyers have had to respond to accusatory letters alleging breaches of security for sending mail in insecure form, charges of contempt of court and a motion to exclude them from a case. All of these rather unsettling actions have been defeated but they still impact on the lawyers' ability to fearlessly defend their clients. In one case a defence lawyer gave an interview on a community radio station which was subsequently raided by police who seized the tapes of the interview – presumably to investigate a possible offence under the NSI Act or a contempt of court.[9]

But at least we know about these acts of scrutiny. There is a belief on the part of some lawyers that they might be subject to covert electronic surveillance. Under recent amendments to the *Telecommunications (Interception and Access) Act 1979* (Cth), ASIO and police have the ability to intercept 'third party' telephone services. If the authorities cannot readily keep track of which telephone services suspects are using, they can obtain warrants to tap the phones of people that the suspects might contact. The suspects' lawyers are prime targets for 'third party' warrants.

Lawyers must leave their phones at the door of the court when appearing in sensitive, closed-session hearings – a measure prompted by government fears that well organised terrorist cells might surreptitiously use lawyers' phones to monitor closed court hearings. But defence lawyers have much greater reason to suspect the state, rather than Al-Qa'ida or Lashkar-e-Taiba, of wanting to listen in on their phone calls.

The application of the National Security Information Act

The Commonwealth's approach to national security information matters seems to be informed and crafted in large measure by ASIO, which is usually jointly represented by counsel for the Commonwealth. The game rules for ASIO on claims for national security are not the same as for elite police squads and investigatory bodies such as the Australian Crime Commission and the NSW Crime Commission, both of which are not shy when it comes to claims for public interest immunity. ASIO, though, leaves its police cousins in the shade.

The ASIO approach relies on the analogy of the mosaic – a device which drives its opposition to the public disclosure of basically any pertinent piece of information about its operations. The argument goes:

> A scrap of information which, in itself, might seem to have no bearing on national security may, when put together with other information, assume a vital significance.[10]

By gathering little pieces of information – like ceramic tiles – the terrorists can assemble a clear picture of significant issues – akin to a mosaic.

As a result of this approach arguments take place about a myriad of details in the evidence. Anything at all that might tend to reveal ASIO's involvement in an investigation is obsessively guarded by its lawyers. This results in a form of trench warfare.

ASIO in fact can play a very significant role in investigating alleged terrorist-related offences. ASIO works in a cooperative relationship with the federal and State police. At times it is difficult to distinguish the roles played by police on the one hand and security officers on the other. But where police officers expect their identities and, in the most part, their day-to-day methodologies to be revealed publicly in criminal prosecutions, ASIO agents jealously guard every aspect of their operations. This leads to a drive for lack of transparency in the courtroom which, in turn, adds to the mystique of power and certainty that the accused faces in these trials.

The use of overseas witnesses

Another factor that adds to the abnormality and lack of transparency of these cases is the frequency of the use of witnesses who have 'rolled over' under inducement in foreign countries and whose continuing welfare is, in one way or another, dependent on the goodwill of a foreign state. In Australia if a witness decides to cooperate with authorities and is utilised by the prosecution as a witness against other accused, the process that leads that witness to the courtroom is open to scrutiny. The DPP must reveal the process in its full detail. The defence must be told what inducements the person was offered, what benefits they received, what cases the person has given evidence in and any other matters that might affect their credit.

But when a witness has been held in custody overseas, it is sometimes difficult to gain access to all of the relevant information and the Commonwealth may have a duty to withhold it from the defence and, indeed, from the DPP. Revelations about the form of questioning that foreign security services have undertaken of a witness, their conditions of custody and the benefits or penalties that the witness might receive for giving evidence (or not) may all be matters that a foreign power may not wish to have made public in a court case in Australia. In that case, the foreign power's interests may well dictate the Australian government's claims for national security information restrictions over such information. Unlike the DPP, the Commonwealth has no duty to disclose to the accused all relevant information touching upon the reliability of a prosecution witness. But, as the definition of 'national security' extends to the need to maintain Australia's international relations,[11] there might be a legitimate basis for the Commonwealth to launch a claim for protection of this information.

There have been some interesting issues concerning overseas witnesses already. In one instance the defence team became aware of the fact that a witness had been arrested in Saudi Arabia and so sought disclosure from the DPP about how this man came to be giving evidence in the Australian proceedings from the United States. The DPP were completely unaware of the mechanism by which the man ended up in American custody. So when he was called to give evidence everyone at the bar table learned for the first time, through defence cross-examination, that he had been arrested by Saudi police in Riyadh, held without warrant and without charge for approximately four weeks in solitary confinement in a cell with the lights on 24 hours a day, and interrogated regularly throughout the night by Saudi police. He was then handed over to the FBI who, after stripping him naked and photographing his genitals, dressed him in prison greens, placed him in irons with dark goggles over his face and transported him from Riyadh to Washington on a special FBI flight. He told the court that it was during this flight that he first confessed to his involvement in Lashkar-e-Taiba activities.

A Singaporean witness who was used in relation to a number of cases in Sydney proved to be even more problematic. He had been held for some years in prison without charge under Singaporean national security laws and was still in custody there. Before he was called to give evidence in one case, the Commonwealth made a successful application to the court that defence counsel be refused the right to cross-examine him on certain specified topics, even though those topics were relevant and probative. At one stage the magistrate closed the court and then ordered the accused to be taken to the cells so that legal argument could be had in his absence because the Commonwealth had argued that the accused's presence in court constituted a national security risk. All of this was, of course, over the defence objection.

The prosecution eventually dropped the witness from the case after the defence subpoenaed documents that it thought would adversely affect his credibility and, in particular, his ability to accurately identify the accused without prompting from his Singaporean handlers. The Commonwealth refused to produce the documents on subpoena even though similar documents had been produced to the defence about the witness in another case. Eventually, it seems that the Singaporean witness became too problematic for the Commonwealth DPP and he was dropped from its witness list.

Conclusion

When an accused is arrested in a blaze of publicity and his detention depicted as an illustration of governmental competence, the conditions for a fair trial involving a jury that is capable of acting free of prejudice and bias are not very favourable. The Commonwealth's approach to handling national security information should be particularly measured in such circumstances. The potential for adding to the risk of miscarriages of justice is high. It is necessary for all participants in these extraordinary proceedings to be exceedingly careful to avoid adding to the climate of fear that understandably exists outside the courtroom.

Notes

1 *National Security Information (Criminal and Civil Proceedings) Act 2004* (Cth) ss 24 and 42.
2 *National Security Information (Criminal and Civil Proceedings) Act 2004* (Cth) s 25.
3 *National Security Information (Criminal and Civil Proceedings) Act 2004* (Cth) ss 24-27.
4 *National Security Information (Criminal and Civil Proceedings) Act 2004* (Cth) s 31.
5 R *v Lodhi* (2006) 163 A Crim R 448, 464.
6 R *v Lodhi* (2006) 163 A Crim R 448, 469.
7 R *v Lodhi* [2006] NSWSC 586.
8 See in particular R *v H;* R *v C* [2004] 2 AC 134; R *(Roberts) v Parole Board* [2005] 2 AC 738; *Secretary of State for the Home Department v Rehman* [2003] 1 AC 153; *PV v Director of Immigration* [2004] HKCFI 386.
9 See Frank Moorhouse, 'The writer in a time of terror' (2006) 14 *Griffith Review* 11, 25.
10 See *Church of Scientology v Woodward* (1982) 154 CLR 25, 51.
11 *National Security Information (Criminal and Civil Proceedings) Act 2004* (Cth) s 8.

PART III

Beyond Guilt or Innocence – Preventative Orders and Counter-terrorism

10

Control Orders and Preventative Detention – Why Alarm is Misguided

Geoff McDonald PSM

As the title to this part of the book suggests, control and preventative detention orders are not to do with guilt or innocence. The orders are to do with imposing restrictions on individuals who are proven to the civil standard, that is, on the balance of probabilities, to be likely to be a risk to others. This is not so different to what the law does in the context of family law, domestic violence and some mental health orders.

This legislation is part of Australia's comprehensive evolution of new laws in response to radical terrorism during the current decade. Federal counter-terrorism preventative orders fall into two categories: control orders and preventative detention orders. In this chapter, I outline the two regimes and explain the rationale behind them and counter-terrorism laws more generally.

Control orders

In essence, a control order is an order made by a court that imposes obligations, prohibitions or restrictions on a person's movements or activities to protect the public from a terrorist act. Division 104 of the *Criminal Code* (Cth) comprises 25 pages of detailed provisions regulating the administration of control orders. The following is a short summary that encapsulates the substance of the provisions for the purposes of the discussion in this chapter.

The making of a control order

Applications for control orders are made by the Australian Federal Police (AFP), not the government. However, the application requires the consent of the Attorney-General. If a control order is made, it is made by a federal court.

The control order regime contemplates that an initial, or interim, control order will be made. The interim order can be made *ex parte* but the court could choose to require the respondent to be present before an order is made. In either case, the interim order does not come into effect until the affected person is provided with a copy, and he or she may contest it when the court is required to confirm, void or revoke the order. The court date is stated in the interim order and must be as soon as practicable but at least 72 hours after the order is made. The AFP must advise the issuing court whether it wishes to seek confirmation of the order at least two days before the specified hearing date. If the AFP does not elect to confirm the interim order, it is no longer in force. Once a control order has been confirmed, the affected person or the AFP Commissioner can apply to the court for it to be revoked or varied.

The AFP can only make an application for a control order if a senior member considers, on reasonable grounds, that the order in the terms to be requested, would substantially assist in preventing a terrorist act. The applicant is required to provide an explanation of why each obligation, prohibition or restriction should be imposed *and* any known facts relating to why they should not be imposed.

The court may only make the order if it is satisfied on the balance of probabilities that the order would 'substantially assist in preventing a terrorist act' or that the person, who would be the subject of the order, has 'provided training to, or received training from, a listed terrorist organisation'. In addition, the court must be satisfied that, on the balance of probabilities, each of the obligations, prohibitions and restrictions to be imposed by the order is 'reasonably necessary, and reasonably appropriate and adapted, for the purpose of protecting the public from a terrorist act'.

A control order can be made for a period of up to 12 months. However, the AFP can apply for further orders if they can be justified.

Prohibition or restrictions in a control order

The types of controls that could be placed on an individual who is subject to a control order include prohibiting or restricting a person from:

- being at specified areas or places or leaving Australia;
- communicating or associating with specified individuals;
- accessing or using specified forms of telecommunication or other technology (including the internet);
- possessing or using specified articles or substances; and
- carrying out specified activities, including in respect of his or her work or occupation.

They may also include a requirement that the person:

- remains at specified premises between specified times each day or on specified days;

- wears a tracking device;
- reports to specified persons at specified times and places;
- allows himself or herself to be photographed; and
- if the person consents, participates in specified counselling or education.

The counselling and education orders recognise that control orders can last for a long period and that the individual may gain some benefit that could take them away from association with terrorists through appropriate counselling or education. For example, lack of literacy skills could be holding the person back from general employment and an opportunity to participate in an education program could address this shortcoming.

Safeguards

The legislation contains a number of safeguards. To my mind, the most significant of these safeguards is the fact that the orders are made and supervised by judges and magistrates. One-time critics of control orders have been found early this year calling on the government to bring David Hicks home from Guantanamo Bay on the basis that he could, on his return, be subjected to a control order. Those calling for this to be done of course did so without much regard to the fact it is not the government that determines who will be subjected to a control order.

Specific safeguards in the control order regime include:

- the order does not commence until it is served personally on the subject of the order;
- the AFP must explain the order to the person, taking into account the person's age, language skills, mental capacity and any other relevant factor;
- the person can apply for the order to be varied, revoked or declared void as soon as the person is notified that an order is confirmed, or at any time thereafter;
- the person and his or her lawyer are able to obtain a copy of the order which contains the summary of the grounds of the order;
- normal judicial review processes apply to decisions to issue or revoke control orders;
- when determining to impose each of the obligations, prohibitions and restrictions on the person, the court must take into account their impact on the person's circumstances, including the person's financial and personal circumstances; and

- control orders do not apply to young people under the age of 16 and may only be granted for a maximum of three months for young people between 16 and 18 years.

Similar regimes in Australia and elsewhere

The Australian control order regime is not unique. The United Kingdom has adopted similar sorts of provisions in its *Prevention of Terrorism Act 2005* and they were also included in Canada's *Criminal Code 1985* by the *Anti-Terrorism Act 2001* under the name 'recognizance with conditions'.

One of the concerns expressed about control orders is that the people who are likely to be subject to them have not been convicted of any criminal offence. There are precedents for placing controls on a person arising from their danger to the community without them having been convicted of a criminal offence.

Recognisances to keep the peace have been available under the law to protect the community from violence for over a hundred years. Persons released on bail are subject to restrictions on their activities which the court making the order feels are appropriate. In addition, State and Territory regimes of non-association orders can be used to break up criminal gangs while apprehended violence orders (AVOs) are used to protect people from violence from a spouse, neighbours, bullies at school or from gang members.

I am aware of a criticism that there are significant differences between, for example, AVOs and control orders. That is correct. There are significant differences brought about by the different nature of the risk; although I note that some measures that are available for control orders, such as tracking bracelets, are used in the context of domestic violence in other jurisdictions. However, the policy rationale behind them is substantially the same. They allow a court to proscribe restrictions on an unconvicted person's liberty. The purpose of the restriction is to protect the community or a particular person or group from the danger they represent.

In discussing the similarities between the issues a court needs to assess with respect to issuing AVOs and control orders, Gleeson CJ, as part of the majority in the High Court's decision in *Thomas v Mowbray*, stated:

> I am unable to accept that there is a qualitative difference between deciding whether an angry person poses an unacceptable risk to his or her family, or to the community or some section of the community, or whether a sexually dysfunctional man poses an unacceptable risk to women, and deciding whether someone who has been trained by terrorists poses an unacceptable risk to the public. The possibility that the person will do what he or she has been trained to do, or will be used as a 'resource' by others who have been so trained, is capable of judicial evaluation.[1]

Preventative detention orders

The preventative detention regime, set out in Division 105 of the *Criminal Code*, provides for the detention of a person without charge in certain circumstances. Preventative detention is a more restrictive measure than control orders but it may only occur where a terrorist act is imminent (within 14 days) and making the order would substantially assist in preventing an attack. It can also be used after an attack for the purpose of preserving related evidence if it is necessary to detain the person to do so. The maximum period of detention under the Commonwealth preventative detention regime is 48 hours, but it can be extended to 14 days under complementary State provisions. Further detail on the process for making preventative detention orders can be found in the following chapter by Justice Margaret White.

In creating preventative detention orders, the government recognised that there will be circumstances where there is no basis for questioning, but there is a real danger the person will engage in a terrorist act and detention will substantially assist in a preventing a terrorist act occurring. In practice, this order will not be easy to get and in most cases candidates will be arrested, questioned and charged with an offence. However, in the case of multiple attacks or a large attack involving many people, it provides an opportunity for law enforcement to catch breath and contain people who are identified as being associated with the attack but who for some reason cannot be arrested and charged.

There are situations where plots are discovered at an advanced stage and agencies can be sure the planned attack is imminent but are not sure whether there are others out there who can pick up where the suspect has left off. It is well publicised that agencies were caught by surprise in the New York and London attacks and most of the plots that have been uncovered in more recent years.

Safeguards

There are many safeguards concerning humane treatment of individuals detained under preventative detention, which are backed up by an offence that applies to law enforcement officers who do not comply with these requirements. As with control orders, the most substantial safeguard is in the issuing process. Only a senior AFP member, superintendent or above, is authorised to make the initial 24 hour order. Extensions after that must be made by a judge, magistrate or senior member of the Administrative Appeals Tribunal (AAT) acting in a personal capacity. The decision about the making of the order can be reviewed by the AAT which may order compensation if it finds the decision was not justified.

Investigative questioning of people in preventative detention is prohibited in recognition that the purpose of the detention is prevention and that detention itself can impact on the quality of evidence. If questioning is necessary, the person can be released from preventative detention and questioned and detained under Crimes Act or Australian Security Intelligence Organisation (ASIO) questioning provisions.

Other safeguards are:

- a person detained will be given an opportunity to contact a lawyer, family members and employers who are not linked to the terrorist activity to let them know that they are safe but not contactable for the time being;
- the detention does not apply to people under 16 and special rules apply for those between 16 and 18, and the incapable;
- the process must be properly explained to the detained person and special assistance must be provided where the person has an inadequate knowledge of the English language or a disability;
- consistent with Australia's international human rights obligations, any person being preventatively detained must be treated with humanity and respect for human dignity and must not be subjected to cruel, inhuman or degrading treatment; any official who fails to treat the detained person in this manner is subject to a specific offence in the legislation; and
- each year the Attorney-General must report to parliament on the operation of the orders.

Similar regimes elsewhere

The UK has similar powers in its *Terrorism Act 2000*, as amended by the *Terrorism Act 2006*, without many of the safeguards found in Australia. The British government tried to extend the maximum period of detention of persons arrested 'without warrant' from 14 to 90 days. It was unsuccessful, but the parliament passed laws allowing detention for up to 28 days. The laws were used at the time of the 2006 plot to blow up aircraft.

The UK law tends to merge the questioning time and preventative detention concepts into a single detention period. Australia's law is more transparent about the purpose. Time limits apply to the amount of actual questioning that is permitted and to the specific allowances for rest, medical care and, in terrorism cases, for the extraction of information from computers to assist the investigation (see Part IC of the *Crimes Act 1914* (Cth)). This can be accompanied by preventative detention which must be justified with reference to the preventative purpose and cannot be used for questioning. If questioning is to take place, it must be justified under Part IC.

While in Britain, the Secretary of the Attorney-General's Department asked law enforcement and security agencies about the rationale for the increase in the period of detention. The explanations they offered were very similar to the rationale behind Australia's laws.

The first point they made was about the difference in the nature of terrorism experienced in England some years ago, particularly attacks by Irish Republican Army, and terrorism today. In the past, the authorities often had warning about a possible attack through good intelligence. And those earlier terrorist attacks were planned and implemented over a period of time. This meant that security and law enforcement agencies had the opportunity to conduct surveillance and other investigations, which had two outcomes. In many cases, it enabled them to disrupt the planned attack and identify and arrest the participants. It also enabled them to gather evidence to put before a court in a criminal prosecution. The final point of difference is that those earlier attacks were intended to achieve a political objective and not just the random killing of innocent citizens in pursuit of an imprecise jihad against Western countries and their values. This political definition gave their attacks some structure and predictability.

Today's terrorist environment is quite different. The British view is that the lengthy task for terrorists is cultivating or identifying a suicide bomber. Once that has been achieved, terrorist organisations move quickly to a terrorist attack before the potential bomber changes his or her mind.

From the State's perspective, the need for an urgent response is increased by the huge range of potential targets in an open, democratic society. We have also seen in Jakarta, for example, the effects of displacement. In other words, because a terrorist attack can have almost any target, if an attack is thwarted against one target, it can easily be redirected to another.

So there can be very limited time for surveillance and investigation. If law enforcement and security agencies acquire intelligence that indicates a terrorist attack could occur, they may have to move almost immediately in order to prevent the attack happening. The dilemma is that, in moving so quickly, they may have very little evidence to substantiate holding, charging and prosecuting the individuals concerned in accordance with traditional criminal law procedures. Preventative detention could both defuse the threat of an attack and allow time for further investigations to be carried out and evidence obtained.

There are a number of other factors that can complicate and delay investigations that the British law enforcement bodies advised justify detention in terrorist cases. They are:

- the fact that the terrorists may be part of a global network crossing national boundaries, therefore requiring international police and security assistance;

- potential difficulties in establishing the identities of the suspected terrorists;
- problems and delays arising from difficulties with foreign languages and the need for interpreter services;
- the fact that valuable information and potential evidence may be buried in the hard drives of computers which can take a long time to find, analyse and, if necessary, translate;
- the material on the hard drives can be encrypted and the encryption may be hard to break;
- precise requirements about the collection of evidence have to be met to allow the presentation of forensic evidence in court;
- many hours of CCTV tapes may have to be inspected; and
- other difficulties can arise as a result of modern technology such as mobile phones.

Extended detention with a preventative purpose is not unique to the UK. A 72-hour period was included in the Canadian *Criminal Code 1985* by the *Anti-Terrorism Act 2001* but those provisions expired under a sunset clause in March 2007. The Netherlands has preventative detention for security reasons for three days in its *Expansion of Competencies in Criminal Investigation and Prosecution Act 2007*. That period can be extended by a court for a further 10 days if certain criteria are met and then for an even longer period if it is authorised by a judge under even stricter requirements. Once again, the view in the Netherlands was that 10 days was too short a period of preventative detention in terrorism cases.

The situation is different in France due to its judicial system. A person of interest, such as Willie Brigitte, can be held for several years while the investigating magistrate pursues detailed investigations.

The United States has invoked its material witness provision in relation to people suspected of being involved in terrorist activity.[2] Those provisions allow a person to be arrested and detained when his or her testimony is material in criminal proceedings but it is impractical to secure his or her presence by subpoena. There is no requirement that the person be charged with a criminal offence. The person's release can be delayed for a reasonable period of time until the witness' deposition can be taken. The Americans have held people for over a year under these provisions.

Many of these reasons for, and justifications of, preventative detention given to us by our overseas colleagues resonated with the rationale for the introduction of preventative detention in this country.

Rationale for counter-terrorism laws generally

The rationale underpinning the legislation introducing control and preventative detention orders is the same rationale underpinning all of the counter-terrorism legislation passed by the Australian parliament since 2001. Put simply, the Australian government, and the State and Territory governments, have a responsibility to protect Australians, wherever they might be, and anyone visiting Australia.

ASIO assesses Australia's threat level at medium, which means that a terrorist attack is possible and could occur. That threat level is expected to continue for many years into the future. Hence, the sunset clause for the orders is 10 years.

While Australia has – fortunately – not had a significant terrorist attack on Australian soil since the Hilton Bombing, there have been attacks against Australian interests in Bali, Jakarta and other places. The convictions of Jack Roche, Faheem Lohdi, and Willie Brigitte in France, and the forthcoming criminal proceedings against more than 20 other defendants indicate that Australia or Australians are not in some way isolated from the impact of terrorism.

As a consequence, much of the argument about our terrorism laws is about the appropriate balance between protecting the community at large and preserving individual rights. A number of commentators have observed that the aim to protect the safety of our community as a whole and, in that process, to protect the rights of individuals within society, is totally consistent with the *Universal Declaration of Human Rights* which states in art 3 that every person has the right to life, liberty and security of person. The same theme is also repeated by some of the judges who have presided over terrorism trials in Australia.

A process of seeking a control order or preventative detention order through a properly defined statutory process, where the order is made by a judge or magistrate and can be challenged on appeal is, to my mind, a more acceptable process than that observable in other countries.

Conclusion

The introduction of preventative order legislation is appropriately not to do with any question of guilt or innocence. Guilt or innocence is the test for determining whether a person spends years in prison and gets a criminal record. The impact of conviction is very significant compared to the impact of preventative orders. Pre-trial detention also has a much more significant impact. A recent Canadian murder trial took five years to just get started.[3] In Australia, about 20 per cent of cases in our higher courts take more than a year to be completed and seven per cent take more than two years. This, combined with the fact that 20 per cent of people in our prison system are on remand, suggests to me that preventative orders are not as significant as they are made out to by some critics.[4]

The idea of someone being in detention awaiting trial for two years compared to a maximum period of 14 days under preventative detention puts things into perspective. Furthermore, since the legislation was enacted in 2005 no one has been detained under preventative detention orders and only one person has been the subject of a control order.[5]

Australia's preventative orders legislation is a carefully considered measure, designed to ensure a fair, judicially supervised process for strictly limited controls on people who could engage in terrorist activity in the broader interest of protecting the community as a whole.

It is quite important for us to acknowledge that every parliament in this country has been party to the enactment of the preventative orders laws and they did so in the knowledge that the legislation is consistent with Australia's obligations under international law, including international human rights law. Freedoms such as freedom of movement and expression are only restricted where it is necessary to protect national security and public order. The measures are in no way arbitrary. In the clear light of experience, the use of preventative orders in Australia to deal with terrorism is very limited, measured and still consistent with the democratic ideals of a society I hope we all believe should be protected.

Notes

1 *Thomas v Mowbray* [2007] HCA 33, [28] (Gleeson CJ).

2 18 USC §3144.

3 Robert Pickton was charged in February 2002. His trial commenced before the Supreme Court of British Columbia in January 2006. Pickton's jury trial did not commence until 22 January 2007.

4 Australian Institute of Criminology, *Crime Facts Info*, No 146 (2007) 5.

5 *Jabbour v Thomas* (2006) 165 A Crim R 32.

11

A Judicial Perspective – The Making of Preventative Detention Orders

Margaret White

Today the soldiers took away one,
Tomorrow they may take away two,
One April they took away Greece,
But surely they would never take you.
So close your eyes and stop your ears,
Close your mouth, take it slow,
Let others take the lead and you bring up the rear,
And later you could say you didn't know.

This song – the *Song of Choice* – was written in 1968 by Peggy Seeger, the British folk singer, a year after the Colonels became dictators in Greece. It prefaced the contribution which the Hon Jim Fouras made to the debate in the Queensland House of Representatives in December 2005 on the Second Reading of the Terrorism (Preventative Detention) Bill 2005.

And, although he spoke passionately and persuasively, drawing on his own family's experiences under the Junta in Greece where two of his brothers were 'made to disappear' for five days by the police, like Duff Cooper in 1938 explaining to the House of Commons why he could no longer support his Prime Minister and remain First Sea Lord (a speech which Churchill described as one of the finest he had ever heard), Jim Fouras carried no-one from his party with him. The Bill was passed with bipartisan support, as was the case around Australia. Two independent members of parliament voted against the Bill. This was reflected in the parliaments of the other States.[1]

The debates in all State parliaments were particularly interesting and rather unusual in Australian parliamentary history because the Honourable Members, more in sorrow than with any enthusiasm, passed the legislation. Its closest analogy was the debate in the Federal House on the Communist Party Dissolution Bill in 1950.

Around Australia Honourable Members who spoke described the legislation as 'draconian'. For example, the Premier of Queensland said:

> It gives me no pleasure to bring this Bill into the House. I do so with a grave sense of duty but no pleasure. As I said when introducing it, these laws are draconian. Unfortunately, they are a sign of the times, tragic as that may be.[2]

No doubt the Honourable Members did not seriously contemplate that the Bill was 'rigorous, harsh, severe or cruel' as the Oxford Dictionary describes the code of law established by Draco, Archon at Athens in 621 BC. But if not, what did they mean when they employed that description? And should this deeply felt sense of unease at what they were legislating for inform the manner in which the legislation is interpreted?

The Public Interest Monitor: an important safeguard in the Queensland scheme

What is of particular interest is that although the debate was concerned, for the most part, with expressing unhappiness at the abandonment of hard-won and valued liberties, consciences were salved because Supreme Court judges were to make the preventative detention orders rather than the executive. In Queensland the Premier and the Attorney-General had been able to secure the inclusion in the Queensland complementary legislation of the participation of the Public Interest Monitor in the process of making control and preventative detention orders. Such an entity is not established in other Australian jurisdictions although legislation to this end is now in place in the Australian Capital Territory.[3] In the debates in other jurisdictions it was mentioned as a desirable safeguard.

The position of Public Interest Monitor was established in Queensland in 1998 and operates under three pieces of Queensland legislation – the *Police Powers and Responsibilities Act 1997*, the *Crime Commission Act 1977* and the *Criminal Justice Act 1989*. The position may not be occupied by a person who is a current or former employee of bodies who are the subject of the legislation (for example, police). The position is or has been held by a current or former member of the private Bar or an academic lawyer.

The role of the Public Interest Monitor in Queensland has been of considerable benefit by adding a layer of scrutiny to applications made to the Supreme Court by police officers and others for covert search warrants and surveillance devices in circumstances where there is otherwise no contradictor. The Public Interest Monitor seeks to examine, among other things, whether the balance of the particular case lies with the public interest in privacy or the public interest in the detection and prosecution of serious criminal offences.

The role of judges in the preventative detention scheme

As a sitting judge who may be called upon to interpret and apply the legislation I can make no suggestions as to how specific expressions may be construed but can, I think, with proprietary make some general observations.

The Commonwealth *Anti-Terrorism Act (No 2) 2005* inserted the Commonwealth's preventative detention regime into Division 105 of the Commonwealth *Criminal Code.* As is well-known, the Commonwealth persuaded the States and Territories to enact complementary legislation at the Council of Australian Governments (COAG) meeting in September 2005 because it was perceived that the Commonwealth was unable constitutionally to enact preventative detention laws operating beyond 48 hours. The State and Territory laws may extend the period of detention to a maximum of 14 days. This is a period which is legislatively described as 'short' but one might query why it was thought necessary to so describe it at all. Fourteen days might not be described as 'short' by the subject of the order. The State and Territory courts cannot exercise their own jurisdiction to make such orders or review Commonwealth-made orders whilst the Commonwealth order is still in force.

An initial preventative detention order is made to a senior police officer. The issuing authority for a continuing or final order is, in the case of the Commonwealth legislation, among others, a person who is a judge of a State or Territory Supreme Court. Under the State legislation the issuing authority is a Supreme Court judge or a retired judge and later provisions expressly state that the function of making an order is conferred on the judge in a personal capacity. All appointees (who must be appointed by the Attorney-General) must give their consent in writing to be appointed.

As will be immediately apparent, the Commonwealth *Criminal Code* makes clear that judicial officers are acting in their personal capacities. And even though it is the opinion of some constitutional experts that there is more latitude open to State judges to perform non-judicial functions, the States too have conferred the power to make orders under the anti-terrorism Acts on a judge in his or her personal capacity and not as a member of a court or on a court. In constitutional terms this is thought to circumvent the Australian Constitution's requirement that the exercise of judicial power be separate from the exercise of legislative and executive powers, and that making administrative orders, which preventative detention orders necessarily are, is not a proper function for a court.

Even though State courts are not thought to be similarly constrained, after *Kable v The Director of Public Prosecutions (NSW)*[4] and other cases considering similar issues about the essential characteristics of a Chapter III court (that is, a court that exercises federal jurisdiction), legislative prudence might suggest that similar considerations apply to State courts. That the designated person happens to be a judge and the holder of judicial office and who is identified as eligible to be an issuing authority because of those characteristics rather than as a member of a court seems a fragile basis for legitimacy and hardly likely to be comprehended by the ordinary citizen. And yet it was this perception of judges performing non-judicial functions by Chapter III judges which lay at the heart of *Kable*. The bright line that divides compatible and incompatible functions can become hazy as seen in *Grollo v Palmer*, *Hilton v Wells* and *Wilson v Minister for Aboriginal and Torres Strait Island Affairs*.[5]

Plainly the legislature wishes to clothe the process of making preventative detention orders with a certain acceptability to the thoughtful members of the community (and judging by the comments made in the parliamentary debates there were many such constituents throughout the country). The observation by the US Supreme Court in 1989 quoted by Gummow J in *Grollo* is informative:

> The legitimacy of the Judicial Branch ultimately depends upon its reputation for impartiality and nonpartisanship. That reputation may not be borrowed by the political Branches to cloak their work in the neutral colours of judicial action.[6]

An issuing authority under the anti-terrorism legislation who is a sitting judge must have consented to act. Accordingly, if that judge concludes, when confronted with an application to issue a preventative detention order, that doing so is incompatible with the function of a judge or with being a judge one might suggest that he or she should withdraw his or her consent.

Judges of State courts have been carrying out the non-judicial function of issuing covert warrants and the like for years. On my court many judges felt unhappy at this activity but equally felt under some collegiate pressure not to shirk the work and that it was preferable that judges did it rather than some administrative tribunal, an argument that found favour with some justices in *Fardon v Attorney-General (Qld)*.[7] However it might be added that those warrants are issued in aid of the gathering of evidence to prosecute a crime whereas the preventative detention legislation is not concerned with ultimate criminal charges at all.

The making and effect of a preventative detention order

There are two bases on which the issuing authority may make a preventative detention order. These apply to both the initial and the continued or final preventative detention order but only the latter concerns a judge. The first basis requires the issuing authority to be satisfied that there are reasonable grounds to suspect that the person subject to the order:

- will engage in a terrorist act; or
- possesses a thing that is connected with the preparation for, or the engagement of a person in, a terrorist act; or
- has done an act in preparation for, or planning, a terrorist attack.

The issuing authority must also be satisfied that:

- the preventative order would 'substantially assist in preventing a terrorist act occurring'; and
- detaining the subject for the period for which the person is to be detained under the order is reasonably necessary to achieve that end for this person.

The 'terrorist act' must be one that is both 'imminent' and 'expected to occur, in any event, at some time in the next 14 days'.

The second basis for making a preventative detention order provides that an order can be made when it is necessary to detain a person for the purpose of preserving evidence relating to a recent terrorist act being one that has occurred in the past 28 days. Such an order may only be made if the issuing authority is satisfied that the period of detention is reasonably necessary for this person.

Persons detained under these orders may be held in a State or Territory prison or remand centre and there are particular provisions for persons under the age of 18 and persons with apparent disability. A person who is detained must be treated with humanity and respect for human dignity and not be subjected to cruel, inhuman or degrading treatment; failure to do so is punishable by a maximum of two years' imprisonment.

Perhaps somewhat surprisingly, all that a detainee is required to provide by way of information is his or her identity and, thus unlike its British counterpart, may not be used as a general tool for gathering intelligence. The powers of the Australian Security Intelligence Organisation may, however, be utilised for that purpose.

Constitutional considerations about the character of preventative detention

I would now like to consider another issue of constitutional interest. The essential characteristics of a court and the nature of judicial power might well be matters which exercise a judge faced with making a preventative detention order. One thing is clear, preventative detention orders are not orders made in the process of bringing a criminal charge against a person or in order to facilitate the bringing of a criminal charge. Judicial power has traditionally been limited to ordering detention after a person has been found guilty of a crime by a trial or plea according to law. That much might have seemed axiomatic after *Chu Keng Lim v Minister for Immigration* in 1992 where Brennan, Deane and Dawson JJ said:

> the involuntary detention of a citizen in custody by the State is penal or punitive in character and, under our system of Government, exists only as an incident to the exclusively judicial function of adjudging and punishing criminal guilt.[8]

This observation merely endorsed a long expressed tenet of the common law found in the writings of the great English jurists Blackstone and Coke. However, after the split decision of the High Court in *Al-Kateb v Goodwin*,[9] if laws ordering detention of an individual can be characterised as something other than punitive they will survive constitutional challenge; for example, the protection of the security of the Australian community or, as in *Re Kruger*,[10] the protection of Aboriginal children. This characterisation test resonates in the judgments in the US Supreme Court in *Korematsu v US* in 1944 concerning the forced exclusion of US citizens of Japanese ancestry from certain West Coast areas which led to their certain incarceration – the majority described the place where they were to go as an assembly point, the dissentients as a concentration camp.[11]

Courts in this country have traditionally detained accused persons before a trial in which their guilt or innocence is to be established by the refusal to grant bail. The adversarial process is at work. Certain legislatively identified criteria are applied and the well-accepted way in which judicial discretion is exercised occurs and may be reviewed.

In most States there is recent legislation to detain violent sexual offenders beyond the expiration of their criminal sentence where they are seen to constitute a serious risk to the safety of the public. Legislation of this kind was considered by the High Court in *Fardon* in 2004. The legislature made plain that in certain specified circumstances the liberty of the individual may be curtailed. In *Re Bolton* Brennan J had said:

> the courts acknowledge that the balance between the public interest and individual freedom is struck not by the courts but by the representatives of the people in Parliament.[12]

The transcript of debate before the High Court in *Fardon* demonstrates that the judges were troubled by legislation which sought to undermine a fundamental legal principle, namely, that the right to personal liberty is the most elementary and important of all common law rights. Gummow J observed, in a much quoted passage, that:

> the 'exceptional cases' aside, the involuntary detention of a citizen in custody by the State is permissible only as a consequential step in the adjudication of criminal guilt of that citizen for past acts.[13]

Ultimately, what was happening to Mr Fardon was characterised not as detention without trial but protection of the public and his rehabilitation.

Under that legislation the court had to be satisfied 'to a high degree of probability' on the basis of 'acceptable, cogent evidence' that was 'of sufficient weight to justify the decision'.[14] But the preventative detention legislation requires the ordinary civil standard which is to be contrasted with the 'high degree of probability' in the *Fardon*-type legislation. My own view is that although there was a six-to-one majority decision in *Fardon* upholding the validity of the legislation it was, nonetheless, a far from foregone conclusion.[15] The Queensland Parliamentary drafter had done a good job of putting in place a high hurdle before confinement could be ordered. The focus was on confining risk and rehabilitation of the offender. The process was fully-informed and adversarial.[16]

A recent enunciation of what is well-established in Australian jurisprudence as the *Bringinshaw* test of the civil burden of proof was articulated in *R (N) v Mental Health Review Tribunal (Northern Region)*:

> the more serious the allegation or the more serious the consequences if the allegation is proved, the stronger must be the evidence before a court will find the allegation proved on the balance of probabilities. Thus the flexibility of the standard lies not in any adjustment to the degree of probability required for an allegation to be proved (such that a more serious allegation has to be proved to a higher degree of probability), but in the strength or quality of the evidence that will in practice be required for an allegation to be proved on the balance of probabilities.[17]

With this firmly in mind, a judge may be correct to be unpersuaded by the strength of the evidence advanced by the applicant for a preventative detention order if it is couched only in broad national security terms and the 'reasonable grounds to suspect' – a test well known – may not be made out.

The Public Interest Monitor's role in preventative detention order proceedings

Only the initial detention order may be applied for and made *ex parte* and that is by a police officer to a senior police officer. In Queensland the Public Interest Monitor must be notified. Applications made to a judge are on notice. To provide otherwise would invite successful challenge. Courts regularly make *ex parte* orders – for example, a number of injunctive orders – but they can be set aside after the order has been served and the affected party brings further evidence into court.

Returning then to the question of the Public Interest Monitor and whether that person should be seen as in some way reassuring those who feel concern about the issue of preventative detention orders. Ours is essentially an adversarial system and, while judges considering and making orders for search warrants or surveillance devices (which are of an administrative or executive, rather than judicial, character and are made without notice) must act judicially, the assistance of a contradictor to the application is significant.

Under the Queensland *Terrorism (Preventative Detention) Act 2005* the Public Interest Monitor can question any witness and present questions for the applicant. The role may bring some safeguards for the detainee under this legislation. A 'neutral' mind will be brought to bear on the key issues of whether there are reasonable grounds to suspect that the person will engage in a terrorist act or in some other way fulfil the preconditions for the making of an order. Where the public interest is the personal safety of members of the community and is the *raison d'etre* for the anti-terrorism legislation, the Public Interest Monitor's role may well be more than symbolic even where the affected person is legally represented.

The role of the court in protecting human rights

This legislation, unlike the detention of serious sexual offenders after the expiration of their sentence, does represent a major departure from accepted notions of how we apply the rule of law in Australia. But it is important to recognise that there has been general acceptance of that change, albeit with disquiet. While judges can demand a high degree of cogent evidence to fulfil the satisfaction that there are 'reasonable grounds for believing' as the basis for making the order and demand exact compliance with the legislation, it is not, might I suggest, to the judges that the community should look in general, for the preservation of civil liberties in a representative democracy. Their record, as exemplified particularly in Germany in the 1930s and South Africa during apartheid as well as in the United Kingdom and the United States of America during World War II, has been rather dismal. Professor Dyzenhaus quotes Bruce Ackerman that judges should not be regarded as 'miraculous saviors of our threatened heritage of freedom'.[18] It is better to rely on a system of political incentives and disincentives, a political economy that will prevent abuse of emergency powers.

Nonetheless as a judge, even a mere *designata*, one might hope to fall within the second category of judges described by Professor Dyzenhaus, namely:

> judges who articulate and follow through on such a duty [that is to uphold the rule of law in the sense of fundamental principles] despite the fact that

they have no Bill of Rights to rely on, and despite the fact that the legislature and/or the Executive claims that there is an emergency situation.[19]

The proper role for the courts in the field of human rights was recently commented on by the Court of Appeal in England in *R (Al Rawi) v Secretary of State for Foreign and Commonwealth Affairs* in its judgment dismissing the claims by non-British detainees at Guantanamo Bay that because they had previously been lawful residents in the United Kingdom the Secretary of State was obliged to seek their release by diplomatic representation to the United States.

The court posed two questions:

(1) How does the law approach the balance of individual claims of right with the general public interest in a context as acute as this?

(2) How big is the court's role as decision-maker?[20]

The court said that the task of striking a balance between the demands of the general interests of the community and the requirements of protecting individuals' fundamental rights is shared by the courts and the elected government. Their Lordships noted that a recurrent theme of public law in recent years has been the search for a principled means of disentangling the functions of these different arms of government. Their Lordships quoted from Lord Hoffmann in *R (Pro Life) v British Broadcasting Corporation*:

> In a society based upon the rule of law and the separation of powers, it is necessary to decide which branch of Government has in any particular instance the decision-making power and what the legal limits of that power are. That is a question of law and must therefore be decided by the courts.[21]

Their Lordships postulated that the rule of law requires not only that a public decision should be authorised by the words of the enabling statute but also that it be reasonable and (generally in human rights cases) proportionate to a legitimate aim. Their Lordships noted that reasonableness and proportionality are not formal legal standards but are substantive virtues on which it may be thought lawyers do not have the only voice or necessarily the wisest. Their Lordships concluded:

> For present purposes, we would approach the matter as follows. The courts have a special responsibility in the field of human rights. It arises in part from the impetus of the Human Rights Act 1998, in part from the common law's jealousy in seeing that intrusive State power is always strictly justified. The elected Government has a special responsibility in what may be called strategic fields of policy, such as the conduct of foreign relations and matters of national security. It arises in part from considerations of competence, in part from the constitutional imperative of elected accountability.[22]

Their Lordships finally quoted from Lord Hoffman in *Secretary of State for the Home Department v Rehman* where his Lordship said that not only did the Executive have access to special information and expertise but that those decisions which have serious potential results for the community require a legitimacy which can be conferred only by entrusting it to persons responsible to the community through the democratic process. If the people are to accept the consequences of such decisions they must be made by persons whom the people have elected and whom they can remove.[23] It is for this important reason that I began with the parliamentary debates on the anti-terrorism preventative detention bills.

Judges must approach their task under this legislation as under any other by employment of the ordinary canons of construction informed by the objects of the Act and with the understanding that parliament (State or Commonwealth) does not intend to derogate from well-understood and accepted precepts of the common law except by the clearest language.

Notes

1 New South Wales, *Parliamentary Debates*, Legislative Council, 30 November 2005, 20246; Victoria, *Parliamentary Debates*, Legislative Assembly, 9 February 2008, 184 and Legislative Council, 1 March 2006, 545; South Australia, *Parliamentary Debates*, House of Assembly, 9 November 2005, 3929 and Legislative Council, 24 November 2005, 3240; Western Australia, *Parliamentary Debates*, Legislative Assembly, 1 December 2005, 8118 and 30 March 2006, 941 and 957 and Legislative Council, 22 August 2006, 4863 and 4880; Tasmania, *Parliamentary Debates*, House of Assembly, 30 November 2005, 98.

2 Queensland, *Parliamentary Debates*, House of Representatives, 2 December 2005, 4694 (Premier Peter Beattie).

3 *Terrorism (Extraordinary Temporary Powers) Act* (ACT) s 62.

4 *Kable v The Director of Public Prosecutions (NSW)* (1996) 189 CLR 51.

5 *Grollo v Palmer* (1995) 184 CLR 348; *Hilton v Wells* (1985) 157 CLR 57; and *Wilson v Minister for Aboriginal and Torres Strait Island Affairs* (1996) 189 CLR 1.

6 *Grollo v Palmer* (1995) 184 CLR 348, 392 referring to *Mistretta v United States* 488 US 361 (1989), 407.

7 *Fardon v Attorney-General (Qld)* (2004) 223 CLR 575, 586 (Gleeson CJ).

8 *Chu Keng Lim v Minister for Immigration* (1992) 176 CLR 1, 27.

9 *Al-Kateb v Godwin* (2004) 219 CLR 562.

10 *Re Kruger* (1997) 190 CLR 1.

11 *Korematsu v US* 323 US 214 (1994).

12 *Re Bolton* (1987) 162 CLR 514, 523.

13 *Fardon v Attorney-General (Qld)* (2004) 223 CLR 575, 612.

14 *Dangerous Prisoners (Sexual Offenders) Act 2003* (Qld) s 13.

15 The High Court has granted special leave to appeal in *Yeo v Attorney-General (Qld)* – where a continuing detention order was made under the same legislation as in *Fardon* – will bring the Act into focus again: [2007] HCATrans 326.

16 There have been some applications for indefinite detention orders against prisoners in far from compelling circumstances. There is significant media pressure and paedophiles are the witches *du jour*. Judges need to be alert to this kind of pressure when national security is the basis for an order.

17 *R (N) v Mental Health Review Tribunal (Northern Region)* [2006] QB 468, 497-8.
18 David Dyzenhaus, *The Constitution of Law: Legality in a Time of Emergency* (2006), 40.
19 Above, n 18, 15.
20 *R (Al Rawi) v Secretary of State for Foreign and Commonwealth Affairs* [2007] 2 WLR 1219, 1246.
21 *R (Pro Life) v British Broadcasting Corporation* [2004] 1 AC 185, 240.
22 *R (Al Rawi) v Secretary of State for Foreign and Commonwealth Affairs* [2007] 2 WLR 1219, 1273.
23 *Secretary of State for the Home Department v Rehman* [2003] 1 AC 153, 162.

12

The Constitutional Validity of Preventative Detention

James Renwick[*]

Introduction

The right to personal liberty – that is, to freedom from arbitrary detention – has been described as 'the most elementary and important of all common law rights'.[1] This is reflective of Blackstone's warning in his *Commentaries on the Laws of England* in 1765. He wrote:

> Of great importance to the public is the preservation of this personal liberty: for if once it were left in the power of any, the highest, … to imprison arbitrarily whomever he or his officers thought proper there would soon be an end of all other rights and immunities.[2]

If the appropriate response in a democracy to the threat of terrorism has become *the* issue of our age, then detention without trial of suspected terrorists or their associates is perhaps the most controversial of all of the laws enacted in Australia in the past six years. Such laws have led to controversy elsewhere, notably in the United Kingdom and in the United States where a number of important cases have considered their application and validity.

Here there are no cases – yet – directly concerning the validity of the anti-terrorism laws, both state and federal, which provide for executive detention without trial, although there are a number of cases concerning that topic outside of the terrorism area which may help predict the fate of those laws when they fall for consideration. In my view the existing precedents suggest both the state and federal terrorism laws for preventative detention orders are valid.[3]

The policy of preventative detention

Before I explain why that is my view, something should be said about the policy behind the laws given the controversy that surrounds them. On the one hand, there are those who regard terrorism as just another matter for the criminal law, and who regard the arguments of necessity made by many governments around the world much as Pitt the Younger did two centuries ago when he said that '[n]ecessity is the plea for every infringement of human freedom. It is the argument of tyrants; it is the creed of slaves'.[4]

On the other hand there are those such as Judge Richard Posner of the US Court of Appeals for the Seventh Circuit who have described terrorism in the 21st century as 'global, diffuse, fanatical, alien, protean, mobile, elusive and indistinct',[5] and as constituting a threat which requires governments to move beyond the traditional paradigms of criminal justice on the one hand, or a World War II model of imprisonment of the enemy for the duration of the conflict on the other, to find a third way, a way beyond guilt or innocence, a way which includes detention without trial, not for punishment but for the protection of the community.

The policy argument in favour of this third way acknowledges that there have been many terrorist groups in the past – they existed even before the revolutionaries who gave France 'the Reign of Terror' from which the word 'terrorism' is derived – but argues that, unlike the anarchists of the 19th century or the assassins of the early part of the past millennium, 21st century terrorists have mutated into something genuinely new and newly dangerous. There are at least two reasons for this:

- modern terrorists' mobility in movement and communication, and thus their ability to strike without warning; and
- the asymmetric effects of the modern weapons available to terrorists, and thus the ability of a small group to cause huge loss of life – the events of September 11, 2001 being a paradigm example.

Because a major terrorist act such as 9/11 or the Bali bombing has such horrific consequences, prevention of the act assumes far greater importance than is the case in the normal law enforcement context.

Thus, as several other chapters in this book discuss, there are a whole series of laws in Divisions 101 and 102 of the Commonwealth *Criminal Code* built about the new notions of 'terrorist acts' and 'terrorist organisations', laws which among other things, seek to prevent such acts by criminalising both terrorist associations and also terrorist planning at an early stage.

In 2005, the Commonwealth parliament pursued this preventive policy further through the enactment of laws which authorised control orders (Division 104 of the *Criminal Code*), and also preventative detention for up to 48 hours (Division 105). The former scheme was unsuccessfully challenged in *Thomas v Mowbray*,[6] a result which has some significance for the validity of the latter type of order. In relation to the preventative detention orders of Division 105, the State parliaments have passed complementary laws which permit executive detention for up to two weeks.[7] The power to detain a person under the Commonwealth and State laws exists in order to prevent a terrorist act or to preserve evidence of a terrorist act.[8]

The constitutional issues

There are really three constitutional issues which arise from consideration of the scheme:

- Why do we need such a law at all?
- Are there any limits on what State parliaments can do – at least in the absence of an inconsistent federal law?
- What can the Commonwealth parliament do? (A question which involves attention to the distinction between punitive and preventative detention.)

The inadequacy of executive power

Clearly, executive power will not suffice for lengthy detention within Australia.[9] The reason for this lies in some old but still vital law and history. As Scalia J stated in his dissent in the United States Supreme Court's decision in *Hamdi v Rumsfeld*, the *Petition of Right* accepted by King Charles I in 1628 expressly prohibits executive imprisonment without formal charges.[10] This provision is no dead letter – it is still the law in New South Wales, and some other Australian jurisdictions.[11]

Furthermore, the Bill of Rights – that is the *Bill of Rights 1688* – which is also, and for the same reason, still the law in NSW provides that the suspension of laws or their execution by 'regal' (that is 'executive') authority and without the consent of parliament is illegal. This provision was among the reasons for the decision of the High Court in *A v Hayden* – the remarkable ASIS Sheraton Hotel raid case – that there was no power in the executive government to authorise a breach of the law, nor was a general defence of superior orders available in Australian criminal law. As Gibbs CJ said, 'It is fundamental to our legal system that the executive has no power to authorise a breach of the law and that it is no excuse for an offender to say that he acted under the orders of a superior officer'.[12] This is why, incidentally, the executive cannot grant anticipatory pardons.[13]

Detention of persons outside of Australia by executive authority is a more obscure topic, being devoid of modern authority. There is old authority suggesting an enemy alien cannot sue in times of war,[14] but both whether that remains good law and what 'war' now means is unclear. The limits of the executive power overseas are equally unclear, and this is an area where the murky relationship between public international law and domestic law is important. It could come up, for example, if an Australian soldier or sailor detained a foreigner on the battlefield, and the detainee sought relief from an Australian court. The Commonwealth would rely, I am sure, on the 'Act of State' doctrine[15] but there is little modern authority concerning the application of that doctrine.

While, unlike the United States, there is, in s 75(v) of the Australian Constitution, entrenched jurisdiction to review actions of officers of the Commonwealth, including as to the lawfulness of detention by such officers,[16] Australia has no Commonwealth bill of rights and very few, and limited, constitutional rights. Thus, there is no equivalent in our Constitution to the fifth and 14th amendments found in the Constitution of the United States which relevantly provide for a right not to be deprived of life, liberty or property by either federal or state laws, without due process of law. As Dawson J pointed out in *Kruger v Commonwealth*, the 1898 Australian Constitutional Convention expressly rejected a proposal to incorporate due process rights, largely based on the 14th Amendment.[17]

Although, 90 years later, in 1988, the Australian Constitutional Commission recommended the insertion of a new s 124J into the Constitution which would have provided that 'everyone has the right not to be arbitrarily arrested or detained', that recommendation was never put to a vote at a referendum, to the lasting regret of the Commission's chairman, Sir Maurice Byers who cited the example of the *Korematsu* case.[18]

Given that legislative authority is required to establish a scheme of detention without trial, what constitutional limits apply?

State laws

There are few if any limits on State legislative powers. Certainly, the strict principles guarding the separation of powers at the federal level are not directly applicable. *Kable v Director of Public Prosecutions (NSW)* establishes that there is an implied prohibition in Chapter III of the Constitution against a State parliament vesting in a Supreme Court a function or a power that is incompatible with the vesting of federal jurisdiction in the Supreme Court.[19] That is a different test to determining whether a Commonwealth law breaches Chapter III of the Constitution, although, if a State law could have been enacted by the Commonwealth parliament without infringing Chapter III, a *Kable* challenge will necessarily fail.[20]

In *Fardon v Attorney-General (Qld)* it was held that the *Kable* principle was not infringed by a law which provided for the annual but, because renewable, possibly indefinite detention in gaol, of serious sex offenders whose term of imprisonment had ended, because they were considered by a court to be an unacceptable risk to society if released.[21] The analogies with the detention law for the prevention of terrorism are obvious.

While, in *Fardon*, both Gummow and Kirby JJ would have struck down the law had it been enacted by the Commonwealth, the other justices did not consider that question. *Fardon* is a strong indication that the State laws providing for detention without trial will be valid – there is nothing to the contrary in the most recent case to consider the application of *Kable* to a State law, *Forge v Australian Securities and Investments Commission*.[22]

Federal laws

Finally, there is the question of federal laws. First, it must be noted that the Commonwealth possesses no general criminal law-making power, nor a specific power concerning terrorism. But possible sources of power include the defence power in s 51(vi), which is clearly of major importance after six members of the High Court found in *Thomas v Mowbray* that this supported the Commonwealth's regime for the issuing of interim control orders under Division 104 of the *Criminal Code*.

Additionally a number of other powers are of significance in this field. Presuming that terrorists will often be agents of a foreign state or organisation, the Commonwealth parliament's capacity under s 51 of the Constitution to make laws, variously, with respect to 'aliens', 'immigration' and the 'influx of criminals', are all of potential utility. The external affairs power is crucial in this context, not only because of the many anti-terrorist treaties to which Australia is a party,[23] but also because of the positive obligations imposed on 'all states' – including Australia – by a number of UN Security Council resolutions passed since 11 September 2001.[24]

There is also the implied nationhood power and the Commonwealth's executive power in s 61 of the Constitution, read in combination with the express incidental legislative power, which have been relied upon to support, for example, the enactment of the *Australian Security Intelligence Organisation Act 1979* (Cth).

Apart from the need for a source of law-making power, what are the essential constitutional principles on the issue of executive detention without trial? In *Chu Kheng Lim v Minister for Immigration and Local Government and Ethnic Affairs* the High Court considered the involuntary detention of aliens pending expulsion or deportation, and held that such detention was not unconstitutional.[25] It was here that Brennan, Deane and Toohey JJ made their well-known statement that:

> It would, for example, be beyond the legislative power of the Parliament to invest the Executive with an arbitrary power to detain citizens in custody

> notwithstanding that the power was conferred in terms which sought to divorce such detention in custody from both punishment and criminal guilt. The reason why that is so is that, putting to one side the exceptional cases to which reference is made below, the involuntary detention of a citizen in custody by the State is … punitive in character and, under our system of government, exists only as an incident of the exclusively judicial function of adjudging and punishing criminal guilt.[26]

Nevertheless, they recognised exceptions to their general rule, for example, '[i]nvoluntary detention in cases of mental illness or infectious disease'[27] and of course the migration detention at issue in that case.

However, their Honours' oft-quoted statement has never received the unqualified support of a majority of the court, either in that case or subsequently. Chief Justice Mason's concurrence in relation to the joint judgment's reasoning concerning aliens did not extend to agreement with this passage,[28] leading Kirby J to say that it is not, therefore, part of the ratio decidendi of the case.[29]

Subsequently, in *Re Woolley; Ex parte Applicants M276/2003*, McHugh J pointed out that it is 'going too far to say that, subject to specified exceptions, detention by the Executive is *always* penal or punitive and can only be achieved as a result of the exercise of judicial power'.[30] This had been the view of Gaudron J in *Lim*, which her Honour repeated in *Kruger v Commonwealth* when she said it 'is not possible to say that, subject to clear exceptions, the power to authorise detention in custody is necessarily and exclusively judicial power'.[31] This approach was followed by Hayne and Heydon JJ in *Al-Kateb v Godwin* [32] and later in *Re Woolley* where, in a similar vein, Callinan J said:

> Detention for purposes other than punitive ones has traditionally been constitutionally acceptable. … Examples are arrest and detention pending trial, detention of the mentally ill or infectiously diseased, and for the welfare and protection of persons endangered for various reasons.[33]

In *Vasiljkovic v Commonwealth* a majority of the High Court held that there was no constitutional difficulty with detaining persons including Australian citizens, for the purpose of extraditing them to foreign countries.[34]

In *Lim*, Brennan, Deane and Toohey JJ had found it 'unnecessary to consider whether the defence power in times of war will support an executive power to make detention orders such as that considered in *Little v Commonwealth*'.[35] (In *Little* the High Court had upheld a broad ministerial discretion to detain persons thought to be prejudicial to security interests.) [36]

This question was, however, considered by some members of the court in the later case of *Al Kateb v Godwin*, in which the court held four to three that a Commonwealth law requiring an unlawful non-citizen to be detained pending deportation was valid even in circumstances where there was no real likelihood of his removal in the reasonably foreseeable future. Justice McHugh, having noted that three wartime cases – *Lloyd v Wallach*, *Ex parte Walsh* and *Little v Commonwealth* [37] – established that preventative detention on security grounds could be supported by the defence power under s 51(vi) of the Constitution in wartime, said 'I see no reason to think that this court would strike down similar regulations if Australia was again at war in circumstances similar to those of 1914-1918 and 1939-1945'.[38] Those careful remarks direct attention to the difference between a war of national survival where the defence power is available to its maximum extent, and the present time 'war on terror'.

Conclusion

Ultimately, the correct test is whether detention under a Commonwealth law is for a legitimate non-punitive object which attracts a head of power.[39] If so, the law will be valid. Once it is determined that there is a non-punitive purpose, there is no additional requirement that the law be reasonably capable of being seen as necessary for achieving that non-punitive purpose.[40] However, the question of proportionality arises at the earlier stage of determining the law's purpose – if it goes beyond what is reasonably capable of being seen as necessary to achieve its non-punitive object, the law may be characterised as having a punitive object.[41] And, as McHugh J also points out in *Re Woolley*, 'it is important to recognise the distinction for Ch III purposes between purpose and effect. … It is not enough that the effect of the law is no different from the infliction of punishment'.[42] The distinction between protective and punitive laws is thus alive and well in this context.[43]

Notes

* This paper draws on previous papers given to the Australian Government Solicitor's Forum in March 2005, the Judicial Conference of Australia in September 2005 and an article, 'Constitutional aspects of detention without trial in Australia, the United States and the United Kingdom' (2006) 9 *Constitutional Law & Policy Review* 37.

1 *Trobridge v Hardy* (1955) 94 CLR 147, 152 (Fullagar J).

2 *Commentaries on the Laws of England* (1765) Book 1, 120–21; 130–31.

3 The recent decision of the High Court in *Thomas v Mowbray* [2007] HCA 33, discussed in Chapter 2 of this book, supports this thesis.

4 William Pitt (Speech delivered in the House of Commons, 18 November 1783).

5 Richard A Posner, *Uncertain Shield, the US Intelligence System in the throes of Reform* (2007) 50.

6 *Thomas v Mowbray* [2007] HCA 33. This decision is discussed in Chapter 2 of this book.

7 For example, *Terrorism (Police Powers) Act 2002* (NSW) Pt 2A.

8 See, for example, *Criminal Code* (Cth) s 105.4.

9 The *Tampa* case – *Ruddock v Vadarlis* (2001) 110 FCR 491 – does not help here. It decided only a limited question, namely that the executive power of the Commonwealth extended to a power to prevent the entry of non-citizens to Australia, and to do such things neces-

sary to effect that exclusion – for example, restraining a person or boat from proceeding into Australia or compelling that person or boat to leave.

10 He noted that this law was the direct result of the King detaining without charge several individuals who failed to assist England's war against France and Spain, and who were denied *habeas corpus* by the courts notwithstanding they had not been charged with any offence. The reason asserted for their detention was the interest of the State in protecting the country. In the United States, that was part of the constitutional background which led to the passage of the due process clauses in the 5th and 14th Amendments to the United States Constitution: *Hamdi v Rumsfeld* 542 US 507 (2004), 557.

11 It is mentioned, for example, in *Imperial Acts Application Act 1969* (NSW), s 6 and Sch 2.

12 *A v Hayden* (1984) 156 CLR 532, 540. See also 562 (Murphy J), 580 (Brennan J) and 592 (Deane J).

13 *R v Stead* [1994] 1 Qd R 665.

14 *Johnstone v Pedlar* (1921) 2 AC 262.

15 See, for example, *Ali v Commonwealth* [2004] VSC 6.

16 This was largely because our constitutional founders had read *Marbury v Madison* 5 US 137 (1803), 175. See, for example, John Quick and Robert Garran, *The Annotated Constitution of the Australian Commonwealth* (1901) 778-80.

17 *Kruger v Commonwealth* (1997) 190 CLR 1, 61.

18 Personal conversation with the author. *Korematsu v United States* 323 US 214 (1944) is discussed in Chapter 2 of this book.

19 *Kable v Director of Public Prosecutions (NSW)* (1996) 189 CLR 51.

20 *HA Bachrach Pty Ltd v Queensland* (1998) 195 CLR 547, 564.

21 *Fardon v Attorney-General (Qld)* (2004) 223 CLR 575. It was apparent from the questions emanating from the bench in that case, that the High Court was looking ahead to the possibility that the Commonwealth might pass a law permitting suspected terrorists to be detained because of the risk and danger they posed to the community.

22 *Forge v Australian Securities and Investments Commission* (2006) 229 ALR 223. The High Court will again consider *Kable* in late September 2007 when it hears *Gypsy Jokers Motorcycle Club Incorporated v Commissioner of Police*, see [2007] HCATrans 297.

23 See the *Report of Australia to the Counter-Terrorism Committee of the United Nations Security Council pursuant to paragraph 6 of Security Council Resolution 1373* (2001).

24 The external affairs power supports legislation to implement treaty obligations and matters of international concern: *Commonwealth v Tasmania* (1983) 158 CLR 1, 131-2, 171, 220, 258.

25 *Chu Kheng Lim v Minister for Immigration and Local Government and Ethnic Affairs* (1992) 176 CLR 1.

26 Above n 25, 27.

27 Above n 25, 28.

28 Above n 25, 10.

29 *Vasiljkovic v Commonwealth* (2006) 228 ALR 447, 492.

30 *Re Woolley; ex p Applicants M276/2003* (2004) 225 CLR 1, 24.

31 *Chu Kheng Lim v Minister for Immigration and Local Government and Ethnic Affairs* (1992) 176 CLR 1, 55; *Kruger v Commonwealth* (1997) 190 CLR 1, 110.

32 *Al-Kateb v Godwin* (2004) 219 CLR 562, 648-51 (Hayne J); 662-3 (Heydon J), a view which both maintained in *Re Woolley; ex p Applicants M276/2003* (2004) 225 CLR 1, 75 (Hayne J); 87 (Heydon J).

33 *Re Woolley; ex p Applicants M276/2003* (2004) 225 CLR 1, 85.

34 *Vasiljkovic v Commonwealth* (2006) 228 ALR 447.

35 *Chu Kheng Lim v Minister for Immigration and Local Government and Ethnic Affairs* (1992) 176 CLR 1, fn 66.

36 *Little v Commonwealth* (1947) 75 CLR 94.

37 *Lloyd v Wallach* (1915) 20 CLR 299; *Ex p Walsh* [1942] ALR 359; *Little v Commonwealth* (1947) 75 CLR 94.

38 *Al Kateb v Godwin* (2004) 219 CLR 562, 589.

39 *Chu Kheng Lim v Minister for Immigration and Local Government and Ethnic Affairs* (1992) 176 CLR 1, 71 (McHugh J).

40 *Re Woolley; ex p Applicants M276/2003* (2004) 225 CLR 1, 32-3 (McHugh J); and *Al Kateb* (2004) 219 CLR 562, 647-51 (Hayne J).

41 *Chu Kheng Lim v Minister for Immigration and Local Government and Ethnic Affairs* (1992) 176 CLR 1, 33 (Brennan, Deane and Dawson JJ); 10 (Mason CJ agreeing). McHugh J, at 71, required the law to be 'reasonably necessary'. See also McHugh J in *Re Woolley; ex p Applicants M276/2003* (2004) 225 CLR 1, 32.

42 *Re Woolley; ex p Applicants M276/2003* (2004) 225 CLR 1, 35.

43 The decision of *Thomas v Mowbray* was delivered just prior to going to print. The court's upholding of the conferral upon the federal judiciary to issue control orders is an important development in the jurisprudence of Ch III generally as well as the scope of the defence and external affairs powers. But the mechanism by which preventative detention orders are made – not by courts but instead by persons acting in an executive capacity – means that the case does not address the issue directly under consideration here and in the decisions of *Lim*, *Al Kateb*, Re *Woolley* and *Vasiljkovic*.

PART IV

Human Rights and Terrorism: is a Trade-off Necessary?

13

When are Restrictions on Speech Justified in the War on Terror?

Katharine Gelber

In the 'war on terror', it is democracy that we are said to be defending. It is in the name of preserving democracy that we have gone to war and passed new legislation combating terror. Our Prime Minister regularly talks of the shared democratic values that are important to Australia's social and political fabric. He has talked of Australians' strength in 'our democratic beliefs', and applauded the fact that Australia is one of the very few countries that has remained 'continuously democratic for the last 100 years'.[1]

In terms of characterising that democracy he has averred that frequent and vigorous disagreement is 'in the nature of participatory democracy, … in the nature of a civilised democratic society which values dialogue and differences of view'.[2] More specifically, he has argued that Australian democracy is composed of three central 'pillars': a robust parliamentary system, an incorruptible judiciary and a free press.[3] These have been described as the 'three situations that prevail against all assaults on political freedom', the 'three title deeds of our democracy', and the 'three great bulwarks of democracy'.[4] My specific interest here is in the third of these characteristics. The Prime Minister has elaborated on his conception of a free press as involving 'very importantly, and sometimes for we [sic] in the practice of politics frustratingly, the existence of an open, robust, free and usually highly critical media'; a 'free and sceptical media, free and sceptical often to the discomfort of us but nonetheless an important and integral part of our society'.[5] He has also elaborated on the idea that democracy involves the expression of different points of view, including criticism of government and robust debate.[6]

In this chapter I investigate the meaning of those views, to move beyond rhetoric or platitudes. If Australian society can claim to be democratic, what do we mean by that claim? If Australians value democracy, what does that mean? In what precisely lies the value and importance of that third bulwark of our freedom, a free and open press? What is it about expressing differing points of view that renders that process 'democratic'? What does it mean, in short, to describe Australia as a democracy, in speech terms?

In order to do this, first I examine a perspective on *why* free and open discussion is important to democratic practice; so that this is not simply an assumption or rhetorical claim but a substantive instantiation of democracy. Secondly, I consider *how* free and open discussion can be facilitated, an important consideration if we agree that it is indeed important. Thirdly, I outline briefly some of the ways in which some of our current anti-terrorism measures might be considered to impact upon freedom of expression. I conclude by arguing the importance of having in mind concrete, informed and rich understandings of what democracy is constituted by, when developing policy to counter terrorism.

Free and open discussion and critical engagement

First, let us consider the idea of a free and open press since the claim is made by our government that this is a crucial institution to our democracy. Let us think here of the role of the press as a conveyor of ideas, as well as an institution of shareholders or profit or a business enterprise. What if we think of the press as having primarily a public function, as a conveyor of ideas throughout a variegated and complex 'public'.

It is possible, indeed probable, that in the public sphere and in public debate, an informed public is able to monitor the activities of government. This would be a public engaged in 'critical reasoning'.[7] To engage in critical reasoning requires knowledge; knowledge of laws for example, or the circumstances under which those laws may be applied. The public in that sense can monitor the authority of representative government, and be able to make judgments as to the rightness of its actions; a truly civic task. In this context, the media are precisely that – the *media* by which a process of critical and informed engagement is able to occur. In this context of consideration of the public sphere, the idea of free and open media has a particular democratic resonance. It could be seen in an ideal model as a key institution by which the process of informing the public to be able to become engaged and critical takes place. It is thus capable of being a key institution of democracy in the sense that it fulfils a function crucial to the maintenance of a critical public sphere, which in turn is crucial to monitoring and checking the activities of a representative and – we may thus describe it so – democratic government.

To be sure, in the contemporary context, the media do and are much more than this. They do not simply provide information to a critical public. The reporting of events and news has been commodified via mechanisms including the rise of electronic forms of media, increased commercialisation, the use of advertising, the fusion of entertainment and information, the concentration of media outlets and increased regulation. This means that rather than an ideally critical public we see evidence of a highly consumerist public and the marketing of news and reporting as 'infotainment'. Under these conditions it is rather more challenging to ensure that ideal deliberation can still occur, although critical potential of course remains in the potential agency of media users – the public. Nevertheless it is crucial that such deliberation is able to occur for a system of representative government to be able to claim authority legitimately, from a diversified and pluralistic people. What is required is a 'political public sphere'.[8] Eminent US First Amendment scholar Robert Post concurs with this view. He argues that public discourse is the communicative structure by which citizens engage in democratic self-rule.[9]

These ideas explain *why* it is that a free and sceptical media and free and open discussion, are important to democratic practice. But they do not yet explain *how* such debate can be facilitated.

Discourse, democracy and the legitimacy of law

How can such critical debate happen? Through dialogue, discussion and debate. We might even call this process 'discourse', by which I mean a communicative interchange. In this communicative interchange speakers make claims that what they are saying is valid. A hearer can accept these claims, or if they do not accept them, debate them further with the purpose of reasoning with hearers to come to a common understanding over time. This is a process of interchange in which differences of opinion are not just stated for the purposes of stating them, or of the speakers making their views heard and known. It is not simply an exchange of views that goes no further, an expression of differing viewpoints. Expressions and points of view are put forward for the express purpose of making claims to their validity. These claims are engaged with by hearers. They can accept or reject them. The purpose is thus not to have a cacophony of ideas presented with no listeners to be persuaded, but rather that the exchange of ideas has a purpose, and that that purpose is for speakers to seek to persuade each other to come to their understanding. This is a concept of speech or expression that is far more comprehensive than simply the expression of one's opinion, and it is what is meant (by Habermas) by 'discourse'. This means that speech is a means of effecting social coordination among speakers.

A feature of this process is that it is not just an exchange of ideas; this process can also be seen as the mechanism by which laws can be regarded as attaining legitimacy. The law as an entity provides a standard for behaviour, a common benchmark, in a world in which people's views are diverse and differentiated, and individuals are generally in pursuit of their own ends. It is enforceable, and subject to sanctions if necessary. It is thus vital that the procedure for the production of law is legitimate. If what I have said thus far holds true, then the process of attempting to establish common ground through exchanging views that claim to be valid, is a means by which that legitimacy can be achieved. Discourse enables free discussion of competing ideas, and simultaneously 'secures a discursive character for political will-formation'. It is through discourse that citizens can become the authors of the laws to which they are subjected. There is thus an internal relationship between the rule of law and democracy such that the 'democratic process bears the ... burden of legitimation'.[10] Indeed, investigating the role of discourse in a democracy allows us to explain how discourse legitimises disagreements over enforceable norms in social organisation.

At this point in the argument, then, we can see two elements clearly: why free and open discussion is important to democratic legitimacy and how free and open discussion instantiates the very processes and procedures that permit us to call ourselves democratic. Without them, our democracy would be impoverished. The elements are closely interrelated in that the purpose of a sceptical media is to provide an institutional mechanism by which free and open and informed discussion can better take place, with a view to establishing and legitimating the norms by which we must all abide, or risk punitive sanction.

This brings me to a third element in the democratic legitimacy framework. The whole mechanism I have already described suggests that discourse is a means by which legitimacy can be secured. Citizens must be able to judge the adequacy of the laws they enact. However, this whole mechanism relies on an as-yet unstated assumption. That is that the forms of communication that make it possible to judge the adequacy of laws enacted by the people must themselves be legally institutionalised, in order to guarantee the social and political conditions required for discourse to occur. That means certain liberty rights and participation rights must be guaranteed because without the recognition of these rights the entire order I have described would fall apart.

Thus we arrive at a justification for the widely-held premise that free speech is a core element of a democratic framework. It is often said that democracy is synonymous with free speech; that without the freedom to express one's thoughts and opinions democracy would be desiccated, lacking in the robustness that our political leaders aver is a defining characteristic of democracy in this country (see above). It is on the ground of democracy that our government has defended the right to freedom of expression.[11] And this premise has been central to the High Court of Australia's finding of an implied freedom of political communication in the Australian Constitution. In the two 1992 landmark cases which established the freedom, the justices held that freedom of communication on political matters derived from the constitutional provisions (ss 7 and 24) that provide that representatives are 'directly chosen by the people'. Representative democracy was the foundation of the freedom because it required public participation in political discussion, indeed such discussion was 'indispensable', 'essential', 'necessary' and 'inherent' to it.[12] Even this freedom, however, can be limited where a law which does so is reasonably appropriate and adapted to serve a legitimate end in a manner which is compatible with the maintenance of the constitutionally prescribed system of representative and responsible government.[13]

Similarly, adopting the democratic legitimacy framework I have outlined does not automatically demand an absolutist position on free speech. It can be argued that speech that, in its very utterance, substantively injures the processes described, is speech that could be limited or restricted. It is the norm in democratic societies that a narrowly conceived range of speech is so limited. In Australia an example is vilification, which can be seen as speech that, in its very utterance, inflicts substantive harm on its targets in such a manner as to prevent or injure their ability to participate in democratic legitimation processes. Thus, in this framework and interpretation of what is required for democracy to flourish I am not suggesting an absolutist protection of all speech, no matter its character.

Freedom of speech under Howard

Yet to say that accusations have been made that during the past decade free speech has been stifled in this country would be to understate matters. Concern has been expressed publicly about increasing government encroachment into academic freedom, the silencing of scientific data on climate change that could be perceived to be critical of government policy, the defunding of and constraints placed on non-government organisations, the curtailment of access by journalists and the media to policy information, the dismissal of advice which counters the objectives of the Prime Minister in relation to nuclear power, and the general suppression of dissent.[14] Measured against the ideal benchmark I have outlined here, these are all clear failures to protect not only the democratic values which Australia is said to hold dear, but the processes, procedures and mechanisms which I have argued ensure democracy is able to be practised. If democratic practice is being emaciated, this is not purely a moral problem, it is a concrete one; it curtails and limits our ability to fix the problems we face, it degrades our collective capacity to improve our world.

If we consider more specifically some of the statutory changes and proposed changes during the war on terror the picture is one of considerable limitations being placed on the processes of discussion, debate and critical engagement. Many of the statutory provisions enacted since September 2001 by the Australian parliament directly and indirectly limit freedom of speech in important ways. The most obvious are the sedition laws, which criminalise urging another person to overthrow by force or violence the Constitution or government, urging another person to interfere by force or violence with lawful election processes for parliament, urging a group or groups to use force or violence against another group distinguished by race, religion, nationality or political opinion, urging a person to engage in conduct which will assist another organisation or country to be at war with the Commonwealth, and urging another person to engage in conduct to assist an organisation or country engaged in armed hostilities with the Commonwealth.[15] I will not comment on the criticisms of these provisions from a free speech point of view further except to acknowledge the recommendations for amendment made by the Australian Law Reform Commission including the addition of a requirement that the person intends that the urged force or violence will occur.[16]

Some other matters relevant to speech considerations include (but are not limited to) the following. 'Advocacy' of terrorist acts has been defined in the criminal law in a manner inclusive of activity which 'indirectly counsels or urges', or 'praises' the doing of, a terrorist act.[17] The relevant definition is where 'the organisation directly praises the doing of a terrorist act in circumstances where there is *a risk* that such praise *might* have the effect of leading a person … to engage in a terrorist act' [emphasis added]. In addition the collection of documents connected with preparation for, or engagement in, or assistance in, a terrorist act – either with knowledge of, or recklessness as to, that connection – has been criminalised.[18]

In July 2006 two radical Islamic books (*Join the Caravan* and *Defence of the Muslim Lands*) were refused classification, or banned, by the Classification Review Board following an application from the Commonwealth Attorney-General, on the ground that they 'promote[d]' and 'incite[d] … in matters of crime or violence'.[19] After this successful banning the Attorney-General launched a discussion paper seeking to amend the Classification Code to refuse material that explicitly 'advocates' terrorist acts.[20] The argument provided for the amendment is that the 'advocacy' of terrorist acts, as defined in the *Criminal Code* (Cth), is inclusive of 'praise' or 'indirect counsel', concepts which are capable of capturing a broader range of activities than the existing classification code is able to do. In the absence of the State and Territory agreement necessary to amend the Code, the Attorney-General subsequently gave effect to these amendments through the *Classification (Publications, Films and Computer Games) Amendment (Terrorist Material) Act 2007* (Cth).

Preventative detention orders include the curtailment of opportunities for contact, and the matters that can be communicated during limited permitted contact, with others. This includes, under Commonwealth law, preventing a person from disclosing that they are subject to such an order, that they have been detained, or the period for which they are to be detained. Their lawyer is similarly prevented from disclosing such or indeed any other information relevant to their client to others.[21] State laws are a little less stringent.[22] Nevertheless, these restrictions limit the ability of the media to report on matters relating to preventative detention orders.

How much speech should be restricted in a 'democracy'?

If we subject these kinds of limitations on speech to the framework I outlined earlier, a despondent view of the fortunes of speech emerges. It is likely that a number of the measures introduced in the context of new anti-terrorism policies would fare poorly when measured against the two requirements outlined earlier: understanding why free and open discussion is important, and how it can occur.

I argued that free and open discussion is important as a constitutive process of an informed and critical public, capable of engaging in the deliberation necessary for democratic legitimacy, and that the way this occurs is through seeking to convince others of one's ideas, coordinating social beliefs and norms through seeking to reach understanding. It is doubtful this framework would for example sanction the inclusion of praise in a definition of criminal acts of terrorism. Similarly, defining the possession of documents as a criminal act of terrorism and limiting books that extol the virtues of terrorism fare extremely poorly. It is also likely that it is only through more open discussion of views that seek to convince others that terrorist acts are warranted, or the ideas contained in books that extol the virtues of terrorism, that people vulnerable to the ideas of terrorism will become less – and not more – convinced that terrorism is a legitimate enterprise.

I also suggested that speech that instantiates a violation of the processes required for legitimation and democracy in its utterance could legitimately be restricted, when we think of speech within a democratic framework. But the kinds of speech that are captured by our present anti-terrorism laws cannot be said to injure substantively the democratic legitimacy framework I have outlined. Rather, it is the extent of the laws themselves which can be seen as substantively injuring processes of democratic legitimacy. The informed, critically engaged public essential to the notion of democracy is prevented from performing its role. Further, if the laws themselves are set up in such a way as to prevent discourse from occurring then the legitimation project fails and the democratic procedure of will-formation, of reaching discursive agreement, is risked.

The line between speech that substantively injures the conditions required for democratic legitimation to occur and speech that does not is, and will always be, difficult to draw. But we can garner a better framework within which to make such judgments by thinking more carefully, exploring in greater depth the great contributions to democratic theory made over the centuries which can help us evaluate the tools we choose to use to fight terrorism.

The point I am trying to make is that we need to move beyond rhetorical platitudes and examine what it is we are defending, and what we are doing in that name, when we claim to be defending democracy. In doing so, we should make use of the wealth of intellectual material that is at our disposal. Democracy literature is diverse and rich. But it shares some common characteristics: the need for legitimacy to derive from the people, the need to create and maintain conditions within which legitimation can occur, the need to enhance opportunities for participation, and the need for criticism to be robust, vigorous and real. It is important that in the name of the war on terror we do not fracture the very practices which enable us to claim the mantle of a democracy. Otherwise what we have left will not deserve the name.

The threat from terrorism is real. But this is not the first time in modern history that democratic nations have felt at risk. This is not the first time they have felt cause to fear for their way of life. May I remind you that at a 'moment unprecedented in … history', when 'security [had never] been as seriously threatened from without' as it was then conceived, the response of Franklin Roosevelt was to think about the 'social and economic problems which [were] the root cause' of the threat he faced.[23] In that context he emphasised that the people expected 'the preservation of civil liberties for all'. He looked forward to a world founded upon the 'essential human freedom'; of 'freedom of speech and expression – everywhere in the world'. So do I.

Notes

1 John Howard 'Address to community morning tea' (Speech delivered at Wantirna, Melbourne, 9 October 2001); John Howard 'Address at the launch of Danna Vale's campaign' (Speech delivered 7 October 2001).

2 John Howard 'Address to ACOSS Congress' (Speech delivered at Melbourne, 25 October 2001).

3 John Howard 'Address at the Opening of the 13th Commonwealth Law Conference and 33rd Australian Legal Convention' (Speech delivered at the Melbourne Convention Centre, Melbourne, 14 April 2003); John Howard 'Address at Ceremonial Sitting to Mark the Centenary of the High Court of Australia' (Speech delivered at the Supreme Court of Victoria, Melbourne, 6 October 2003); John Howard 'Address to the National Press Club' (Speech delivered at the Great Hall, Parliament House, Canberra, 25 January 2006); John Howard 'Address at the Opening of the Commonwealth Law Courts' (Speech delivered at Adelaide, 2 February 2006).

4 Howard 'Address at the Opening of the 13th Commonwealth Law Conference and 33rd Australian Legal Convention', above n 3; Howard 'Address to the National Press Club', above n 3; Howard 'Address at the Opening of the Commonwealth Law Courts', above n 3.

5 Howard 'Address at the Opening of the 13th Commonwealth Law Conference and 33rd Australian Legal Convention', above n 3; Howard 'Address at Ceremonial Sitting to Mark the Centenary of the High Court of Australia', above n 3.

6 Howard, above n 2; John Howard 'Election Night Speech' (Speech delivered at Sydney, 10 November 2001); John Howard 'Address at the Ryde Business Forum Luncheon' (Speech delivered at Sydney, 21 February 2003); John Howard 'Address at the Queensland Press Forum' (Speech delivered 9 April 2003); John Howard 'Address at the Opening of the Police Federation of Australia Offices' (Speech delivered at Manuka, Canberra, 16 September 2003); John Howard 'Address at Australia Day Citizenship Ceremony' (Speech delivered at Commonwealth Park, Canberra, 26 January 2007); John Howard 'Address to the Menzies Research Centre' (Speech delivered at the Theatrette, Parliament House, Canberra, 18 April 2006).

7 Jürgen Habermas, *The Structural Transformation of the Public Sphere* (first published 1962, 2003 ed) 25-6, 52, 162. This and the next section of this chapter rely on ideas developed in great depth by Habermas. See also Jürgen Habermas, *The Theory of Communicative Action, Volume 1: Reason and the Rationalization of Society* (1984): especially 38-42, 279-337; Jürgen Habermas, *The Theory of Communicative Action, Volume 2: Lifeworld and System. A Critique of Functionalist Reason* (1987); Jürgen Habermas, 'Further Reflections on the Public Sphere' in Craig Calhoun (ed), *Habermas and the Public Sphere*, (2nd ed, 1993): especially 425, 436-7, 441, 445-46; Jürgen Habermas, *Between Facts and Norms: Contributions to a Discourse Theory of Law and Democracy* (first published 1992, William Regh trans, 1996) 448, 455. Note also the changes in Habermas' views over time, in that in his 1993 work he concedes his account of a transformation of a 'culture-debating' to a 'culture-consuming' public was 'too simplistic'. He maintains the idea that critical inquiry could exist in the form of intra-associational, collective spheres (at 438, 440).

8 Habermas, 'Further Reflections on the Public Sphere', ibid, 446.

9 Robert Post, *Constitutional Domains: Democracy, Community, Management* (1995) 7, 273.

10 Habermas, *Between Facts and Norms: Contributions to a Discourse Theory of Law and Democracy*, above n 7, 448-50.

11 John Howard, 'Address at the NSW Liberal Party State Council' (Speech delivered at Homebush Bay, Sydney, 23 November 2002).

12 Gerald N Rosenberg & John M Williams, 'Do Not Go Gently Into That Good Right: The First Amendment in the High Court of Australia' (1997) *Supreme Court Review* 439, 448-50.

13 *Coleman v Power* (2004) 220 CLR 1, 66.

14 Stuart Macintyre, 'Universities', Ian Lowe, 'The Research Community' and Helen Ester, 'The Media' in Clive Hamilton and Sarah Maddison (eds) *Silencing Dissent* (2007); Linda Weiss, Elizabeth Thurbon and John Mathews *National Insecurity: The Howard Government's Betrayal of Australia* (2007), 37-38 and 40-44; Sarah Maddison, and Richard Denniss, 'Democratic constraint and embrace: implications for progressive non-government advocacy organisations in Australia' (2005) 40(3) *Australian Journal of Political Science* 373; David Marr, 'In His Master's Voice: The Corruption of Public Debate Under Howard' (2007) *Quarterly Essay* 26.

15 *Criminal Code* (Cth) s 80.2.

16 Australian Law Reform Commission, *Fighting Words: A Review of Sedition Laws in Australia*, Report 104 (2006) 176.

17 *Criminal Code* (Cth) s 102.1(1A)(c).

18 *Criminal Code* (Cth) s 101.5.

19 Norman Abjorensen, 'Strike up the ban: Censor joins the war on terror', *Democratic Audit of Australia Discussion Paper* 26/06 (2006); see also Phillip Coorey, 'Book Ban Anger: It Will Hinder Freedoms', *Sydney Morning Herald*, 4 October 2006, 2.

20 Australian Attorney-General's Department, *Material That Advocates Terrorist Acts: Discussion Paper* (2007) 3-5.

21 *Criminal Code* (Cth) ss 105.34-105.41.

22 For example, *Terrorism (Police Powers) Act 2002* (NSW) Div 5.

23 Franklin Roosevelt, 'Four Freedoms Speech' (Speech delivered at Congress, 6 January 1941).

14

Torture: The Fallacy of the Ticking Bomb

Sarah Joseph

Torture is absolutely forbidden in all circumstances in international law. Yet some commentators argue that, in light of the exigencies of the current 'war on terror', torture should be allowed in certain circumstances in order to attempt to extract information concerning future terrorist attacks. This chapter summarises and responds to such arguments.

The definition of torture

The most universally accepted definition of 'torture' is found in art 1 of the United Nations *Convention Against Torture and Other Cruel, Inhuman or Degrading Treatment or Punishment.* There are several elements to the convention definition. First, torture entails an extremely high level of physical and/or mental pain and suffering. Secondly, torture must be intentional. There is no notion of negligent or reckless torture. Thirdly, torture is inflicted for a particular purpose, including obtaining information from the victim. Fourthly, torture is an act of state: the definition requires some involvement of a public official in the act of torture.

Finally, and perhaps most intriguingly, is the rider to the definition in the last sentence of art 1: '[torture] does not include pain or suffering arising only from, inherent in or incidental to lawful sanctions'. Strangely, the UN Committee against Torture, the international body that monitors and supervises implementation of the Convention Against Torture, has said little about the meaning of this important sentence. It seems to indicate that an act, no matter how heinous, can escape classification as torture if it is authorised under a State's domestic law. If so, this rider seems like a classic get-out clause for the most unscrupulous of governments. However, such a scenario is unlikely. Such laws would not be permitted under many domestic constitutions. Furthermore, a trend in UN human rights jurisprudence has been to interpret the word 'lawful' in similar contexts to mean 'lawful in international law', rather than 'lawful in domestic law'. International law (in the convention and other sources) prohibits severe ill treatment and punishment, so it is likely that the rider only saves laws that authorise reasonable treatments and punishments. For example, the imprisonment of a person upon conviction of a serious crime is probably a punishment saved by the rider, notwithstanding the pain and suffering it might cause to a detainee.

The prohibition on torture and other ill treatment

Torture is prohibited under numerous international human rights treaties, along with other forms of ill treatment, namely 'cruel and inhuman treatment' and 'degrading treatment'. These latter prohibitions entail bad treatment that is not as severe as torture. Furthermore, other elements of the torture definition, such as the requirements of intention and purpose, do not apply.

All of these forms of ill treatment are absolutely prohibited. That is, they are non-derogable rights that cannot be compromised in any situation. For example, art 2(2) of the Convention Against Torture states:

> No exceptional circumstances whatsoever, whether a state of war or a threat or war, internal political instability or any other public emergency, may be invoked as a justification of torture.

This absolute prohibition is extended to other forms of ill treatment under other treaties, such as art 7 of the *International Covenant on Civil and Political Rights*.

Torture is also absolutely prohibited under customary international law. The status of the prohibition of other forms of ill treatment under customary law is more questionable.

Therefore, the international law on torture is clear. It may never be perpetrated, ever. Arguments in favour of its use in any circumstance are therefore arguments in favour of reform of international law.

Arguments in favour of the use of torture

The terrorist attacks on the US on 11 September 2001 have prompted arguments that torture is a legitimate weapon to combat terrorism. These arguments have tended to focus on the hypothetical 'ticking time bomb' scenario. The scenario typically has the following elements: a powerful device is set to explode and kill many people; the police have a suspect in custody who knows where the bomb is; the police know the suspect knows; the suspect will not tell the police where the bomb is under conventional interrogation techniques; time is running out for the police to plausibly discover the location of the bomb by conventional means. In that situation, would it not be reasonable, even appropriate, for the police to subject the suspect to torture to force him or her to give them the information they need to save lives?

One type of pro-torture argument is the utilitarian argument, exemplified in articles published by Australian academics Mirko Bagaric and Julie Clarke.[1] The utilitarian argument simply holds that torture should be allowed in the above scenario as the greater good is served by torturing the suspect and saving the lives of many innocent people. Bagaric and Clarke go further and seem to advocate the use of torture outside the catastrophic ticking bomb scenario – perhaps even in a case where torture could plausibly save just one life. This contention is based on the idea that it is illogical for the freedom from torture to be absolute when the right to life is not. The right to life is a fundamental right, but it can indeed be limited in exceptional circumstances – for example one may kill someone who imminently threatens one's own life or the life of another. Bagaric and Clarke believe that the freedom from torture should give way to the right to life when torture is likely to save lives.

A variant argument is the accountability argument, exemplified by Harvard Professor Alan Dershowitz.[2] Dershowitz is normatively opposed to torture. However, he argues that it happens regardless of its absolute prohibition, and that it will inevitably happen in a ticking bomb situation. In that circumstance, he believes that it is appropriate in democratic societies for such torture to come out from under the radar and be regulated and controlled, rather than denied and silently sanctioned. Dershowitz proposes that torture warrants be available from judicial officers in exceptional situations. Such a system would ensure that torture only occurred in the most extreme of circumstances, and would remove the crucial decision on whether to torture from the hands of potentially inexperienced or overly emotional field agents or police officers into the hands of dispassionate senior judicial officers. The torture itself would be regulated to only allow certain 'safe' techniques, such as the administration of a sterilised needle under the fingernail. Dershowitz believes that such a system promotes greater accountability, which accords with the values of liberal democracies, and will lead to less torture. Bagaric and Clarke also support the idea of a torture warrant.

Arguments in favour of maintaining the absolute prohibition

The utilitarian and accountability arguments are flawed for a number of reasons. A simple deontological, or non-consequentialist, argument is that torture should be prohibited because it is a complete affront to and negation of the human dignity of both the victim and the perpetrator. The world has finally evolved into a place where no government openly argues in favour of torture. Though torture is undoubtedly still practised throughout the world, no government admits it and all governments at least purport to condemn it. Surely we cannot step back towards that particular precipice, and water down the prohibition.

What then of the idea that the deontological argument cannot stand when the freedom from torture comes up against the right to life? Is the deprivation of life not a greater affront to one's dignity than torture?

First, that contention is debateable. I once made the throwaway comment during a class discussion of torture that of course one would rather be tortured than killed. The sudden intake of breath alerted me that I had said something very controversial. It was clear that many in the class felt differently.

Secondly, the comparison of killing in self-defence to torturing in self-defence or defence of others is flawed. Self-defence killing arises in a situation where the victim poses a realistic and imminent lethal threat to the perpetrator or to others. Similarly, soldiers who are lawfully killed in war represent realistic lethal threats, though there is no requirement that the soldier victim be an imminent threat. The situation is fairer in that the victim has the means to defend him or herself; torture can only arise when the victim is helpless.[3] Self-defence killing can occur without State involvement; torture is necessarily perpetrated with at least the acquiescence of a State official and represents the ultimate abuse of State power. Killing can involve a split second decision; torture involves an intentional deliberative process. Finally, as noted below, it is highly speculative in any situation to infer that torture is likely to save lives. In contrast, it is possible to infer with reasonable certainty that the killing of a person in self-defence will likely save a life or lives imminently threatened by that person.

The utilitarian and accountability arguments are essentially consequentialist arguments – both maintain that good overall consequences will result from their proposals; that is, the saving of lives, or less and more accountable torture. It is therefore appropriate to point out some of the many bad consequences that could well arise from these proposals, and how the bad outweighs the good.

Both arguments misrepresent or underestimate the effects of torture on its victims. Bagaric, Clarke, and Dershowitz all talk of torture with no lasting effects or damage. John Conroy has written a disturbing account of the effects of detainees in Northern Ireland under British internment laws in the 1970s.[4] The treatment inflicted was found to amount to inhuman treatment rather than torture by the European Court of Human Rights.[5] Some of the victims suffered the following after-effects: extreme paranoia, insomnia, uncontrollable shaking, twitching, and poor memory (including inability to remember the names of their own children). A number died of early stress-related illnesses. Given the after-effects of this 'non-torture', one cannot underestimate the after-effects of even a medically supervised 'safe' insertion of a sterilised needle.

The authorisation of torture, even in the most narrow (or fantastical) of circumstances, inevitably equates with a limited acceptance of torture and its consequent (limited) legitimation. If such a chink in the armour of the absolute prohibition was to be inflicted by a state as influential as the US (about whom Dershowitz was arguing), its lead would likely be enthusiastically taken up by states with less credible checks and balances. While it is perhaps conceivable that the US federal judiciary could independently administer a torture warrant system, can the same be said for the Burmese or Zimbabwean judiciaries? One could well find that the 'narrow permissible circumstances' for torture would be administered in totally self-serving and contemptuous ways by abusive governments. Though such governments might already torture, there would be lesser need to hide and cover up, and therefore greater opportunity for more torture. There would consequently be more rather than less torture, contrary to Dershowitz's assertions.

The potential slippery slope consequences from any erosion of the prohibition are perhaps already apparent in the war on terror. It is an open secret that torture has been used by the US in offshore detention centres. Extraordinary rendition has also been used in contravention of art 3 of the Convention Against Torture. This apparent tolerance of torture at the highest levels probably helped create a climate where US personnel in Abu Ghraib could commit atrocities against inmates and brazenly photograph themselves doing so. Even the constant use of torture in ticking bomb situations by the hero in the popular fictional TV series, *24*, has reportedly had a 'toxic effect', and 'has adversely affected the training and performance of real American soldiers'.[6] The possible floodgates effects of a limited acceptance of torture cannot be underestimated.

Dershowitz bases much of his argument on the contention that torture occurs, so we must regulate it rather than tolerate it. This argument is somewhat strange: we do not regularly change our laws to accommodate illegality. While it seems torture might have been supported at high levels in the US administration, Dershowitz's assumptions regarding tolerance for torture are challenged by a 2004 news poll which found that two-thirds of Americans opposed the use of torture in the war on terror.[7] It is a mockery of constitutional law to argue that government toleration of torture necessitates a change in the law to accommodate its wish for fewer constraints on its own power.

In addition, as Dershowitz concedes, torture already occurs when it is completely illegal. Why would the legalisation of torture within certain parameters reduce torture outside those parameters? If the authorised needle under the thumbnail does not work, it seems highly likely that the desperate interrogator will break protocol and try something more barbaric to 'break' the victim, such as the torture of the suspect's children. A mundane analogy is to raise the speed limit in a 60 zone to 70 to accommodate those who commonly do 70: the result will likely be more cars going at 80.

Furthermore, a torture warrant is seeking to regulate what is inherently non-regulable. Torture is premised on the idea that the victim is under the complete power of the perpetrator, who could choose to flay or kill the victim if he or she chooses. The power of torture, and therefore its potential utility as an interrogation device against committed terrorists, is undermined if the perpetrator can only go so far. Accountability and openness could simply mean that terrorists would train to withstand the authorised techniques.[8]

A final theoretical argument in favour of preserving the absolute prohibition on torture is the need to maintain the moral high ground. The crude utilitarianism that justifies torture also justifies terrorism; terrorists justify their actions as ends justifying means. If it is true that terrorists hate our freedoms and our way of life in our liberal democracies, as has been commonly asserted by leaders such as US President Bush, the dismantling of the prohibition on torture would give terrorists a victory that they cannot achieve by themselves.

Does torture actually work?

Is torture a useful way of eliciting information in the ticking bomb situation? First one may note that the level of certainty attributed in a ticking bomb situation is very unlikely to exist in real life. How can the police *know* that the suspect *knows* the location of the bomb, *know* that the suspect will give the correct information if tortured, and *know* that terrorist affiliates will not switch to a plan B prompted by the suspect's capture? How, for example, can the police know that the suspect will not give bogus information designed to lead them to a booby trap that might set off the very explosion that they are trying to avert?[9] There are simply too many variables in the ticking bomb scenario. As an aside, one may note that such variables do not normally exist in the typical 'killing in self-defence' scenario.

There is, of course, no empirical data on the utility of torture as an interrogation device. Bagaric and Clarke argue that it must work, or governments would not use it. It depends on what it is being used for: torture is probably more often used as a technique of social control than interrogation.[10] In the short term, it is probably a useful way of intimidating a population (though it may also lead to a hardening of opposition to the torturing government). Torture was once a common part of the European criminal law system, and was used to elicit confessions. It was abolished as it became clear that too many confessions were unreliable. The European experience indicates that torture is not a reliable road to the truth.[11]

Torture of course might, on occasion, lead to eliciting information that saves a life, or many lives. Israel claimed before the Committee against Torture that its use of 'moderate pressure' on terrorist suspects had averted 90 bus bombings.[12] In that respect, the relevant interrogation procedures had good outcomes. Nevertheless, the interrogation techniques were condemned by both the committee and the Israeli Supreme Court. Such a statistic is, however, only part of the story: another unknown is how many were tortured needlessly. And what of the long-term consequences? How many more willing bus bombers volunteered, perhaps sparked by outrage over torture inflicted on a friend or relative or neighbour? Was the backbone of the insurgency significantly strengthened by the injustice of torture?

And what of the ticking bomb?

That leaves us with the thorny question: what to do in the ticking bomb scenario? Perhaps the law already permits torture in such a scenario, on the basis of the defence of necessity. Bagaric, Clarke and Dershowitz believe so, and indeed argue that their proposals would in fact limit the amount of torture actually allowed under law. The Israeli Supreme Court, while confirming the prohibition on torture and ill treatment in Israeli law, left open the possibility of applying the defence of necessity in an interrogation situation.[13] The defence is however unlikely to apply. This narrow defence applies when a person acts reasonably in committing a criminal act to avoid a graver consequence. There must be a high level of certainty before one can state that torture could ever be a reasonable response to any situation.[14] There are, as stated above, simply too many variables in the ticking bomb situation for such certainty to ever exist. Furthermore the Committee against Torture has confirmed that a necessity defence would breach the international prohibition on torture.[15]

That leaves one possibility: mitigation. That is, the circumstances of the torture are taken into account after conviction in determining sentence. Mitigation, unlike the defence of necessity, does not necessarily breach international law; there are no requirements of mandatory sentences. Indeed, human rights law supports the consideration of individual circumstances in criminal sentencing. A first-time torturer could expect a lighter sentence than a serial torturer. The mastermind who orchestrates a torture should get a heavier sentence than the lowly henchman perpetrator. Shouldn't a ticking bomb torturer get a lesser sentence than one who tortures for fun?

Nevertheless, even mitigation has to be applied with care, to ensure that it is not applied routinely. Courts must ensure that they are not seen to be lenient in the face of brutal law enforcement behaviour, and that they do not indirectly endorse the unacceptable use of short cuts in terrorism investigations. The precedent effects of mitigation decisions would always have to be considered to ensure that the green light for torture is not apparently given, either domestically or internationally. A sentence must reflect the gravity of the offence of torture.

Which may all seem unfair to the apocryphal good citizen cop who tortures a suspect as a last resort in order to save a city, only to end up with a conviction and significant jail time. But hard cases, in many instances and certainly in this one, do in fact make bad law.

Notes

1 Mirko Bagaric and Julie Clarke, 'Not enough Official Torture in the World? The Circumstances in which Torture is Morally Justifiable' (2005) 39 *University of San Francisco Law Review* 581; Mirko Bagaric and Julie Clarke, 'The Torture Debate: Tortured Responses (A Reply to our Critics)' (2006) 40 *University of San Francisco Law Review* 703.

2 See Alan Dershowitz, *Why Terrorism Works* (2003) ch 4 ('Should the Ticking Time Bomb Terrorist be Tortured?'); Alan Dershowitz, 'Tortured Reasoning' in Sanford Levinson (ed), *Torture: A Collection* (2004) 257.

3 See Henry Shue, 'Torture' in Levinson, above n 2, 47.

4 John Conroy, 'The Internment', *Granta*, Spring 1992.

5 *Ireland v UK* (1979-80) 2 EHRR 25. The relevant treatment was a combination of the following five techniques: hooding, sleep deprivation, subjection to white noise, deprivation of food and drink, and forcing victims to stand for long periods in uncomfortable positions ('wall-standing').

6 The contention comes from US Army Brigadier General Patrick Finnegan, dean of the US Military Academy at West Point in Jane Mayer, 'Whatever it Takes', *The New Yorker*, 19 & 26 February 2007, 66, 72.

7 David Morris and Gary Langer, *Terror Suspect Treatment: Most Americans Oppose Torture Techniques* (2004) ABCNEWS.com <http://abcnews.go.com/sections/us/Polls/torture_poll_040527.html> at 26 July 2007.

8 See Desmond Manderson, 'Another Modest Proposal' (2005) 10 *Deakin Law Review* 640.

9 I am grateful to Neil James, author of Chapter 15 of this book, for this suggestion.

10 See Mika Haritos-Fatouros, 'The Official Torturer: A Learning Model for Obedience to the Authority of Violence' (1988) 18 *Journal of Applied Social Psychology* 1107.

11 John H Langbein, 'The Legal History of Torture' in Levinson (ed), above n 2, 93.

12 Israel's second report to the Committee against Torture: UN Doc CAT/C/33/Add.2/Rev.1 (1997).

13 *Public Committee Against Torture in Israel v Government of Israel* (HCJ 5100/94), decision of Israeli Supreme Court of 6 September 1999, [39].

14 See Paolo Gaeta, 'May Necessity be available as a Defence for Torture in the Interrogation of Terrorist Suspects?' (2004) 2 *Journal of International Criminal Justice* 785, 791-92.

15 Convention Against Torture Concluding Observations on Israel: UN Doc. CAT/C/27/Concl 5 (2001), para 6(a)(iii).

15

Torture: What is it, Will it Work and Can it be Justified?

Neil James

The terms interrogation and torture are often wrongly confused or conflated in public discourse, due in part to commonplace fears about learning enough detail to tell them apart. A failure to adequately distinguish between the two has detrimental consequences for the legitimacy, authorisation and control of effective interrogation and indeed for the outlawing of torture. Most importantly, this failure needlessly hampers practical attempts to enforce the universal prohibition of torture embodied in the United Nations *Convention Against Torture and Other Cruel, Inhuman or Degrading Treatment or Punishment.* Almost as importantly it complicates effective discussion as to whether the universal prohibition could or should ever be relaxed in certain circumstances.

Many of the moral, legal and practical issues involved when discussing torture and its perceived role in questioning, if any, are not new and debating them is assisted by some general observations from history. But first, we need to examine the background to contemporary calls for relaxing the universal prohibition in dire emergencies such as large-scale terrorist attacks, not least because they seem to be largely based on three unspoken, and highly questionable, assumptions.

The first assumption is that torture is technically possible in the circumstances described, is necessarily effective in obtaining the specific information desired within the time constraints supposedly justifying its special use, and incurs no countervailing factors. The second assumption is that interrogation not involving torture is less effective, or is so less effective that torture should be used instead during dire emergencies. The final assumption is that the dire emergency scenarios used in arguments to relax the universal prohibition on torture are realistic, or likely, enough to justify such a step.

Questioning the assumptions

The last assumption is worth examining first as the other two depend on it completely and objections on both moral and practical grounds readily spring to mind. A commonly cited example to justify torture is the so-called 'ticking bomb' scenario where a captured terrorist, almost invariably described as a fanatic, supposedly knows where the bomb in question is located. There is said to be no time for other methods to extract the information and the consequences are inevitably pronounced in terms of casualties. A moment's reflection on the variables and methodologies involved raises obvious doubts about such scenarios, including:

- How can we know or confirm there is actually a bomb, and with such a short timescale, or that the captured terrorist knows where the bomb is?
- How can we know or confirm that only this particular terrorist can provide all the information needed? Can the bomb be disarmed or the area evacuated in time anyway?
- How can we assess, and do so with the urgency supposedly required, whether this particular terrorist will succumb to torture?
- How can we know or confirm that his or her apparent confession under torture will be accurate enough to use, and not just a stratagem to delay proceedings until the bomb detonates or searchers are led into a trap?
- How can we know or confirm the number of potential casualties with enough certainty to justify torture in order to help prevent them?

The overall problem with such ticking bomb scenarios is that they are generally simplistic even for the thin plots of lawyer-led television programs posing idealistic hypothetical dilemmas. They usually preclude, for example, the alternative or even contemporaneous use of other forms of intelligence gathering or criminal investigation. They also tend to pose a sequential chain proposition of events (such as only one terrorist knowing all the information needed and then being captured) where the breaking of any one link renders the whole scenario highly unlikely at best and usually quite unrealistic.

When the first assumption is also examined the above questions from the third one become even starker. How could we be certain, for example, that torture would work and work in time, or that it might not result in the person being tortured saying anything to avoid further severe pain? Or, to the contrary, how could we determine that they were not just deliberately lying in reaction to the torture and the hatred and contempt it would naturally engender? Moreover, just in terms of the time constraints there are obvious problems. Is a 'suitably qualified' torturer available, and with the right tools and conditions? If not, might an 'amateur' torturer only make things worse by either killing the prisoner, rendering them unconscious and unable to answer questions or, conversely, by inadvertently strengthening their will to resist?

This is where the weaknesses of the second assumption also come into play. How can we be certain that legitimate interrogation might not be just as effective or even more effective in the circumstances? Understanding what interrogation is and how it differs from torture is therefore vital in both philosophy and practice.

Questioning the universal prohibition on torture

Recent calls for relaxing the universal prohibition on torture essentially fall into two schools of thought. Both deplore the use of torture but are prepared to sanction its use in specific dire emergency situations such as where mass-casualty terrorism results in a ticking bomb scenario.

The first school, led by an American lawyer and academic, Alan Dershowitz,[1] basically argues that while torture is always abhorrent, the pressures of a ticking bomb scenario, especially in a situation of mass-casualty terrorism, would mean torture would probably be used anyway on the ground. It is therefore less destructive to the rule of law to regulate its non-lethal use rather than pretend it will not occur in any circumstances. A variation of this school is the belief that torture should remain illegal but that the relevant Head of State could subsequently pardon the torturers if they prevent a dire mass-casualty catastrophe.

The second school of thought is not necessarily in complete or partial contradiction to the first, but tends to argue for the moral legitimacy and practicality of torture on first principles. As advanced, for example, by Australian academics Mirko Bagaric and Julie Clarke in their book *Torture: When the Unthinkable Is Morally Permissible*,[2] five factors are cited as justifying investigative torture under what they term 'controlled conditions':

- the number of lives at risk;
- the immediacy of the harm threatened;
- the possibility of acquiring the life-saving information sought by alternative means;
- the level of wrongdoing of the person to be tortured; and
- the likelihood that the person to be tortured does possess the information needed.

The arguments of both schools are obviously controversial.[3] One interesting aspect has, however, gone virtually unnoticed in the clamour. In Australia, and largely across the globe, the calls for rollback of the absolute prohibition against torture have come from lawyers, and predominantly academic ones at that. Such calls have not come from the ranks of those professions which involve the systematic questioning of often uncooperative individuals in order to gain information for legally prescribed purposes. This latter group essentially comprises two categories:

- officers of police, other law enforcement and security intelligence agencies who are required to question people as authorised by domestic law; and
- professional interrogators within a defence force who could be called upon to practise their profession, primarily under the strictures of international law in circumstances of armed conflict.

The reasons for this apparent stark juxtaposition of professional as well as moral opinion are worth exploring.

Now a confirmed cynic might argue that the reason why police or military interrogators might not be arguing for the use of torture by warrant is because they do not know it is banned. Those with less of a cynical disposition, but perhaps still with somewhat of a suspicious mind, might even believe that interrogators and police know torture is illegal but reckon they can get away with it, at least from time to time. Those honestly interested in the truth instead should listen to what professional interrogators are saying.

Three factors are important in any informed discussion of torture: what is it, will it work and can it ever be justified? Professional interrogators have much to offer such discussion, especially with regard to the far from simple matter of what constitutes genuine torture as opposed to questioning that exploits mere hardship, discomfort or annoyance. They also have much to contribute to debates on whether torture works or can ever be necessary. The profound silence from interrogators in support of the idea of torture by warrant clearly indicates where professional opinion lies.

Torture by warrant in the 17th century

Some perspective and practical lessons can also be gained from a brief examination of the law and practice of torture by warrant when it was last used within our criminal justice system.[4] This provides useful insights into the potential nature of the 'controlled conditions' specified by advocates of a modern version of torture by warrant.

In 1215 torture was expressly forbidden in the *Magna Carta* but not defined. In an age where you had a right at trial to demonstrate your innocence by appeal to supernatural means, where there was trial by ordeal or judicial combat, and when an indicted person who 'stood mute in malice' (refused to answer) could be starved or pressed to death, the express prohibition of the Great Charter was problematic in practice.

There was also the issue of the legal jurisdiction of the King's Council (a body with constitutional roots before the Norman Conquest). For centuries this body constituted a court, claimed the authority to supersede other courts, and argued it could in some circumstances employ methods otherwise banned by statute. An evolving parliamentary system sought to limit this jurisdiction by various statutes from 1331 onwards. Under Edward IV, around 1468, torture although regarded as 'foreign to the law' was claimed as a royal prerogative for offences brought before the King's Council. In 1487 parliament effectively agreed to the council, by then operating as the Court of the Star Chamber, investigating and trying those accused of certain heinous offences such as treason.

Excluding physical punishments such as branding, or those forming part and parcel of a graduated execution process when sentenced to death – such as being hung, drawn and quartered or burnt at the stake – torture was limited to the questioning of those under indictment. After developments under the Tudors, the mature legal and procedural bases for torture at the time of the Gunpowder Treason in 1605 are worth noting. These embodied a range of moral, legal and practical controls in keeping with community standards of the time:

- Torture was practically distinguished from physical punishments in that it was commonly accepted as constituting the deliberate and direct application of extreme pain, however gradually, rather than indirect practices such as 'pinching' whereby prisoners under indictment could be incarcerated without food and water until they co-operated with their investigators.
- Torture could only be used in exceptional circumstances and for the most serious crimes, such as treason, where speed of investigation was essential to protect the realm.
- The employment of torture could only be authorised by warrant of the King or the Privy Council (in practice it was usually a King-in-Council decision) once a strong *prima facie* case had been made.
- Torture could be undertaken only on prisoners detained in the Tower of London, although other physically coercive practices such as 'pinching' were more widespread.
- The methods of torture authorised at the Tower were prescribed and limited, and chiefly comprised the Manacles and the Rack.[5]
- Prisoners had to be given ample opportunity to answer questions truthfully first before torture could be used.

- The application of torture had to be graduated. In practice this usually meant starting off with the Manacles before progressing to the Rack.
- Prisoners were not meant to be tortured to death.
- Crippled, maimed and mutilated people were not meant to be tortured because it was thought they might be so weak that torture risked killing them.
- A prisoner under investigation was meant to be tortured only once for the same information. The principle here was that to torture someone over and again in pursuit of the same information meant someone telling the truth under torture had no means to end their suffering. This was considered both unjust and inefficient, and likely to lead to those being tortured agreeing with mistaken or false accusations merely to end the torture. Exceptions to this precept were made in serious cases, as with Guy Fawkes and some of his co-conspirators, but this had to be explicitly authorised by the King.

The reign of James I was effectively the end of the period where torture was commonly authorised. Two principal factors led to the decline. First, general constitutional, legal and political developments, and the increased powers of parliament after the civil war and the revolution of 1688, meant a consequent decline in both the incidence of treason and in the royal prerogative that underwrote the use of torture in such circumstances. Second, the simple fact that torture tended to elicit incorrect information as much as it resulted in the truth coming out was widely accepted.

This summary of law and practice concerning judicial torture, the last time English-speaking peoples used it extensively, illustrates most of the key issues that would need debating today were the debate on resurrecting torture by warrant really serious. The first point to consider is that even in the early 17th century the moral justification for torture warrants was very shaky and not popularly accepted. A second point is that the procedures for reintroducing torture by warrant would need to be quite complex. The third, and most important, however, is that even if all the other problems could somehow be surmounted, 'investigative torture' is simply an impractical, unreliable and unnecessary means of discerning the truth.

Problems of polemic and definition

In domestic law numerous legal precedents over many years have established what can and cannot be done during the incarceration and questioning of those arrested. Often referred to as the 'Judges Rules' they can be summarised as the criteria that govern questioning, and which exclude the use of force, threats of force or dishonest trickery to coerce confessions or other admissions from those being questioned.

In terms of international law, Australia is a signatory to the four Geneva Conventions of 1949 and their two Additional Protocols of 1977 which cover, among other things, the treatment of people during armed conflict. In August 1989 Australia also ratified the Convention Against Torture, which defines torture in art 1 as:

> any act by which severe pain and suffering, whether physical or mental, is intentionally inflicted on a person for such purposes as obtaining from him or a third person information or a confession, punishing him for an act he or a third person has committed or is suspected of having committed, or intimidating or coercing him or a third person, or for any reason based on discrimination of any kind, when such pain or suffering is inflicted by or at the instigation of or with the consent or acquiescence of a public official or other person acting in an official capacity. It does not include pain or suffering arising only from, inherent in or incidental to lawful sanctions.

The prohibitions and definitions seem clear enough but, as with debate about the definition of genocide, there is always someone (often an academic or activist lawyer) trying to stretch the definition beyond its genuine and useful limits. This results in an unfortunate irony in the debate against torture. The moral and practical arguments against it are frequently frustrated by too wide a definition of torture being applied by some of those seeking to stamp it out. This does little to help eliminate real torture as it causes confusion and dissipates effort. It also demeans the victims of genuine torture by needlessly belittling the horrific experiences they have endured.

A further irony of the torture debate in this regard is that while some academic lawyers are advocating a return to torture by warrant, some 'human rights lawyers' are unintentionally helping them. The latter achieve this by wrongly branding legitimate and morally justifiable interrogation methods and techniques as somehow falling within the legal definitions of torture. The essential element in the convention definition of severity, and the specific exclusion of inherent or incidental pain or suffering, are too often forgotten or discounted.

Among professional interrogators in countries abiding by the rule of law the common working definition of interrogation is 'the systematic extraction of information from an individual, either willing or unwilling, by the use of psychological attack only'.[6]

Thus, interrogation is essentially an intellectual process not a physical one. No physical or mental pain or severe suffering is involved. The subject is convinced to cooperate by reasoning and by overcoming their will to resist. Many variables are involved but the time available, the professional skill of the interrogator and the condition, intelligence, education and willingness to co-operate or otherwise of the subject are important.

One or both of two legal regimes govern interrogation depending on whether it occurs during an international armed conflict or is a criminal or protective security matter covered by domestic law. An additional consideration, especially in terms of counter-terrorism, is the object of the information sought. Does the questioning concern a crime already committed, with the purpose of gaining evidence to be tested in a court of law, or is it for the purposes of general intelligence gathering to deter or prevent future terrorist activities? In practical terms, interrogations to gather intelligence are generally less onerous procedurally and quicker than ones undertaken to collect evidence.

In a situation of armed conflict, a variety of safeguards necessarily apply to the interrogation process under the Geneva Conventions and Protocols. In domestic law a similar situation applies under the 'Judges Rules'. In the United Kingdom in the early 1970s, however, a series of higher court decisions concerning security force operations against terrorists in Northern Ireland reinforced the important legal principle that a reasonable degree of temporary hardship during detention and questioning, involving no application of force, is not torture or illegal coercion.

This principle is important because it confirms that it is normal and reasonable for those being questioned in such circumstances to experience degrees of discomfort, annoyance or other hardship, and that detention and questioning methods that result in such hardships are not necessarily abusive of a prisoner's human rights. Furthermore, measures or conditions of discomfort or annoyance designed to encourage cooperation during questioning are not unreasonable in the circumstances and in many cases are inherent in the circumstances of capture, arrest or detention anyway.

With obvious safeguards such conditioning may, for example, legally include the strictly controlled and temporary use of measures such as isolation, sensory deprivation or sleep deprivation. Such factors, if not prolonged or otherwise carried to extremes, do not constitute severe pain or suffering, or have long-term effects.

The problem of the enemy

The debate on torture by warrant in cases of terrorism is also complicated by the moral and political positions of the terrorist enemy. Much heat but little light is generated during many public debates on the detention and interrogation aspects of the campaign against transnational Islamist terrorism. One key problem involved is that international law tends to lag well behind the circumstances of international conflict. In the conflict with internationally proscribed terrorist groups, for example, the terrorists are covered by art 3 of all four Geneva Conventions (and perhaps art 75 of Additional Protocol 1). But they do not qualify for full prisoner-of-war status under the Third Geneva Convention because they do not abide by wider international humanitarian law in their prosecution of conflict. They are, of course, fully covered by the Convention Against Torture.

The other key problem in the struggle with Islamist terrorism, in particular, is the perennial paradox the liberal democracies have faced over the past century. Once again we are fighting an enemy who does not, and will not, abide by international law. As in our previous conflicts, these enemies fully understand their immoral advantage in this regard and are quite willing to exploit it.

In case of capture, for example, terrorists know their questioning will not involve torture or maltreatment and that liberal democracies will bend over backwards to act honourably. The isolated and infrequent instances where some maltreatment has illegally occurred do not alter this overall situation. Captured terrorists also know that if they make false claims that they have been tortured or abused then a whole raft of oversight processes will swing into effect, however imperfectly at first. We know from Al-Qa'ida training manuals captured in Afghanistan in 2001 and 2002 that extensive use of false claims of torture is highly recommended. The terrorists also know there are now plenty of gullible people in Western societies only too willing to believe the worst and criticise the way their own governments detain and interrogate captured terrorists or terrorist suspects.

The perspective of the professional interrogator

Any professional interrogator, after noting that torture is both illegal and immoral, and that this is just a 'given', will go on to stress that it is also unnecessary. It is unnecessary for the three principal reasons that it is generally counter-productive, that given the right conditions the same information can almost invariably be gained by legal and morally acceptable means of investigation and interrogation, and that the theoretical scenarios cited as justifying the use of torture are generally so unrealistic and unlikely as to not warrant serious consideration.

After a moment's thought, professional interrogators are also likely to add further objections. These might include, for example, the problem of where would you find people educated and capable enough to be interrogators but who would be somehow also willing to become torturers. And in any case, how would you train them and how would occupational health and safety standards be set and monitored? Another key moral and practical matter, even ignoring the overall slippery-slope risk, is how could you really control or eventually halt an institutionalised process of judicially sanctioned torture, or even be able to recognise when you should do so?

Any member of the profession of arms, after noting the same legal, moral and practical objections to torture, is likely to add one further strong objection. The international law intended to ameliorate the suffering of those captured in combat or otherwise affected by it is too often ignored by the types of regimes and groups Australia has had to fight. In the past 70 years the examples of the Japanese in World War II, the Chinese and North Koreans in the Korean War, the North Vietnamese in the Vietnam War, and now various types of Islamist terrorist in Afghanistan, Iraq and elsewhere, present a clear trend – pluralist liberal democracies often have to fight quite unsavoury, immoral and ruthless enemies who ignore international law. We should give no enemy, actual or potential, any excuse to mistreat Australian prisoners-of-war on the ostensible grounds that our adherence to international humanitarian law in general, and the laws of war in particular, are somehow questionable.

The arguments against torture by warrant are not just legal and moral. They are also practical in that professional interrogators know that torture is both unlikely to work and unnecessary as a purported form of intelligence gathering.

Notes

1 Alan M Dershowitz, 'Want to torture? Get a warrant', *San Francisco Chronicle*, 22 January 2002, A19.

2 Mirko Bagaric and Julie Clarke, *Torture: When the Unthinkable is Morally Permissible* (2007).

3 For further discussion of these arguments see Chapter 14 in this book.

4 Frederic William Maitland, *The Constitutional History of England* (1926).

5 The Manacles was a method whereby the prisoner was stood against a wall, atop wooden blocks, and hung up by their wrists using a form of iron glove which could be tightened. The blocks were then removed until the prisoner was hanging by the wrists and then left there for several hours at a time. The Rack in the Tower was the only one in England. It comprised a large oak frame resembling a double bed without a base. The prisoner (facing upwards) was tied with cords around the hands and ankles to rollers at each end. These could then be rotated to stretch the arms, legs and finally the torso. Dislocation of limbs was common and permanent damage virtually inevitable. The reputation of the Rack was such that it was often shown to those accused of crimes serious enough to merit its use as the next step in their questioning. This often elicited cooperation by the threat alone.

6 Australian Defence Force, *Interrogator's Handbook*. Most NATO countries employ the same or similar definitions. A related definition is the difference between an interview and an interrogation. In the latter the person being questioned is under some form of legal and physical constraint (such as arrest or capture in war) and is not free to end the questioning by simply leaving.

PART V

Australia's Response Compared

16

Counter-Terrorism Law in New Zealand

Alex Conte

Counter-terrorism law in New Zealand is principally set out within six items of legislation, and amendments to other enactments made under those six legislative instruments. Law before 11 September 2001 can be categorised in two ways: three pieces of legislation incorporating New Zealand's obligations under the international terrorism-related treaties to which New Zealand was then a party;[1] and the legislative response to the Rainbow Warrior bombing of 10 July 1985, which saw the enactment of the *International Terrorism (Emergency Powers) Act 1987*.[2] Post 9/11, New Zealand has adopted two legislative packages: legislative reform leading up to the *Terrorism Suppression Act 2002*, including reform of that Act under current consideration; and the parcel of reforms initiated under the Counter-Terrorism Bill 2003. It should be mentioned at this early stage that there are numerous other pieces of New Zealand's domestic legislation that can be treated as contributing to countering terrorism. This chapter restricts itself to consideration of the Terrorism Suppression Act and the Counter-Terrorism Bill.

Post-9/11 legislative developments on counter-terrorism

The Terrorism Suppression Act is a significant piece of legislation, currently containing 81 sections, five schedules and running to over 120 pages. It contains definitions of the term 'terrorist act'. It creates offences and provides for associated issues of jurisdiction, prosecution and extradition. It establishes a process by which persons or entities may be designated as terrorists and contains various provisions aimed at suppressing the financing of terrorist activities. The Act has undergone a long and somewhat unusual transformation from its original form and content as the Terrorism (Bombings and Financing) Bill to what now appears as the *Terrorism Suppression Act 2002*.

Following the executive's decision to become a party to the *International Convention for the Suppression of Terrorist Bombings* and the *International Convention for the Suppression of the Financing of Terrorism*, the Terrorism (Bombings and Financing) Bill was introduced in early 2001. National interest analyses were prepared, with the Foreign Affairs, Defence and Trade Committee subsequently lodging treaty examination reports with the House of Representatives. The reports did not bring any matters to the attention of the House, but the analyses each noted that domestic implementing legislation would be needed to create new criminal offences, establish extraterritorial jurisdiction and facilitate the prosecution or extradition of alleged offenders.[3]

After the preparation of the national interest analyses and the presentation of reports required by parliamentary standing orders, the horrific events of 11 September 2001, transpired. The Security Council subsequently adopted resolution 1373 (2001), imposing both binding and non-binding obligations on New Zealand as a member of the United Nations. The resolution was adopted when the Terrorism (Bombings and Financing) Bill was in its final stages of the select committee process. Compliance with the obligations under the resolution was thus the second aim of the 2001 Bill, as amended. To achieve that objective, the reasonably unusual step was taken of adding a considerable number of new substantive provisions to the Bill, seeing the Bill almost double in size. Due to these circumstances, the Foreign Affairs, Defence and Trade Committee presented an interim report on the Bill to the House, drawing its attention to the new provisions in the Bill, with explanatory notes.[4] The committee also called for public submissions on the draft amendments and received 143 submissions from interest groups and individuals. In contrast, the committee had received no submissions on the original Terrorism (Bombings and Financing) Bill.

The next stage in the development of the Terrorism Suppression Act came through amendments to the legislation enacted under the Counter-Terrorism Bill 2003. The purpose of the Bill, and the nature of legislative amendments achieved under it, is discussed in more detail below. What should be noted at this stage is that Part 2 of the Counter-Terrorism Bill was directed towards amending the Terrorism Suppression Act. The primary purpose of those amendments was to incorporate obligations under the *Convention on the Physical Protection of Nuclear Material* and the *Convention on the Marking of Plastic Explosives for the Purpose of Detection*. The amendments also added substantive provisions concerning the search and seizure, and related issues, by the Customs Service of goods owned or controlled by terrorist entities or associated persons.

On 14 December 2004, further amending legislation was introduced to the House: the Terrorism Suppression Amendment Bill (No 2). The amendments to the Terrorism Suppression Act under this Bill achieved two things: the creation of a new offence of providing financial support to all terrorist organisations (including those that might not yet be formally designated under the Act); and an increase in the length of time that designations remain in force without further extension by High Court order (from three years to five), pending anticipated amending legislation (now introduced under the Terrorism Suppression Amendment Bill 2007).

The most recent addition to the international legal framework on counter-terrorism is the *International Convention for the Suppression of Acts of Nuclear Terrorism.* New Zealand is an original signatory to the Convention. At the same time as the negotiation of the Convention, work was being undertaken by the International Atomic Energy Agency (IAEA) towards adopting amendments to the Nuclear Material Convention. One of the purposes of the Terrorism Suppression Amendment Bill 2007 is consequently to allow New Zealand to implement obligations under, and take treaty action in respect of, both the Nuclear Terrorism and Nuclear Material Conventions. The 2007 Bill looks to make changes for two further purposes. It includes a set of amendments concerning the regime under the Terrorism Suppression Act for the designation of terrorist and associated entities. It also looks to make changes to existing offences, relating to 'avoidance of doubt' provisions and the offence of participating in a terrorist group, as well as introducing a new offence of committing a 'terrorist act'.

Terrorist acts and corresponding offences

Section 5 of the Terrorism Suppression Act, combined with definitions contained within s 4(1) and the conventions listed in Schedule 3, provides for three distinct types of 'terrorist acts'. The term is significant for various reasons. First, it is linked to offences such as the financing of terrorist acts. It also plays a role in the designation of terrorist or associated entities, which include those entities that have perpetrated terrorist acts. Finally, if enacted without change, the 2007 Bill will create a new offence of engaging in a terrorist act (as defined in s 5(1)).

Definition of 'terrorist act'

The first type of terrorist act defined reflects the international obligations assumed by New Zealand under the various international terrorism-related conventions. Sections 4(1) and 5(1)(b) prohibit acts that constitute an offence under one of the nine terrorism conventions listed in Schedule 3 to the Act. Schedule 3 does not list the Financing Convention, the Plastic Explosives Convention nor the *Montreal Convention on Offences and Certain Other Acts Committed On Board Aircraft.*

The second type of terrorist act defined is that of a 'terrorist act in armed conflict', established under ss 5(1)(c) and 4(1) as conduct that:

- 'occurs in a situation of armed conflict';
- has the purpose of intimidating a population, or compelling a 'government or an international organisation to do or abstain from doing any act';
- 'is intended to cause death or serious bodily injury to a civilian or other person not taking an active part in the hostilities in that situation'; and
- 'is not excluded from the application of the Financing Convention'.

Finally, a more general 'catch-all' definition is provided within the balance of s 5, under which a terrorist act is conduct that is carried out:

- 'for the purpose of advancing an ideological, political, or religious cause';
- with the intention of inducing 'terror in a civilian population', or unduly compelling or forcing 'a government or an international organisation to do or abstain from doing any act'; and
- with the intention of causing:
  - death or serious injury to other people;
  - 'a serious risk to the health or safety of a population';
  - serious interference with, or disruption to, an infrastructure facility that is 'likely to endanger human life';
  - 'destruction of, or serious damage to', valuable or important property, or 'major economic loss, or major environmental damage', that is likely to result in one or more of the above three outcomes; or
  - 'a disease-bearing organism' to be introduced or released that is 'likely to devastate the national economy of a country'.

Regrettably, all three definitions fall outside the scope of conduct to be suppressed in the fight against terrorism, as characterised by the Security Council in its resolution 1566 (2004) and endorsed by the UN Special Rapporteur on counter-terrorism.[5] The current definitions are overly broad and capture conduct which, while certainly criminal, falls outside the scope of terrorism.[6]

Terrorism-related offences

The Terrorism Suppression Act, and amendments made to it, establishes the following offences:

Terrorist bombing

Section 7 prohibits the intentional and unlawful delivery, placement, discharge or detonation of an explosive or other lethal device with the intention to cause death (or serious injury) or extensive destruction. The provision does not specify that such conduct be aimed at inducing fear or influencing an organisation or government, nor does it specify that this be for the advancement of any particular cause. The offence is thus not one of *terrorist* bombing, it is simply one of bombing where death or serious injury results, or where extensive damage to public facilities results.

Financing of terrorism

Section 8 prohibits the wilful provision or collection of funds (directly or indirectly), intending (or knowing) that those funds are to be used to carry out a 'terrorist act', 'without lawful justification or reasonable excuse'. The Terrorism Suppression Amendment Bill (No 2) 2004 added to this prohibition by extending it to a person who provides or collects funds to benefit an entity knowing that it carries out terrorist acts. The explanatory notes to the Bill referred to doubt that the offence, as originally enacted, was enough to prohibit general financial support to an organisation involved in terrorism (whether designated or not), such as the payment of routine expenses such as rent. In explaining the need for this extension, the Bills Digest and General Policy Statement for the Bill pointed to the requirement to comply with international standards set by the Financial Action Task Force on Money Laundering. Minister of Justice Phil Goff added:

> Given the fluidity of terrorist movements, and the unpredictable emergence of new terrorist groups, this change is the most workable way of ensuring that New Zealand will always remain compliant with international obligations prohibiting the funding of terrorist organisations.[7]

The extended prohibition is not limited to funds provided to designated terrorist entities but applies to any entity carrying out terrorist acts. Consequently, its application may well be problematic since there will not be the same element of notice to the public as is achieved through gazetting designations under the Act. Prosecution of such offending conduct, where the entity is not designated, will have the added difficulty of establishing knowledge in the mind of the accused that the entity was a terrorist entity.

The 2007 Amendment Bill proposes removing the 'avoidance of doubt' provisions in the terrorist financing offences. Section 8(2) currently provides that, for the avoidance of doubt, it is not an offence to provide or collect funds 'intending that they be used, or knowing that they are to be used, for the purpose of advocating democratic government or the protection of human rights'. The explanatory note to the Bill explains that this provision – as well as the similar provision in s 10(2) – has created uncertainty and that removing it will remove ambiguity. This proposal seems questionable, however, since neither the explanatory note nor the Bills Digest provides reasons as to how or why the avoidance of doubt provisions have created uncertainty.

Dealing with terrorist property

Section 9 of the Act makes it an offence to deal with property known to be owned, controlled or derived by a 'terrorist entity', 'without lawful justification or reasonable excuse'. To 'deal with' terrorist property:

- 'means to use or deal with the property, in any way and by any means'; and
- 'includes allowing the property to be used or dealt with, or facilitating the use of it or dealing with it'.

Making property, or financial or related services, available

Prohibited under s 10 is the provision (direct or indirect) of 'any property, or any financial or related services, either to, or for the benefit of', a terrorist entity, 'without lawful justification or reasonable excuse'. Section 11 limits the operation of this prohibition, where the Prime Minister permits, by notice in writing, any particular dealing. The terms 'make available' and 'property' are defined within the Act, but the phrase 'financial or related services' is not. As considered in the above discussion of the financing of terrorism offence, the Terrorism Suppression Amendment Bill 2007 proposes removal of the 'avoidance of doubt' provision in s 10(2).

Recruiting members of terrorist groups

Section 12 makes it an offence to recruit another person into an organisation or group, knowing that the organisation or group is either a 'terrorist entity' or participates in 'terrorist acts'. This is much broader in its scope than the previous three offences, since it goes beyond conduct relating to a 'terrorist entity' as designated under the Act by also prohibiting conduct relating to entities that participate in 'terrorist acts'. As seen already, there are three categories and definitions of terrorist acts under the combination of ss 4 and 5.

Participating in terrorist groups

Prohibited under s 13 is participation in an organisation or group for the purpose of enhancing the ability of the group to carry out terrorist acts, knowing that the organisation or group is either a 'terrorist entity' or participates in 'terrorist acts'.

Harbouring or concealing terrorists

Intentionally providing assistance to a person to avoid arrest, escape custody or avoid conviction where it is known (or ought to be known) that the person has carried out, or intends to commit, a 'terrorist act' is itself an offence under s 13A of the Terrorism Suppression Act. Clause 12 of the Terrorism Suppression Amendment Bill 2007 seeks to amend this offence by including the element of recklessness.

Using or moving unmarked plastic explosives

Section 13B prohibits the possession, use, manufacture, importation or export of unmarked plastic explosives, except as allowed by the *Hazardous Substances and New Organisms Act 1996* or by the Environmental Risk Management Authority.

Offences involving nuclear material

The final terrorism-related offence under the Terrorism Suppression Act is to be found in ss 13C and 13D, prohibiting a range of conduct relating to nuclear material, including its importation and its use to intimidate. As a result of changes adopted by the IAEA to the Nuclear Material Convention, a further set of offences, involving radioactive material and radioactive devices, is to be introduced under clauses 14 to 16 of the Terrorism Amendment Bill 2007.

Engaging in terrorist acts

The 2007 Bill will also create a new offence of engaging in a terrorist act. The offence is linked to the definition of 'terrorist act' in s 5 of the Terrorism Suppression Act. It is highly problematic that this offence, punishable by a maximum of life imprisonment, is linked to the overly broad definition of terrorist acts under s 5.

The designation of 'terrorist entities'

As seen from the foregoing discussion, a number of offences under the Terrorism Suppression Act concern conduct in support of or related to a 'terrorist entity' or 'associated entity'. The Act establishes a regime by which organisations, groups or individuals may be designated as such. The designation process, governed by ss 20 to 42, empowers the Prime Minister to designate terrorist entities based on information from the United Nations Security Council or 'any relevant information, including classified security information'. The Terrorism Suppression Amendment Bill 2007 proposes to change this system so that all those listed by the Security Council resolution

1267 (1999) Sanctions Committee are automatically prohibited under New Zealand law. The Attorney-General, in place of the Prime Minister, will retain the ability to make designations under New Zealand law.

The current regime allows the Prime Minister to make an interim designation, after consulting with the Attorney-General and the Minister of Foreign Affairs and Trade, if he or she has good cause to believe that the entity has undertaken one or more 'terrorist acts' or is knowingly facilitating such acts. An interim designation automatically expires after 30 days, during which time certain notice must be given about the designation. The Act contemplates that a final designation, if appropriate, will be made before the expiry of the interim designation. Again, steps are required to notify and, in addition, publish the designation.

A final designation currently expires after three years, unless the High Court extends the designation. The period of final designation was extended under the Terrorism Suppression Amendment Bill (No 2) 2004. To allow consideration of the Select Committee's review of the Terrorism Suppression Act (as required under s 70), part of which was to address the designation process, current designations are to continue for two years after presentation of the committee's report to the House, which took place in November 2005.[8] Minister of Justice Phil Goff explained:

> At the time the original Bill was first introduced, there was uncertainty as to the nature and extent of the terrorism phenomenon. An assumption that some designations might be short-lived has since proved to be false … [9]

He continued:

> Provisions in the existing Act mean that New Zealand's designations of terrorist organisations, including several hundred organisations listed by the United Nations Security Council, expire after three years unless renewed by order of the High Court. The drafting of that provision created the unintended need for each designation to be renewed individually, meaning that it would be impossible to renew the first 318 United Nations Security Council-listed designations that New Zealand has listed before they expire in October. That would put New Zealand in breach of Security Council Resolution 1373, which was passed unanimously by the United Nations in the wake of September 11, and related resolutions.

Both the interim and final designation processes are open to judicial review. A designated entity may at any time apply to the Prime Minister to revoke the designation. New Zealand has thus far only designated as terrorist entities those identified by the United Nations Sanctions Committee. The lack of any non-UN listed terrorist entity has been criticised as a failure by New Zealand to 'add its considerable moral and symbolic voice to the international chorus against terrorist violence'.[10]

The Terrorism Suppression Amendment Bill 2007 proposes three main changes to the designation regime. The first, as mentioned, concerns entities that have been designated by the United Nations Sanctions Committee as terrorist or associated entities. The listing of such entities by the committee is currently subject to subsequent designation by the Prime Minister before they are prohibited entities under New Zealand law. Under the proposed changes, this designation process would no longer apply to entities listed by the committee. Instead such an entity would automatically be a 'designated terrorist entity'.

The next set of changes relates to the extension of designations made by the Prime Minister. Final designations currently expire after three years, unless extended by the High Court. The Bill proposes that this extension be made by the Prime Minister, instead of the High Court, and that the extension procedure only apply to non-UN-designated entities.

The final change proposed under the 2007 Amendment Bill concerns the protection of classified security information. The current Act sets out two procedures by which such information may be protected, whereas the Bill is to establish one single procedure. There are considerable problems with the protection afforded to classified information which, while important, currently interferes with the rights to natural justice and fair trial in an unjustifiable and disproportionate way.[11]

Other mechanisms under the Terrorism Suppression Act

Financing of terrorism

In aiming to suppress the financing of terrorism, the Terrorism Suppression Act impacts on both individuals and institutions in two ways. First, by the creation of offences (financing of terrorism, dealing with terrorist property and making property or financial or related services available) and by the designation of individuals or groups as terrorist or associated entities (resulting in prohibited dealings with such entities as a result of the offences just mentioned). The second means by which the Act seeks to suppress the financing of terrorist activities is through the establishment of a financial transactions reporting regime and providing for the forfeiture of terrorist property. The power of forfeiture is vested in the High Court under s 55. The Attorney-General can apply for an order for forfeiture in respect of property owned by a designated terrorist entity where the mere prohibition against dealing with such property is not enough by itself. The entity must be the subject of a final, and not interim, designation. The Terrorism Suppression Amendment Bill 2007 proposes to change the freezing and forfeiture provisions so that they are automatic on interim or final designation.

In terms of financial transactions reporting, s 43 of the Terrorism Suppression Act requires financial institutions and other people in possession or control of suspected terrorist property to report that suspicion to the police. The provision was enacted to ensure that the mere *holding* of terrorist property, without necessarily dealing in it, is detected and made unlawful. The process for reporting suspicious property is aligned with the process for reporting suspicious transactions in the *Financial Transactions Reporting Act 1996*, which is limited to reporting for the purposes of money laundering offences or for proceeds of crime action. Double-reporting is avoided by deeming a report under the Terrorism Suppression Act to be notice under the Financial Transactions Reporting Act.[12]

Review mechanism

Following receipt of public submissions on the November 2001 version of the Terrorism (Bombings and Financing) Bill, the Foreign Affairs, Defence and Trade Committee recommended including a review mechanism for provisions that implemented resolution 1373. Section 70 of the Terrorism Suppression Act was the result, requiring a select committee to consider the operation of those provisions and whether they should be retained or amended. The review was to take place as soon as practicable after 1 December 2004, with the committee required to report to the House by no later than 1 December 2005. Due again to the timing of elections and the consequent uncertainty as to membership of the Foreign Affairs, Defence and Trade Committee, the committee was unable to undertake a comprehensive review of the Act. The committee recorded in the opening section of its report that it had not had sufficient opportunity to consider the evidence and advice received on the review and that:

> We have not made specific recommendations on how the legislation might be amended. In the time available to us we have focussed on recording those issues that we consider warrant further scrutiny.[13]

This is a most unfortunate result and undermines the integrity of legislative review mechanisms such as this. Their intention is to allow parliamentary committees, made up of elected representatives, to review the operation of legislation based on public submissions and advice from relevant government departments. What instead happened was that the committee was forced to speedily consider issues and note them within just eight substantive pages, without proper debate and commentary. Albeit that the committee will have an opportunity to examine the issues again in its consideration of the Terrorism Suppression Amendment Bill 2007, the reality is that the proposed amendments have now been drawn up entirely by government officials without input from the committee, whereas a proper review process would have seen the reverse occur. Rather than leaving the committee with the limited time it was given, s 70 should instead have been amended to allow the committee to undertake a proper review of the legislation.

Counter-Terrorism Bill 2003

The Counter-Terrorism Bill 2003 was a multi-purpose piece of legislation: primarily enacted to allow New Zealand to become party to the Plastic Explosives and Nuclear Material Conventions; to implement the remaining obligations under resolution 1373; and to establish supplementary powers and investigative measures 'designed to combat terrorism and address miscellaneous problems encountered by agencies in the investigation and enforcement of [terrorism-related] offences'.[14]

Purposes of the Counter-Terrorism Act

Treaty implementation

Within the scope of the first objective, to allow treaty accession, national interest analyses were presented to the House on 22 February 2002 with the accompanying reports of the Foreign Affairs, Defence and Trade Committee. The analyses noted that implementing legislation would need to create new criminal offences prohibiting the movement or use of unmarked plastic explosives and nuclear materials.[15] The Counter-Terrorism Bill achieved this through introduction into the Terrorism Suppression Act of ss 13B (use and movement of plastic explosives), 13C (physical protection of nuclear material) and 13D (importation and acquisition of radioactive material).

The national interest analyses also considered the question of reporting, registration and monitoring obligations under the relevant treaties. It was noted that the transport safety standards within the Nuclear Material Convention would not require implementation, since New Zealand had already incorporated IAEA regulations, which contain more stringent requirements than those under the Nuclear Material Convention.[16] The analysis on the Plastic Explosives Convention concluded that:

> A reporting and registration regime needs to be put in place adequately to control the existing stock of unmarked plastic explosives in New Zealand. This administrative function is already carried out in relation to other explosives under the *Hazardous Substances and New Organisms Act 1996*. Slight modifications to the operational procedures under that Act would be required to facilitate plastic explosives of the type covered by the Convention being captured by the tracking and reporting mechanisms of the HSNO Act.[17]

The Counter-Terrorism Bill did not, however, address this issue. To that extent, the plastic explosives reporting and registration regime has not been fully implemented into New Zealand law.

Resolution obligations and investigative/supplementary powers

The explanatory notes to the Counter-Terrorism Bill identify two further objectives of implementing the remaining obligations under resolution 1373 and establishing investigative powers to assist in the detection of terrorists, terrorist acts and terrorist or associated entities. In that regard, several clauses pertaining to interception warrants, tracking devices and computer access were identified by New Zealand as adding to its compliance with paragraph 2(b) of the resolution. The new offence of harbouring or concealing terrorists was said to add to New Zealand's compliance with paragraph 2(d) of the resolution. New sentencing directions were further identified as being in furtherance of the requirements of paragraph 2(e) of the resolution.

Material provisions of the Counter-Terrorism Bill

It should be noted that the Counter-Terrorism Bill, once passed through parliament, did not establish an independent Act with its own life. As introduced, the Bill was to become a stand-alone Act. Following submissions during the select committee process, however, its provisions were instead incorporated into other existing legislation. Those provisions relating to treaty implementation, under Part 2 of the Bill, have already been discussed. Reflecting the second and third stated purposes of the Counter-Terrorism Bill, to further implement resolution 1373 and to establish supplementary powers and investigative measures, Parts 1 and 3 of the Bill amended various items of legislation.

First, new terrorism-related offences were created under the *Crimes Act 1961*. New ss 298A, 298B and 307A make it an offence to cause disease or sickness in animals; contaminate food, crops, water or other products; or make threats of harm to people or property to achieve terrorist ends. Associated provisions provide extraterritorial jurisdiction over these offences and restrict the ability to prosecute by requiring the consent of the Attorney-General. The second feature of Parts 1 and 3 was to extend the ability of police to obtain warrants to intercept private communications relating to terrorist offences, by amending s 312 of the *Crimes Act 1961* and s 26 of the *Misuse of Drugs Act 1978*. These appear unproblematic.

A controversial part of the Bill concerns the creation of a new s 198B of the *Summary Proceedings Act 1957*, allowing police to demand assistance to access computer data by requiring any data protection codes necessary to effect access to that data to be provided. Where such a demand is made subsequent to a person's arrest, there must be an identified and pressing objective in order to satisfy s 5 of the *New Zealand Bill of Rights Act 1990* that it is a justified limit on the right to silence guaranteed under s 23(4) of that Act. By operation of s 4 of the Bill of Rights Act, however, it is 'not invalid'. While this does not breach the International Covenant on Civil and Political Rights (ICCPR), since there is no comparable provision in the Covenant to s 23(4), it fails to comply with the international guidelines on counter-terrorism and human rights.[18]

A further troubling aspect of amendments to the Summary Proceedings Act under the Counter-Terrorism Bill concerns a new regime authorising police or customs officers to obtain a warrant to attach a tracking device to any property or person where it is suspected that an offence has been, is being or will be committed. In this case, there is a lack of safeguards against the arbitrary or unlawful interference with privacy by use of tracking devices, rendering the regime both in breach of Article 17 of the ICCPR and of international standards on counterterrorism and human rights.[19] Common to both this regime, and the new police powers of questioning mentioned in the preceding paragraph, is the fact that these new powers are not restricted to countering terrorism but are in fact applicable to the investigation of any offence carrying a sentence of imprisonment.

In introducing the Counter-Terrorism Bill in 2003, it was said that the Bill:

> reflects the need for New Zealand, in a new, more dangerous era of international terrorism, to ensure we have a comprehensive legislative framework in place to help to prevent, and to deal with, terrorist offending.[20]

The establishment of broad legislative provisions like these within the umbrella of a 'Counter-Terrorism' Bill was a matter of regular criticism in submissions to, and evidence before, the Foreign Affairs, Defence and Trade Committee.[21] Such legislative tactics are also contrary to international guidelines on counter-terrorism. Although these guidelines can be characterised as 'soft law' recommendations, they are nevertheless highly influential given the consistency between the various sources of the guidelines. They represent the standards generally accepted by international society as being applicable to the countering of terrorism in democratic states. As stated in the latest *Draft Principles and Guidelines* within the report of the Special Rapporteur to the Sub-Commission on the Promotion and Protection of Human Rights:

> Counter-terrorism measures must directly relate to terrorism and terrorist acts, *not* actions undertaken in armed conflict situations or *acts that are non-terrorist crimes* [emphasis added].[22]

The fifth feature of the Counter-Terrorism Bill is a minor amendment of the *New Zealand Security Intelligence Service Act 1969*, but with major potential effect. The amendment concerns the definition of the term 'security' within s 2 of the Act. Terrorism was already a matter within the ambit of the Act, but not in as wide terms as it is now. Prior to the Counter-Terrorism Bill, 'security' included the protection of New Zealand from acts of terrorism. The term now includes 'the prevention of any terrorist act and of any activity relating to the carrying out or facilitating of any terrorist act'. This is significant since interception and seizure warrants may now be authorised for the purpose of detecting activities prejudicial to 'security' or for the purpose of gathering foreign intelligence information essential to 'security'.[23]

Finally, the *Sentencing Act 2002* has been amended so that conduct forming part of, or involving, a terrorist act is to be treated as an aggravating feature under s 9 of that Act. Where murder is committed as part of a terrorist act, s 104 has been amended to provide for a minimum period of 17 years imprisonment.

Conclusion

Examination of legislation post-9/11 has revealed that New Zealand appears to have, other than in some very minor and usually technical ways, fully implemented its international anti-terrorism obligations. What that analysis did not identify, however, was the failure of New Zealand's general criminal law to properly prohibit the incitement to terrorism, a matter addressed separately elsewhere.[24] By reviewing the structure and operation of the Terrorism Suppression Act and Counter-Terrorism Bill, various provisions have been identified as having the potential to impact on civil and political rights, not least of which is an unsettling movement by the state to extend its powers under the guise of counter-terrorism.

Notes

1 *Aviation Crimes Act 1972*; *Crimes (Internationally Protected Persons, and United Nations and Associated Personnel, and Hostages) Act 1980*; and *Maritime Crimes Act 1999*.

2 For consideration of those items of legislation and their operation, see Alex Conte, *Counter-Terrorism and Human Rights in New Zealand* (2007) 83-92. It is available online at <http://www.lawfoundation.org.nz/awards/irf/conte/index.html>. Significant parts of this chapter are adapted from ch 5 of this text.

3 New Zealand Ministry of Foreign Affairs and Trade, *National Interest Analysis, International Convention for the Suppression of Terrorist Bombings* (2001) para 9, and *National Interest Analysis, International Convention for the Suppression of the Financing of Terrorism* (2001) para 12.

4 Foreign Affairs, Defence and Trade Committee, New Zealand Parliament, *Interim Report on the Terrorism (Bombings and Financing) Bill* (2001).

5 *Report of the Special Rapporteur on the promotion and protection of human rights and fundamental freedoms while countering terrorism*, UN Doc E/CN.4/2006/98 (2005) ch III.

6 For a detailed consideration of this assessment see Conte, above n 2, 361-72.

7 Phil Goff, 'Amendments to Tighten Terrorism Suppression Act' (Press Release, 14 December 2004).

8 Foreign Affairs, Defence and Trade Select Committee, New Zealand Parliament, *Statutory Review of the Terrorism Suppression Act 2002* (2005).

9 New Zealand, *Parliamentary Debates*, House of Representatives, 10 February 2005, vol 623, 18566 (Phil Goff, Minister of Justice and Minister of Foreign Affairs and Trade).

10 John E Smith, *New Zealand's Anti-Terrorism Campaign: Balancing Civil Liberties, National Security, and International Responsibilities*, (2003) 3.

11 For a detailed discussion of this assessment see Conte, above n 2, ch 15.

12 See ss 44(4) and 77 of the *Terrorism Suppression Act 2002* and (amended) s 15(1) of the *Financial Transactions Reporting Act 1996*.

13 Foreign Affairs, Defence and Trade Select Committee, above n 8, 1.

14 Explanatory note to the Counter-Terrorism Bill, presented to the House 1 April 2003, 1.

15 New Zealand Ministry of Foreign Affairs and Trade, *National Interest Analysis, Convention on the Marking of Plastic Explosives for the Purpose of Detection* (2002) para 13, and *National Interest Analysis, Convention on the Physical Protection of Nuclear Materials* (2002) para 21.

16 New Zealand Ministry of Foreign Affairs and Trade, *National Interest Analysis, Convention on the Physical Protection of Nuclear Materials* (2002) para 20. Incorporation was effected through the Radiation Protection Act 1965.

17 New Zealand Ministry of Foreign Affairs and Trade, *National Interest Analysis, Convention on the Marking of Plastic Explosives for the Purpose of Detection* (2002) para 14.

18 For a detailed discussion of this assessment see Conte, above n 2, ch 18.

19 For a detailed discussion of this assessment see Conte, above n 2, ch 17.

20 New Zealand, *Parliamentary Debates*, House of Representatives, 1 April 2003, vol 607, 4619 (Phil Goff, Minister of Justice and Minister of Foreign Affairs and Trade).

21 Including submissions and evidence by this author, the Privacy Commission and the New Zealand Law Society: see *Submissions to the Foreign Affairs, Defence and Trade Committee on the Counter-Terrorism Bill 2003*, Parliamentary Library, Wellington.

22 Kalliopi Koufa (as Special Rapporteur to the United Nations Commission for Human Rights Sub-Commission for the Promotion and Protection of Human Rights), *A Preliminary Framework Draft of Principles and Guidelines Concerning Human Rights and Terrorism*, UN Doc E/CN.4/Sub.2/2005/39 (2005) para 33.

23 *New Zealand Security Intelligence Service Act 1969* s 4.

24 See Conte, above n 2, ch 13.

17

The United Kingdom's Anti-Terrorism Laws: Lessons for Australia

Clive Walker

The agenda set by the foregoing title is daunting. To describe and analyse the immense catalogue of United Kingdom anti-terrorism laws is alone a monumental task. The further possibility that the United Kingdom should act as role model would seem implausible to anyone familiar with the doleful tales of miscarriages of justice and summary shootings which have emanated from their implementation. Nevertheless, the Australian Commonwealth government has occasionally found inspiration for anti-terror laws from the United Kingdom, and so some respectful pointers for another jurisdiction will be mentioned as a subsidiary task.

Are United Kingdom anti-terror laws necessary?

The question may be answered descriptively and prescriptively. A descriptive answer is that there exists a high degree of factual reliance on anti-terror laws by successive United Kingdom governments and parliaments. Unlike many jurisdictions where no serious attention was accorded to terrorism until the shock of 9/11, the United Kingdom has regularly experienced and legally responded to terrorism during three centuries or more. The legal results first reflect the experiences of terrorism in colonial conflicts of the bygone British Empire. Further legal impact was achieved by the sporadic campaigns of Irish Republicans, as well as their Loyalist opponents, both in Ireland and sometimes in mainland Britain. Finally, there has emerged since the 1970s a growing attentiveness to the mounting spectre of international terrorism.

Just before 9/11, the *Terrorism Act 2000* marked an important new phase in the legal framework. That Act launched a more unified and permanent regime in recognition that it is wistful or unrealistic, in the light of this history, to depict terrorism laws as 'temporary provisions', a lesson which other jurisdictions with more recent experiences may be yet to face. The Act also reacted to the decisive paramilitary ceasefires in Northern Ireland in 1998 and so refocused effort further towards international terrorism. Though intended as a turning-point, the *Terrorism Act 2000* was not the end of legal history. The attacks of 9/11 produced the *Anti-terrorism, Crime and Security Act 2001*, and, since that time, the *Prevention of Terrorism Act 2005* and the *Terrorism Act 2006* have responded to jihadist violence. Overall, the contemporary panoply of specialist anti-terrorism legislation is configured as follows.

Terrorism Act 2000

The Act is divided into eight parts, with six reflecting its substantive themes: proscribed organisations; terrorist property; terrorist investigations; counter-terrorism powers; and miscellaneous offences (such as possession of items useful to terrorism). Some of the most eye-catching changes are structural rather than substantive. For the first time ever, anti-terrorism laws are stated comprehensively and permanently in one code. An exception was Part VII, a collection of special measures (including non-jury 'Diplock' trials)[1] relating to Northern Ireland alone. This Part is being phased out, but many aspects continue or can be reinserted by the *Justice and Security (Northern Ireland) Act 2007*.

Anti-terrorism, Crime and Security Act 2001

This substantial supplement, a response to the fears instilled by 9/11, is organised into 12 operative parts. The first three address the forfeiture of terrorist property and seizure of terrorist cash, replacing and adding to measures in the *Terrorism Act*. Part III of the *Anti-terrorism, Crime and Security Act 2001* treads into new territory, dealing with the freezing of foreign property held by United Kingdom institutions.

Part IV addressed immigration and asylum matters. By far the most controversial element was the detention without trial of 16 foreign persons denied asylum on national security grounds or because of their international crimes.[2] A Privy Counsellor Review Committee depicted the system as objectionable in principle because of the lack of procedural safeguards and also because it provided no protection against resident terrorists.[3] The Home Office Consultation Paper in response regarded Part IV as essential and shelved the alternatives as unworkable.[4] There the matter rested until, as described later, the judges intervened.

Parts VI to IX govern dangerous substances (the kinds of materials which make up weapons of mass destruction) and acute vulnerabilities such as nuclear and aviation facilities. The measures bolstering their security also encompass the specialist police forces assigned to their protection (Part X).

Other aspects of Part X, as well as extracts from Part XI, mainly consist of amendments to *Terrorism Act* policing measures as well as pervasive surveillance powers such as the retention of communications data.

Next, there are various new criminal offences spread around the *Anti-terrorism, Crime and Security Act 2001*. More controversial is the sentencing enhancement in Part V concerning offences motivated by religious hatred, which were officially depicted as necessary to send a signal that Muslim communities were not to be victimised, a theme now reinforced by the *Racial and Religious Hatred Act 2006*.

Prevention of Terrorism Act 2005

This Act replaces the regime of detention without trial under Part IV of the 2001 Act with restrictions on liberty by way of control orders. The effect is that those suspects previously detained have been subjected to this new type of executive order – at least until August 2005, when many were detained again pending deportation. The Act allows for two types of order, depending on their severity, namely derogating orders and non-derogating orders, both subject to scrutiny by a court. The orders issued in 2005 were 'not very short of house arrest',[5] and several were subsequently struck down by the courts as incompatible with art 5 of the *European Convention on Human Rights* (ECHR) in the absence of any derogation notice.[6] Because of this substantial level of judicial intervention, the government depicts control orders as having 'holes all through them'.[7] It has hankered after either a new derogation or a return to detention without trial but, fearing judicial condemnation and political unpopularity, has hesitated to strive actively for either.

Terrorism Act 2006

The origins of this Act can be located in the London bombings of July 2005, which sparked the Prime Minister into presenting new measures against terrorism on the basis that 'the rules of the game are changing'.[8] There were two major motivations behind the legislation. The first agenda item was to implement the *Council of Europe Convention on the Prevention of Terrorism* of 2005, though there are major discrepancies between the Act and the Convention. The second, and more prescient, issue was the concern about the radicalisation of British Muslim young men, such as the bombers from Leeds. The analysis of these bombings and their causes is far from complete or certain. The lead bomber, Mohammed Sidique Khan, speaking on a video released a few months later, stated: 'Until you stop the bombing, gassing, imprisonment and torture of my people we will not stop this fight'.[9] But many fellow Muslims and most of the electorate also oppose the war in Iraq and condemn the lack of action in protecting Palestinian people. So, it is not certain whether terrorism is an emanation of a perceived war of aggression in Iraq, or a more deep-seated form of social anomie amongst certain strata of minority communities, or a mixture of both. The government is inevitably quick to deny the causal impact of the 'war on terror' and has instead emphasised the malign influence of radical preachers such as Abu Hamza, Omar Bakri Muhammed and Abu Qatada, who have been either imprisoned or deported.[10]

As for their would-be emulators, there are new offences against the 'encouragement' of terrorism. The principal offence in s 1 relates to the publication of statements that are 'likely to be understood' by their audience 'as a direct or indirect encouragement or other inducement to [it] to the commission, preparation or instigation of acts of terrorism' or specified offences. The publisher must either intend 'members of the public to be directly or indirectly encouraged or otherwise induced, by the statement to commit, prepare or instigate acts of terrorism' or specified offences, or be reckless as to whether members of the public will be so directly or indirectly encouraged by the statement.

Indirect encouragement of terrorism includes a statement that 'glorifies' the commission or preparation of acts of terrorism or specified offences (either in their actual commission or in principle) but only if 'members of the public could reasonably be expected to infer that what is being glorified' in the statement 'is being glorified as conduct that should be emulated by them'. There were furious debates about whether this offence might criminalise anyone who glorified the armed opposition to the Apartheid regime in South Africa (such as the saintly Nelson Mandela), and there were calls for the future prosecution of Cherie Booth, the wife of the then British Prime Minister Tony Blair, for stating in a speech that 'I can well understand how decent Palestinians become terrorists'.[11] The lessons for other jurisdictions are that, while the causes of radicalisation should be vital subjects of official examination, the incarceration of Muslim preachers and students who share the vicarious excitement of jihadist websites should not be the prime or sole mode of engagement with an alienated community.

The 2006 Act further imparts additions to offences of training and preparations, and the widening of proscription powers. The police powers of detention after arrest are also extended – though only by doubling the period to 28 days and not 90 days after Parliament rejected that proposal as an unacceptable and factually unjustified negation of liberty.

Yet more laws have recently been announced for 2008 – including, extra pre- and post-charge detention powers, a register of terrorism offenders (for supervision when they are released), further data-sharing powers and consideration of the admissibility of intercepted communications.[12]

Principled validations for anti-terrorism laws

The fallacy of transition from description to prescription must be avoided. Nevertheless, principled validations for distinct anti-terrorist laws can be mounted at three levels. The first level recognises that it is justifiable in international human rights law for liberal democracies to defend their existence and their values. This position is endorsed by arts 4 (derogation) and 5 (forbidden use of rights to undermine rights) of the United Nations *International Covenant on Civil and Political Rights*. Aside from the power to take action, there is a state duty to act against political or paramilitary violence in order to safeguard the right to life of its citizens (as under art 6). In addition, states should more generally ensure the enjoyment of rights and democracy (under art 2) and, according to other United Nations instruments, must not harbour or condone terrorism.[13] The second level of justification points to the illegitimacy of terrorism in international criminal law – many of its emanations are almost certainly universal crimes of war or crimes against humanity.

Thirdly, terrorism is a specialised form of criminality that poses peculiar difficulties in terms of policing and criminal process arising from its transnational organisation, capacity to intimidate and sophistication. Just as variations in criminal justice have been successively adopted against, for example, rapists, serious fraudsters and drug traffickers in order to secure the public good, so terrorists warrant differential treatment because of atypical methods and targets. There are therefore good reasons to accept that the specific protection of constitutional values is a legitimate practice.

The alternative stance – 'business as usual', on the basis that 'normal' laws suffice to combat terrorism – comes in two guises, but both suffer from naivety. First, those who contend for business as usual because they say normal laws can achieve all we need to achieve are naïve on several grounds. They simplistically believe that there is a clear and fixed concept of 'normal' law and that it is uniquely immutable in the face of terrorism and cannot be shaped by social events unlike the rest of criminal justice. Second, those who contend for business as usual in law but with the fall-back of extra-legal measures *in extremis* are imprudent because they fondly assume officials will act in the public interest and will own up to their extra-legal activities. Most inquiries into misdeeds in Northern Ireland over the past 40 years demonstrate otherwise.

If special legislation can in principle be justifiable, the next question is whether the laws in the United Kingdom adopted over time are actually working.

Are United Kingdom anti-terror laws working?

Rather than providing a tediously nit-picking dissection of the legislation mentioned so far, the remainder of this chapter will relate to several policy themes – presented as binaries – around which many of the controversies and debates concerning the efficacy of the United Kingdom legislation have become entwined. In this way, a more dynamic sense of policy development will be conveyed. Other jurisdictions can then draw appropriate lessons.

A holistic approach – hearts and minds, not just police and crimes

The argument here is that anti-terrorism laws are often conceived narrowly in terms of police and crimes. A more strategic approach opens up the agenda, including the legal agenda. In my estimation, the United Kingdom government has engaged in serious strategic thinking over the past few years by developing a so-called 'CONTEST' strategy for countering international terrorism. The strategy is divided into four principal strands: prevent, protect, prepare and pursue.[14]

'Preventing' terrorism is achieved by tackling the radicalisation of individuals through tackling disadvantage and supporting reform, including the reduction of inequalities and discrimination, by taking action against the radicalisers, but also by more positively engaging in the battle of ideas. 'Protecting' against terrorism means action to protect the public, key national services and UK interests overseas, such as by strengthening border security and by protecting key utilities, transport infrastructure and public assemblies. 'Preparing' for the consequences of terrorism concentrates on risk identification, target hardening, testing and contingency planning.

In terms of implementation, the 'Protect' and 'Prepare' aspects have been significantly advanced through the *Civil Contingencies Act 2004* and work around the Critical National Infrastructure. By contrast, the 'Prevent' aspect has involved a lot of initiatives and noise, especially through a Home Office initiative, 'Preventing Extremism Together', but its impact is more chimeral, perhaps as it unduly emphasises security and underplays social factors.

This leaves the familiar 'Pursue' strand. There should be two outcomes in mind. The most obvious is criminalisation. A criminal justice response should be prioritised as one that carries the important moral platform of legitimacy and fairness,[15] whilst also offering a practical response to danger. Criminal justice is also constitutionally limited by the need for open and substantial evidence. However, the more pervasive objective is control, which responds to anticipatory risk. The anticipatory risk of terrorism has for a long time equally triggered broad disruptive policing such as stop and search and, most radically, executive-based alternatives to criminal justice resolutions so as to allow preventive or even pre-emptive intervention. An inevitable consequence will be an emphasis on an intelligence-led approach and rather more shaky foundations in legitimacy because of the jettisoning of aspects of due process such as open hearings and evidential standards.

A rational code not panic legislation

One lesson which the United Kingdom partially learned is the importance of devising a rational legal code and not panic legislation. As indicated earlier, the *Terrorism Act 2000* was intended to establish a comprehensive and permanent regime, based on independent review by Lord Lloyd and a long legislative process, and therefore represented an attempt to break away from the cycle of emergency 'laws of the last atrocity'.[16] But it is a hard precept to follow. Terrorism is about political drama designed to engender emotions. The resultant danger of ill-considered panic legislation is manifest. Is it fair to depict the legislation subsequent to the 2000 Act as panic measures?

In the case of the 2001 Act, the nature and scale of the 9/11 attacks by Al-Qa'ida suggested that terrorism had developed a new 'Third Millennium' format. So, there was an argument for a legislative response to a new phenomenon, especially since, out of the 19 hijackers, 11 had links with the United Kingdom. The threat of mass casualties through suicidal attack has since been underlined by the 7/7 bombers. The legislative focus is therefore a reinforcement of the logical switch away from reactive policing towards proactive policing and management of anticipatory risk.[17] But having made these excuses, many of the measures in the 2001 Act go well beyond these considerations and represent opportunistic changes in policing and other aspects which are barely related to terrorism.

One can seek to justify the *Prevention of Terrorism Act 2005* as a wish to react appropriately to the case of *A v Secretary of State for the Home Department*.[18] In this case the House of Lords made a 'declaration of incompatibility' with an ECHR right (under the *Human Rights Act 1998*) in relation to the UK's scheme of indefinite detention of non-nationals suspected of terrorism.[19] The controversy in essence surrounded the derogation under art 15 lodged on 18 December 2001 concerning the contravention of art 5 incurred by the instigation of the power to detain foreign nationals under Part IV of the 2001 Act. Detention without trial had been instituted under Part IV out of the fear that there were dangerous foreigners at large against whom there was strong intelligence of involvement in terrorism but either not enough evidence for a criminal prosecution or evidence of a very sensitive nature the revelation of which in open court might compromise security techniques or might even imperil the lives of informants and agents.

This model of detention was eventually found to be incompatible with the *Human Rights Act 1998* in December 2004 in *A v Secretary of State for the*

Home Department. In the leading judgment of Lord Bingham, while a public emergency sufficient to warrant the issuance and continuance of the derogation notice had been demonstrated, detention without trial could not be said to be a proportionate response because of two main features within Part IV. One was that Part IV only applied to deportable aliens but ignored the considerable threat posed by British citizens, a threat which became a tragic reality with the 7/7 bombings. This position was disproportionate and also discriminatory. The other was that the model still allowed the foreign suspects to depart the country if they could find a receiving state willing to let them in and unwilling to apply torture. But the creation of this 'prison with three walls' made no sense in security terms since it invited the enemies of the state to plot abroad.

After stern expressions of disgruntlement, the government responded by way of 'control orders' in the *Prevention of Terrorism Act 2005*. These are certainly preferable to indefinite detention without trial, especially as the official intention is to keep within the bounds of the right to liberty and not to rely on further derogation notices. What should be less the subject of commendation is the dubious way in which control orders have been applied. They have been issued with such extensive restrictions on rights that they undoubtedly infringe rights to liberty, presumably in the cynical hope that litigation will take months or years to offer a response. Several orders have been quashed on this basis. Next, the procedures allow only minimal levels of challenge – described in one case as no more than a 'thin veneer of legality', albeit not to an extent that it breaches due process rights.[20] Third, the government has not taken seriously the possibility of prosecution, making no effort to gather more evidence from subjects and not reviewing files when evidence arrives from abroad, despite a statutory reminder about the superiority of criminal justice.[21]

Is the *Terrorism Act 2006* a panic reaction to the London bombings of July 2005? It is certainly reactionary against the offensive speech of extreme preachers of jihad, as already indicated, but whether it is in panic must be tempered by the fact that it took months, not days, to pass. Another important feature is the salutary defeat of the government proposal for a 90-day precharge detention period. The assumed equation hitherto, that the more draconian the law the more political popularity accrues to its sponsor, may now be fading. The public may have begun to appreciate, not least with the memory of how the Peace Process in Ireland required dialogue and compromise, that the endless ratcheting up of repression may not solve terrorism.

How to avoid panic legislation in the future? There are some institutional features which have secured better designed legislation in the United Kingdom in recent times and which might be considered as adaptable elsewhere. Within Parliament, specialist committees, such as the Joint Committee on Human Rights and the House of Commons Home Affairs Committee, have enhanced the quality of scrutiny which can then command cross-party support in plenary debate. Of course, for these mechanisms to work effectively, parliamentarians must show the courage to demand adequate resources (including researchers and pre-legislative scrutiny) and to loosen party loyalties – otherwise they will remain in the business of legitimisation and not scrutiny.

The courts have also signalled a greater willingness to intervene, and a major influence has been the culture change and the principled arguments fostered by the *Human Rights Act 1998*, a form of bill of rights still absent nationally in Australia. But one must not exaggerate judicial power. It depends on litigation which may conclude years after the event. The presence of sensitive information often produces deference. Even in the House of Lords' decision, there was no finding against the declaration of emergency, and it was fortuitous that the disproportionate and discriminatory policies were evident on the face of the Act.

The other mechanism by which rational policy-making is fostered is the independent review function currently undertaken by Lord Carlile. Lord Carlile provides information on the working of the legislation and some thoughtful recommendations from time to time about its reform. A device of this kind is certainly worthwhile, but Australia could improve on the United Kingdom model in three ways. First, the reviewer should have statutory terms of appointment, authority to investigate and staff to assist. Second, there should be a panel of multiple reviewers to gain a spread of expertise and a fresh look. Third, the reviewer should have explicit links to a parliamentary select committee and thereby would not have to await the pleasure of the government as to the terms on which debate takes place.

A criminal justice model not a war model

The inventory of United Kingdom laws responding to political violence has often adopted the distinctly militaristic approach prevalent in colonial campaigns and in Northern Ireland up to 1972. However, a more criminal justice-oriented slant was heralded by the review undertaken by Lord Diplock in 1972,[22] which formed the basis for the Northern Ireland (Emergency Provisions) Acts 1973-98. This transformation reflected revulsion at internment without trial, the inhuman treatment of detainees and lethal confrontations such as Bloody Sunday in 1972. It has been an article of faith since that time that, at least on the domestic front, sustainability and legitimacy are enhanced by the criminal justice approach which can better adhere to principles of constitutionalism. It follows that President Bush's invocation of 'the first war of the twenty-first century',[23] with its legal black hole at Guantanamo Bay, and its extraordinary renditions and dalliance with brutality, has been condemned by the English Attorney-General.[24]

Yet, there are several tensions in the attainment of this policy. It is not reflected abroad, and the British government, as the most ardent ally of the United States (alongside Australia), has supported military interventions in Afghanistan and Iraq. Even at home, measures such as detention without trial and control orders do not reflect the ideal.

Another tension concerns the development of 'precursor' special offences. These are offences which do not rely on the *actus reus* of a traditional crime – in other words, harm to a person or damage to property. Instead, they facilitate intervention against risk at an earlier preparatory stage, on the grounds that to await the commission of terrorism is too dangerous. Thus, one sees the development of offences such as s 57 of the *Terrorism Act 2000*, the possession of materials useful to terrorism, or s 58 of the same Act, the possession of information useful to terrorism – the most frequently applied special offences. The other development along these lines concerns the development of a war of words with terrorism, now illustrated by the offence of 'encouragement of terrorism' in s 1 of the *Terrorism Act 2006*. The problems with these types of offences are manifold. As well as the dangers of over-breadth from vague drafting terms, the offences penalise equivocal actions or mere speech.

A further tension is the reliance within criminal justice measures – whether in special offences or police powers – on the terminology of 'terrorism' as a useful shorthand but one which is imprecise and value-laden. The United Kingdom continues to struggle with the term, which is defined by s 1 of the *Terrorism Act 2000*:

> (1) In this Act 'terrorism' means the use or threat of action where –
> (a) the action falls within subsection (2),
> (b) the use or threat is designed to influence the government or to intimidate the public or a section of the public, and
> (c) the use or threat is made for the purpose of advancing a political, religious or ideological cause.
>
> (2) Action falls within this subsection if it –
> (a) involves serious violence against a person,
> (b) involves serious damage to property,
> (c) endangers a person's life, other than that of the person committing the action,
> (d) creates a serious risk to the health or safety of the public or a section of the public, or
> (e) is designed seriously to interfere with or seriously to disrupt an electronic system.

The three conjunctive legs in s 1(1) are intentionally broad, since the definition serves as the platform for investigative police powers where there must be some margin of error. But the more flexible the term, the more room for abuse and perceptions of abuse, as exemplified by complaints about the use of stop and search powers under s 44 of the *Terrorism Act 2000* against young males of Asian ethnicity.[25]

Since this usage now seems irreversible, and will grow with the *Terrorism Act 2006*, the definition should be reformed.[26] In terms of *definition* in s 1(1), relevant measures should be designed around a combination of specified seriously threatening and destabilising offences. In terms of *context and remit* as in s 1(2), what is important is the presence of collectives that carry them out and that render less capable normal criminal justice processes. In this way, the emphasis should be upon severe and collective political violence, rather than terrorism per se. The other constraint should relate to the application of the definition. The definition has a proper role in the tasking of ministers and security organisations in the execution of their powers but should not enter the courtroom within a criminal offence – by that stage, there should be more precision and more legitimacy for process and penalties.

The language of constitutionalism, not the language of balance

Terrorism as a strategy seeks to cause deep conflicts which destabilise and delegitimise governments. According to the characteristically exaggerated words of Lord Hoffman in the case of *A v Secretary of State for the Home Department*: 'The real threat to the life of the nation, in the sense of a people living in accordance with its traditional laws and political values, comes not from terrorism but from laws such as these'.[27] A persistent policy strand which seems to fall into this trap alludes to a conflict between public safety and individual rights to liberty, privacy and expression in which there can be some balance or trade off between these values. This concept of balance is commonplace but largely spurious. It is spurious because it assumes a loss of rights makes us per se more secure. It also assumes some kind of universal scale by which we can measure the gains and losses. If the argument is pitched instead in terms of a balance of rights – rights versus rights – rather than a balance of values – rights versus security – more principled and sustainable decisions will ensue. A language of rights and not of balance produces four palatable conclusions.

The first is that this balance within rights discourse is politically possible. There are important rights to security, including the right to life, just as there are rights to liberty or speech. It follows that respect for rights does not demand that special laws against terrorism should not exist at all or cannot be effective, a point already explored.[28]

The second conclusion is that absolute rights can and should be treated as absolute. This observation applies with special force to rights against torture or ill-treatment, despite the musings by some commentators that the ticking bomb justifies torture[29] and despite apparent official willingness to abandon suspects to their fate in the clutches of regimes wedded to torture with the flimsy excuse of a diplomatic assurance.[30] Absolute rights mean that states should never plan to sacrifice absolute rights, though one can understand that in the heat of battle people might get killed or hurt.

A third conclusion is that rights are to be viewed as universal. They apply to foreigners as well as citizens, a vital point understood well by the House of Lords in the case of *A v Secretary of State for the Home Department* but wholly fudged to date by the US Supreme Court. It also means that, wherever the British flag flies and there is effective control by British forces, rights must be respected and there is no point in trying to create a British Guantanamo.[31]

A fourth conclusion is that this emphasis on rights neatly matches the government's own strategic objectives. Going back to the estimable CONTEST document, the overall goal is 'to reduce the risk from international terrorism, so that people can go about their daily lives freely and with confidence'.[32] Freedom cannot be delivered by legislation which substantially diminishes civil, political, economic or social life. Confidence cannot be secured if people are fearful of the arbitrary and ineffective impact of security measures.

Appropriate structures not empty acronyms

Terrorism has long shaped security organisations in the United Kingdom, from the formation of the Metropolitan Police Special Branch in 1883 onwards. Now, the pressures of terrorism have sparked the reorganisation of this leading Special Branch to join up with the Anti-Terrorism Squad to form a new Counter Terrorism Command. There are also new regional Counter Terrorism Units, and local police Special Branches have been coordinated into regional clusters. The lesson learnt is to consider the policing structures for dealing with terrorism – what worked against nationalist or anarchist violence may need revision in the light of the globalisation of terrorism. But the extent of reform can be overdone, as when the Home Secretary insisted in 2006 that local police forces should be merged so as to cope with the threats from organised criminality, international terrorism and domestic extremism.[33] This was an inappropriate overreaction – most policing responds to local, unsophisticated crime, and breaking its local bonds is dangerous folly.

Moving from policing to intelligence agencies, there are two evident trends in the United Kingdom from which lessons can be learnt. The first is the breaking down of barriers between crime and intelligence. The police have emphasised intelligence through their National Intelligence Model. Equally, secret agents have been ushered into the world of terrorism policing since 1992, when the Security Service (MI5) assumed the Metropolitan Police Special Branch's role as the main Irish Republican terrorism intelligence-gathering agency. These trends away from local policing towards national agencies and, increasingly, away from policing to intelligence agencies have implications for democratic accountability that have not been adequately addressed. Another concern is the observance of individual rights; for example, will privacy be properly respected either during surveillance or in data retention?[34] The other issue is efficiency. Have the quality control problems uncovered by the Butler Report in the grand strategy of war been averted in the smaller skirmishes over the repression of individuals?[35] Is it helpful to fragment intelligence work across several major units, including the Secret Intelligence Service (MI6) and the Government Communications Headquarters? The arguments about the focus of work and local connections are not so evident here, and one wonders whether the rivalries discovered by the 9/11 Commission have been miraculously avoided in the United Kingdom. These questions deserve a thorough and independent review, but none has been commissioned in the United Kingdom.

By contrast, there has been governmental reform. The United Kingdom has not adopted the Department for Homeland Security (DHS) model but instead made recent reforms to the Home Office, which has sought to concentrate its efforts on counter-terrorism by shedding some functions in 2007 to a new Ministry of Justice and by reinforcing the Office for Security and Counter-Terrorism. This process is an object lesson in how not to reform structures. There was no public or parliamentary consultation, and as a result it failed to consider all aspects of security and may not achieve its goals.

International cooperation not unilateralism

There has been progress on securing international laws and cooperation against terrorism, and, given its global reach, this aspect is vital. The progress is exemplified by the greater sweep of later treaties, which have moved on from specific tactics such as hijacking into broader subjects such as the United Nations Conventions for the Suppression of Terrorist Bombings and for the Suppression of the Financing of Terrorism. At European Union level, the Council Framework Decision on a European arrest warrant was implemented in the United Kingdom by the *Extradition Act 2003* and secures a quick, no-questions-asked riposte to any qualms about political offence exceptions.

Three difficulties abound in this field. The first is that politicians seem to favour signing new documents but are far less assiduous at following up and ensuring there is universal implementation. The second is that too much of the negotiations remain hidden and secret. But the third problem is perhaps the most serious – when international agreement is viewed as problematic, unilateral or bilateral action will be taken (such as the 2003 war in Iraq), the consequences of which have been to squander the unity and support which followed the 9/11 attacks.

Conclusion

Terrorism legislation will continue both to proliferate and to generate controversies along the foregoing binaries. However, its impact will remain peripheral. The official estimates of active terrorists within the United Kingdom record a rising trend between March 2005 and November 2006.[36] Whether even more have been deterred, prevented or captured though anti-terrorism laws is hard to judge, save that in 2006, for example, 65 persons were charged under the terrorism legislation, 185 were arrested and around 17 were subject to control orders.[37] About 30,000 were stopped and searched.[38] More important factors than special legislation comprise normal police powers and criminal offences, and regular techniques of investigation and securitisation. These must operate alongside cooperation and vigilance on the part of the public who provide much of society's policing capability. Given this dependence of democracies on the mobilisation of the masses, both at political and practical levels, care must be taken to avoid alienating the public by counter-terrorism measures which appear disproportionate or senseless.

So, perhaps the greatest challenge is to maintain the trust and support of the public through adherence to the precepts of constitutionalism. The need to do so may be broadly appreciated. But even after three centuries of grappling with the problem of terrorism, the attainment of these precepts can still be blown off course in the face of the distress and emotion of the terrorist spectacular. To defeat terrorism is necessary if our democratic and humane values are to be preserved. Anti-terrorism laws are necessary, but the lessons of history show that laws can work for good or for ill.

Notes

1 See Northern Ireland Office, *Replacement Arrangements for the Diplock Courts System* (2006).

2 For details, see Lord Carlile, *Reviews of Pt IV of the Anti-terrorism, Crime and Security Act 2001* (2003, 2004, 2005).

3 See Privy Counsellor Review Committee, UK Parliament, *Anti-Terrorism, Crime and Security Act 2001 Review* (HC100, 2003) para 193.

4 Home Office, *Counter Terrorism Powers* (2004) Pt I paras 8, 34, Pt II para 31.

5 Lord Carlile, *First Report of the Independent Reviewer pursuant to Section 14(3) of the Prevention of Terrorism Act 2005* (2006) para 43.

6 See Clive Walker, 'Keeping control of terrorists without losing control of constitutionalism' (2007) 59 *Stanford Law Review* 1395.

7 Richard Ford, 'Terror Controls Full of Holes, Says Reid', *The Times*, 25 January 2007, 2.

8 Rosemary Bennett and Richard Ford, 'Row over tougher rules on preachers of hate', *The Times*, 6 August 2005, 1.

9 For a transcript of excerpts, see *London bomber: Text in full* (2005) *BBC News* <http://news.bbc.co.uk/2/hi/uk_news/4206800.stm> at 15 August 2007.

10 See Clive Walker, 'The treatment of foreign terror suspects' (2007) 70 *Modern Law Review* 427.

11 United Kingdom, *Parliamentary Debates*, House of Commons , 2 November 2005, vol 438 col 844, 2 (Bob Marshall-Andrews).

12 See *New counter-terrorism proposals announced* (2007) Home Office <http://www.homeoffice.gov.uk/documents/ct-discussion-document.pdf> at 15 August 2007.

13 See especially UN Security Resolution 1373 of 28 September 2001.

14 See Home Office, *Countering International Terrorism* (2006) paras 5-9.

15 See Lucia Zedner, 'Securing Liberty in the Face of Terror: Reflections from Criminal Justice' (2005) 32 *Journal of Law & Society* 507.

16 See Michael Humphrey, *The Politics of Atrocity and Reconciliation* (2002).

17 See Richard Ericson and Kevin Haggerty, *Policing the Risk Society* (1997).

18 *A v Secretary of State for the Home Department* [2005] 2 AC 68.

19 See further Clive Walker, 'Prisoners of "War All the Time"' [2005] *European Human Rights Law Review* 50.

20 *Re MB* [2006] EWHC 1000 (Admin), [103]; reversed by the Court of Appeal: [2006] EWCA Civ 1140.

21 See *Prevention of Terrorism Act 2005* s 8; *Secretary of State for the Home Department v E* [2007] 3 WLR 1.

22 *Report of the Commission to consider Legal Procedures to Deal with Terrorist Activities in Northern Ireland* (1972).

23 Duncan Campbell, 'Attack on America' *The Guardian*, 14 September 2001, 5.

24 Neil Rose, 'Goldsmith calls for US to close down Guantanamo and back the rule of law' (2006) 103 *Law Society's Gazette* 6.

25 See Home Affairs Committee, UK Parliament, *Counter-Terrorism and Community Relations in the aftermath of the London bombings* (HC 165-I, 2005).

26 Limited suggestions for reform were made by Lord Carlile, *The Definition of Terrorism* (2007). See further Clive Walker, 'The Legal Definition of "Terrorism" in United Kingdom Law and Beyond' [2007] *Public Law* 331.

27 *A v Secretary of State for the Home Department* [2005] 2 AC 68, 132 (Lord Hoffman).

28 See further UK Department for Constitutional Affairs, *Review of the Implementation of the Human Rights Act 1998* (2006).

29 See Chapter 14 of this book for discussion of these musings.

30 See Clive Walker, 'The treatment of foreign terror suspects' (2007) 70 *Modern Law Review* 427; UK Intelligence and Security Committee, *Rendition* (2007).

31 *Al-Skeini v Secretary of State for Defence* [2007] 3 WLR 33.

32 Home Office, above n 14, para 5.

33 Her Majesty's Inspectorate of Constabulary, *Closing the Gap* (2005).

34 See R v *Secretary of State for the Home Department; ex p Ruddock* [1987] 1 WLR 1482.

35 Committee of Privy Counsellors, UK Parliament, *Review of Intelligence on Weapons of Mass Destruction* (HC 898, 2004) ch 4.

36 Compare John Stevens, 'Forget human rights … kick out the fanatics' *News of the World*, 6 March 2005, 13 and Dame Eliza Manningham-Buller, 'The al-Qaeda challenge' *The Times*, 10 November 2006, 1.

37 Lord Carlile, *Report on other Operation of the Terrorism Act 2000 in 2006* (2007).

38 UK Metropolitan Police Authority, *Report of the MPA Scrutiny on MPS Stop and Search Practice* (2004).

PART VI

The Politics of Australia's Terrorism Debate

18

Muslim Communities: Their Voice in Australia's Anti-Terrorism Law and Policy

Waleed Aly

My task, to examine the voice of Muslim communities in Australia's anti-terrorism law and policy, may be interpreted in two ways. The first is to examine how Muslim voices are reflected in anti-terrorism legislation. The trouble with such an approach is that it would make for a very brief discussion. It is probably fair to say that the extent to which Muslims find their concerns reflected officially in this area approximates none. If Australia's counter-terrorism initiatives can be understood as the expression of a range of community voices, those belonging to Muslims are so quiet as to be negligible.

An alternative, and for the above reasons, preferable approach is to consider the responses and contributions of Australian Muslim communities to anti-terrorism law and policy debates. In the interests of containing the discussion, I will focus on the anti-terror law amendments originally proposed in September 2005, some two months after the London bombings, and finally passed in December of that year. These amendments took the form of the *Anti-Terrorism Act (No 2) 2005* (Cth).

From the outset, it is crucial to note how irredeemably problematic it is to conceive of there being a Muslim response to, or a Muslim view of, anything. No such singular thing exists. Muslim Australia is an amorphous mass of many varied people and communities. It comprises some 70 different nationalities, with a corresponding profusion of cultures, sub-cultures and languages. There are often parallel differences in religiosity. For example, Albanian Australian Muslims, many of whose families lived through repressive communist rule, have often lost connection with much religious practice, and tend to be significantly less devout than, say, many newly arrived Muslim refugees from Somalia.

The congregations that habituate most Australian mosques tend to be divided along ethnic lines. We may speak of the Turkish mosque in Auburn or the Pakistani mosque in Doncaster with considerable coherence. Sermons may be delivered in the non-English language corresponding to the dominant cultural background of the congregation, thereby making the preaching inaccessible to masses of other Australian Muslims. Among first-generation migrants, particularly those whose English is limited, various pockets of Muslim Australia may be unable to communicate verbally. This is obviously less true of the Australian-born second generation, but here, too, there emerge generational, cultural, political and especially sectarian differences that are no less significant and often more intense. Ultimately, this entity, called the 'Australian Muslim community', that so regularly makes an appearance in the Australian public conversation is in fact a horrible political fiction. Taking account of the cultural, experiential and theological diversity within Muslim Australia, it is only a slight exaggeration to say that to collect three Australian Muslims in a room is to collect simultaneously at least five different opinions.

Broad agreement among Australian Muslims is therefore extremely rare. So perhaps the most astonishing achievement of the Commonwealth's anti-terrorism laws is that they managed to generate something of an Australian Muslim consensus at the grass roots level. There is no scientific polling to demonstrate this, but my experience during my time at the Islamic Council of Victoria (ICV) led me to conclude that Australian Muslim attitudes to these laws have, in fact, been unprecedentedly uniform. That is no mean feat.

Australian Muslim concerns

I do not propose to outline in detail the major objections of Australian Muslims to specific provisions in the 2005 Act, or other Acts in the suite of anti-terror legislation. Many of them – such as association provisions, expanded questioning and preventative detention powers, sedition laws and the authorised use of tracking devices – will be familiar and have been discussed elsewhere in this book. However, it is worth noting one particular concern I encountered regularly from Muslims in my time at the ICV that clearly failed to capture the popular imagination and scarcely featured in the public conversation.

This concern surrounds the offences of financing terrorism. There are two offences that are relevant here. The first, which predates the 2005 Act, is the crime of financing a terrorist organisation. However, in the federal government's estimation, this left a loophole where terrorist fundraising is done, not by an organisation, but an individual.[1] It sought to rectify this deficiency through the 2005 Act, which created the following new offence of 'financing a terrorist' in s 103.2 in the *Criminal Code* (Cth):

(1) A person commits an offence if:
  (a) the person intentionally:

(i) makes funds available to another person (whether directly or indirectly); or

(ii) collects funds for, or on behalf of, another person (whether directly or indirectly); and

(b) the first mentioned person is reckless as to whether the other person will use the funds to facilitate or engage in a terrorist act.

Penalty: Imprisonment for life.

(2) A person commits an offence under subsection (1) even if:

(a) a terrorist act does not occur; or

(b) the funds will not be used to facilitate or engage in a specific terrorist act; or

(c) the funds will be used to facilitate or engage in more than one terrorist act.

In order to commit the crime of financing terrorism, you need not know you are giving money to a terrorist. You do not even need to give money to someone who ultimately uses it for a terrorist attack. You need only be 'reckless' as to whether the recipient will use the funds for terrorism, even if ultimately they do not. By virtue of s 5.4, you are deemed reckless in financing a terrorist if you are aware of a 'substantial risk' of the money being used for terrorism, which, in the circumstances, is 'unjustifiable to take'.

So, how likely must the realisation of a risk be before it is 'substantial'? And under what circumstances is taking such a risk 'unjustifiable'? That, it seems to me, is a quite nakedly political question. If one is inclined to regard terrorism as the definitive existentialist threat of our age, then it is arguably 'unjustifiable' to take any risk whatsoever – which may mean the end of charity. Alternatively, if one considers terrorism to be not significantly more threatening than any other crime, a greater degree of risk may be justifiable. In either case, whether or not a risk is 'unjustifiable to take' is likely to depend on the often inherently political assumptions one brings to the inquiry.

Moreover, that inquiry, according to s 5.4(3) of the Code, is not a question of law, but of fact. This underlines the degree of subjectivity in the offence and makes it harder to appeal a conviction. It also means each case is unique, so that there is limited judicial guidance available for people to predict which risks are unjustifiable and which are not. The maximum penalty, meanwhile, is life imprisonment.

This level of uncertainty in such a serious offence is deeply worrying for Australian Muslims. Charity is one of the five pillars on which Islamic practice is built, and is religiously mandated at certain times of the Islamic year.[2] Muslim charities also fulfil an important function in providing relief to parts of the Muslim world many other charities forget. Muslims are understandably keen to donate to them, especially after a disaster. Countless fundraising efforts followed the 2004 Indian Ocean tsunami and the 2005 Pakistan earthquake.

But terrorist organisations, or even individuals associated with them, have been known to source funding via disingenuous charitable bodies. Al-Qa'ida itself was active after the Pakistan earthquake. In the United States, for instance, the government has shut down several Muslim charities for security reasons (though very few investigations have resulted in charges being laid).[3] Like all Australians, Muslims want to be able to give charity in good faith without facing the prospect of a lifetime in prison for something they did not intend. And there is a very keen sense that these provisions will fall disproportionately on them.

This example underscores the first of the two dominant themes that characterise Muslim objections to Australia's anti-terrorism laws: that the measures are designed to, and will, target Australian Muslims. Here, it is oft-noted that the only groups listed as banned terrorist organisations under Australian law are connected to Muslims and Islam. This contrasts notably with the situation in Britain or the United States where non-Muslim – often South American and European – terrorist groups such as Peru's Sendero Luminoso and Spain's Basque Fatherland and Liberty (ETA) organisation are also proscribed.

The second prevailing thematic objection, which emerges from the first, centres on a feeling of deep suspicion of law enforcement and intelligence agencies. As Waleed Kadous of the Australian Muslim Civil Rights Advocacy Network (AMCRAN) told ABC radio, 'I still think that it's an adversarial environment, rather than a cooperative one'.[4] For some, this suspicion arose from the fact that a number of counter-terrorism raids had been conducted across Australia for several years, almost without ever having led to arrests. Particularly unhelpful in this context were the remarks of 'a senior federal source' in the aftermath of raids in Sydney and Melbourne in June 2005, that they were conducted for the purposes of 'rattling the cages' to deter people from taking the 'next step', rather than to gather evidence that would support a conviction.[5] The inference is that raids were being used as a tool to scare people.

It is true that over a dozen arrests did follow the raids of November 2005 in Melbourne and Sydney, but this was after substantial new anti-terror laws had already been announced and passed as a response to the London bombings. In particular, there was a fear that racial and religious profiling was at work in these operations, such that innocent people were having their rights violated on the basis of suspicion by association. This perception was not helped by voices such as that of former ASIO officer Michael Roach, who told ABC Television's *Lateline* that law enforcement and intelligence agencies should be targeting:

> somebody standing in the corner, somebody who's holding onto their backpack, somebody who looks really concerned and anxious. Somebody

> who's clean shaven or somebody wearing a vest that looks so unusual – the jumper is bulky, the vest is bulky not fit with other clothing. *And Middle Eastern appearance* … Unfortunately, Middle-Eastern people are going to be approached more often than not and that's just the way it goes at the moment. We can't do anything about it … And I'm sure their communities, their community leaders have mentioned that they may be more likely to be approached because of their beliefs, their dress and their colour and unfortunately now that is just what's happening [emphasis added].[6]

The federal government has repeatedly recorded its opposition to such profiling, and reiterated that it would not sanction it. That reassurance, however, was roundly ignored when Mark Burgess, chief executive of the Police Federation of Australia, requested that the federal government indemnify police for civil liability in the event that they are accused of resorting to racial profiling in the application of anti-terror laws. For Burgess, a focus on Muslims, or people of Middle Eastern appearance might be 'inevitable'.[7] The implication was that these laws could only be implemented in practice with the use of such profiling. Moreover, the request signalled some kind of intent to implement these increased powers in that fashion. Whatever the pragmatic necessities of counter-terrorism, for present purposes it is sufficient to note that this kind of discourse profoundly supported the fear of many Australian Muslims that broad anti-terrorism powers, implemented by distrusted law enforcement and intelligence agencies, would fall disproportionately and unfairly on them. That they would be targeted.

Muslim responses

So Muslim Australia reacted, at the grass roots level, with near-unanimous negativity to the 2005 Act. By contrast, however, Muslim community organisations did not. Between them, they provided varied responses.

The most dominant response was silence. Several reasons might be postulated for this. AMCRAN suggests it reflects the chilling effect of the counter-terrorism landscape in Australia: that some Australian Muslims are 'now afraid to speak out on political issues, and even, ironically, the anti-terrorism laws themselves'.[8] This is possibly true, but I do not find it comprehensively persuasive. It is far more likely in my view that the organisational silence in much of Muslim Australia stems from a skill shortage within the relevant organisations. Put simply, those who fill such positions are often not familiar with the political process, and are unable to contribute coherently to public debate on sometimes difficult and subtle law and policy issues.

This silence was broken, principally by four interventions:

- the sustained advocacy against the 2005 Act of AMCRAN;

- the media work of the ICV;
- public statements made by Ameer Ali, then president of the Australian Federation of Islamic Councils (AFIC); and
- one public statement entitled 'United Stand: Muslims Oppose Proposed Anti-Terror Laws' signed by 33 unrelated Muslim groups including AMCRAN.

I will briefly outline these responses in turn. From this, it will emerge that these responses most commonly proceeded, broadly speaking, from two familiar arguments: first, that the anti-terror laws will target Muslims; and second, that these laws constitute an unacceptable erosion of Australians' civil liberties.

Australian Muslim Civil Rights Advocacy Network

Perhaps fittingly for a dedicated civil rights organisation, AMCRAN was perhaps the most prolific and creative of Australia's Muslim organisations in responding to the 2005 Act. Naturally, this included a substantial number of appearances in media, and before parliamentary committees. Uniquely, though, AMCRAN produced and published an information booklet, *Terrorism Laws: ASIO, the Police and You*, designed to inform people of their rights and responsibilities under the new laws. By AMCRAN's own admission, this booklet was more information than advocacy, but it is nonetheless an important response.

Substantively, however, AMCRAN's advocacy adhered to the familiar themes identified above. It devoted much energy to arguing that the laws were intrinsically adapted for selective application and that Muslims were being targeted. Perhaps its most troubling allegation in this regard was that authorities were threatening to use their detention powers as a way of coercing Muslims to answer questions. AMCRAN's Agnes Chong said:

> There is evidence to suggest that the powers are being used as a coercive measure in the community, particularly in light of the provision that requires a person's passport to be surrendered when the Director-General [of ASIO] seeks the Attorney-General's consent to request for the issuing of a warrant.[9]

The evidence for this remains anecdotal. It is an allegation that the relevant agencies would be likely to deny strenuously. I am in no position to adjudicate on it, but there is no doubt it deserves greater official scrutiny.

AMCRAN also relied on a suite of familiar civil liberties arguments that focused particularly on the looseness of the definitions used in anti-terrorism legislation, especially of key terms such as 'terrorist act'. In this, they echoed the arguments used widely by civil libertarians that organisations like Nelson

Mandela's African National Congress and protesting trade unions may well fall within the new legislative definition of terrorism:

> The laws are so broad that they cover not only the acts commonly understood to be terrorist actions, but legitimate resistance movements. Under the new regime, the African National Congress or Fretelin would be considered terrorist organisations. In the case of Muslims, resistance to the brutal dictatorship in Uzbekhistan [sic], or even financial support to Palestinian families who lost their houses due to Israeli policy of demolishing homes of suspected – not convicted – suicide bombers, would be considered acts of terrorism.[10]

The implication of AMCRAN's argument was that the vagueness of crucial definitions would necessitate the selective application of anti-terror laws, and that this selectivity would fall disproportionately on Australian Muslims. Thus, a connection was made between AMCRAN's civil liberties arguments and its concerns of discriminatory targeting.

Islamic Council of Victoria

I do not propose to discuss the response of the ICV in any great detail, mainly because I was the ICV's spokesperson during that time and cannot reasonably expect others to accept my account as sufficiently objective.

For present purposes therefore, I note that the ICV's advocacy, while also asserting that Muslims would feel targeted and that civil liberties would be eroded, attempted additionally to articulate its opposition to the anti-terror laws on more pragmatic grounds: that it was not yet demonstrated that the new laws would work. An example of this approach can be found in this passage from the ABC's *Lateline* in September 2005:

> I think the Prime Minister himself actually said in the preamble to outlining these proposed laws that this was really a response to [the] London [bombings], that London has changed things. And I think that really should lead us to ask quite stringently, would any of these measures have prevented an event like London? Now I'm not entirely convinced they would have ... Part of the problem with London was that the people who were alleged to have carried this out were actually not on the radar at all. So we wouldn't have put tracking devices on them. Law enforcement, or the type of measures we're talking about, probably wouldn't have been adequate to confront something like this and I think we actually expose ourselves to significant risk if we reduce the whole security debate to equating security with law enforcement. It's about a lot more than that. There's much more to the sociological dynamics that underlie behaviour like terrorism, for example. We're not discussing these things at the moment.[11]

Australian Federation of Islamic Councils

By far the most intriguing response came from then AFIC president Ameer Ali, principally in his capacity as the chairman of the Howard government's Muslim Community Reference Group (MCRG), which was established temporarily in the aftermath of the London Bombings. Ali's response was intriguing, mainly for its incoherence.

On 6 October 2005, the MCRG had the benefit of a private briefing organised by the Attorney-General on the 2005 Act. A doorstop interview followed with Ameer Ali as MCRG chairman, Attorney-General Philip Ruddock and then Minister for Citizenship and Multicultural Affairs John Cobb, in the course of which Ali declared:

> We were rather concerned about the way these laws are going to be implemented. Having listened to the Attorney-General and Minister John Cobb, we are being more comfortable in these assurance provided, and the safeguards that are engraved in these laws. And therefore we think that we can now sell these to our community with much easier, with much more comfort, because we think that there's adequate, is balanced laws; it has enough safeguards and it protects us from any incident that might happen in this country.[12]

Given the pervasive opposition to the 2005 Act among Australian Muslims, this was a fairly generous endorsement from Ali. Pushed further, he would only become more emphatic:

> Journalist: Dr Ali, can you say that every representative at the meeting today has accepted these laws as you have?
>
> Dr Ali: It was unanimous. Not one single disappointed person.[13]

Ali's statement was a misrepresentation, and it troubled several other members of the MCRG. 'His comments were wrong and they upset a lot of people', said MCRG member and president of the Muslim Women's National Network Aziza Abdel-Halim. She went on to say:

> We had taken no decision on the laws, we were just listening to Mr Ruddock's explanation. He jumped the gun. If we had just jumped in and said we accept the laws before we fully understand them or are fully convinced of them, then we would lose credibility with our community.[14]

The ICV, whose then president Malcolm Thomas was also a member of the MCRG, swiftly issued a media release, in which Thomas said:

> Our position on these laws has remained unchanged. We have grave concerns about these laws and cannot support or endorse them until we have seen them in their final form … This is a view which has broad support in the community. We note with concern Dr Ameer Ali's comment that the

> members of the Muslim Reference Group had unanimously accepted the new laws. This statement was unauthorised and totally misrepresents our position.[15]

A similar objection was registered by AMCRAN:

> Waleed Kadous (AMCRAN): Unfortunately Ameer Ali may not be in contact with the grassroots and may not have seen the effects of existing legislation the way we have. And so I think he may be more willing to put forward a position without going back to his community and consulting them.
>
> Karen Barlow (ABC Radio): Are you angry with Dr Ali?
>
> Waleed Kadous: I just wish that he would consult his community more, and before making major decisions like this, at least come back to us and explain to us what the situation is.[16]

Ali then attempted to deny he had ever lent his support, or that of the MCRG, to the 2005 Act.[17]

'United Stand' public statement

On 27 September 2005, 33 unrelated Muslim groups signed a joint statement titled *United Stand: Muslims Oppose Proposed Anti-Terror Laws*, which insisted that the legislation was 'an over-reaction and should be opposed without compromise'. In my view, the statement is best interpreted as a frustrated response to the silence of many peak Muslim representative bodies.

As with any heavily subscribed public statement, the sentiments it expressed were necessarily simplified. Accordingly, it echoed the most common arguments against new counter-terrorism legislation. It begins by asserting that 'Muslims are bearing the brunt of tougher anti-terror laws worldwide', before going on to argue that:

> The unjustified heavy-handed approach to anti-terrorism will inevitably target Muslims and act to further marginalize us as a community. Such an outcome is counter-productive to the tolerance and inclusiveness of our society. Many Muslims already foster reservations with regard to the current laws. A further toughening of the laws will only serve to create a feeling of victimization.
>
> Of equal concern to us is the impact these proposals will have on the civil liberties of every Australian. The proposed laws impact upon the core of our 'free and fair' society, threatening to undermine the values underpinning the foundation of our country. A correct balance must be achieved between our security and freedom.[18]

The key themes of Muslims being targeted, and the erosion of civil liberties are explicit here. No other basis for opposing the legislation is provided in this statement, and certainly no argument is made that the laws might be inappropriate on pragmatic, counter-terrorism grounds.

Why so ineffective?

It is clear that, in spite of the responses outlined above, Australian Muslims have been widely unsuccessful in having any intended impact on Australian anti-terrorism law and policy. Perhaps the most tempting explanation for this is that the federal government, and indeed the State and Territory governments that passed cooperative legislation as part of an integrated legislative response, was determined for the legislation to proceed such that no amount of protest from Australian Muslims would alter its course. However, this is only partly true. The federal government did demonstrate the capacity to make concessions, particularly on controversial provisions that would have empowered the police to shoot-to-kill suspects in certain circumstances.[19]

In my view, it was more fatal to Australian Muslim advocacy that the dominant arguments made – that Muslims would be targeted and that civil liberties would be eroded – were, and remain, very difficult ones for Muslims to make in the present climate.

To begin with, in the immediate aftermath of the London bombings, it is difficult to imagine the Australian public having any significant sympathy for local Muslim populations. Put simply, statements by Muslims asserting that the federal government's counter-terrorism initiatives were targeting and victimising them, were unlikely to arouse any great public concern. The raw aftermath of a terrorist attack lends itself more to overreaction, to a preparedness to accept the targeting and victimisation of a sector of the community in the apparent interests of security. If anything, Australian Muslims were more likely to be viewed with public suspicion at this moment. One may even be so crude as to suggest that a substantial proportion of the public would have been perfectly happy to see them targeted.

Such imperatives also blunt any civil liberties criticisms of counter-terrorism measures. Opinion polls have repeatedly demonstrated that the Australian public is quite prepared to forego some civil liberties for security, particularly where there appears little prospect of the laws being applied to most people.[20] Additionally, civil liberties arguments are often inaccessible to the wider public because they draw on occasionally subtle legal concepts that are not readily understood by the general populace. Certainly, they demand a level of nuance beyond what is available on commercial television news – where these battles of persuasion are so often fought.

Particularly in a time of insecurity, civil liberties arguments are not compellingly attractive coming from any source. And coming from Muslim advocates, they become positively repulsive. The heightened public suspicion of Muslims provides them with an enormous credibility problem when defending civil liberties. This was most sharply demonstrated in the United Stand statement. The identities of three of the 33 signatories provide the best illustration:

- Ahlus-Sunnah wal Jama'ah Association of Australia: This association is headed by Melbourne-based Sheikh Mohammed Omran, who only months before this statement had appeared on *Lateline* proclaiming that Osama bin Laden was a great man who was not responsible for the 11 September attacks. In the following weeks, he elaborated on *60 Minutes* that 'there is a mastermind behind these things and the mastermind, 100 percent he is from the US Government'.[21]
- Hizb ut-Tahrir: This organisation's *raison d'être* is to re-establish a pan-Islamic Caliphate and, at the time of the statement, it was facing sustained calls for its banning in Britain and Australia after allegedly having connections with the London bombers. Those calls have not yet ceased.[22]
- Global Islamic Youth Centre: Based in Liverpool, Sydney, this centre is run by Sheikh Feiz Mohamad, who infamously asserted that a woman in skimpy clothing who gets raped has 'no one to blame but herself'. Later, a tape emerged in a British documentary of him exhorting Muslims to teach their children a love of martyrdom.[23]

Naturally, members and supporters of these groups will insist they are wildly misunderstood and unfairly maligned in the above descriptions. Such protestations may even be legitimate. For the purposes of this discussion, however, they are irrelevant. The above is an accurate reflection of how these groups are perceived in the public consciousness. And on that basis, the credibility crisis confronting such Muslim advocates becomes clear. The Australian public, already resistant to civil liberties arguments in the post-London environment, would be even less accepting of them coming from supporters of bin Laden or alleged militant groups. Needless to say, the fretting for civil liberties from such organisations rings more than a little hollow in the circumstances.

Indeed, in purely political terms, it is difficult to imagine a greater fillip for the anti-terror legislation's public support than for such organisations to oppose it. The popular imagination of them embodies the very feelings of insecurity on which tough counter-terrorism measures rely. To put it crudely, it may well be a case of 'if these people are complaining, then these laws must be doing something right'.

That is not to say that the more pragmatic approach taken by the ICV was markedly more successful. Ultimately, whatever argument is offered, it appears against a background of public suspicion, of guilt by association. Accordingly, similar credibility problems arise. If Muslims are suspected, *en masse*, of conspiring to terrorise Australia, why should the public be persuaded by a Muslim – any Muslim – who suggests a particular counter-terrorism measure should be abandoned?

This points to more stubborn, structural impediments to effective Muslim public advocacy. With the landscape so definitively shaped by discourses of terrorism, Muslim populations have involuntarily and artificially politicised public identities. It is increasingly unthinkable that Australian Muslims might be chaotically diverse human beings. They do not have mundane struggles and aspirations. And certainly, they have no spiritual dimension. Rather, they are an inhuman abstract; a singular political entity: nameless and faceless, except where punctuated by the image and speech of some villainous radical caricature who shoots rapidly to symbolic infamy. No longer do Muslims subscribe to a rich and varied religious tradition, or indeed any religious tradition at all. They are imagined instead as members of a political party called Islam; one that, in Australia at least, is perpetually in opposition.

Moreover, it is a public identity that is nearly impossible to shed. The publicly visible Muslim can be seen as nothing else. Every other facet is stripped away by political solvent. They cannot comment as lawyers or parents, and certainly not as citizens. This is especially so when the speaker acts on behalf of a community organisation. Conceptually, such organisations stand apart from civic society. They exist for no interest other than that projected onto them by a suspicious public conversation. The result is that Muslims do not have the luxury of having their arguments assessed alone on their merits. They must be assessed primarily on the basis of the identities of those advancing them. Within these confines, Muslim advocates will always struggle to articulate a view – particularly in opposition to counter-terrorism measures – that allows them to be taken seriously.

Notes

1 See Explanatory Memorandum to the *Anti-Terrorism Bill (No 2) 2005*, 13.

2 The best example here is the Islamic obligation of *zakāt*, in which each Muslim must provide approximately 2.5 per cent of their saved wealth every year for charitable purposes.

3 OMB Watch, *Muslim Charities and the War on Terror* (2006).

4 ABC Radio, 'Guide to Terrorism laws aimed at all Australians', *The World Today*, 26 July 2004.

5 Brendan Nicholson, John Silvester and Selma Milovanovic, 'ASIO raids aim to spook suspected extremists', *The Age*, 28 June 2005, 3.

6 ABC Television, 'Former ASIO officer claims Islamic extremists are living in Australia', *Lateline*, 2 August 2005.

7 Simon Kearny, 'Police Alarm on Racial Profiling', *The Australian*, 27 September 2005, 1.

8 Vicki Sentas, *Rattling the cage* (2005) Signature, August 2005, <http://www.spinach7.com/signature/sig-stories.php?id=489> at 6 July 2007.

9 Above n 8.

10 Above n 8.

11 ABC Television, 'New laws could alienate Muslims', *Lateline*, 8 September 2005. It has since emerged that the London bombers could well have been known to police had they shown greater vigilance – see Intelligence and Security Committee, UK Parliament, *Report into the London Terrorist Attacks on 7 July 2005* (2006) – but this was not publicly known at the time of the interview, and does not alter the point for which this passage is produced here: namely to demonstrate that the arguments invoked were of a pragmatic tone.

12 'Joint Doorstop Interview Following Australian Muslim Reference Group Meeting' with Philip Ruddock, Attorney-General, John Cobb, Minister for Citizenship and Multicultural Affairs, and Ameer Ali, Chair, Muslim Community Reference Group (Canberra, 6 October 2005).

13 Above n 12.

14 Cameron Stewart, 'Muslims deny they support new laws', *The Australian*, 13 October 2005, 6.

15 Islamic Council of Victoria, 'Islamic Council of Victoria clarifies reports on proposed security laws' (Press Release, 7 October 2006).

16 ABC Radio, 'Cracks in Muslim endorsement of anti-terror laws', *AM*, 8 October 2005.

17 Stewart, above n 13.

18 'United Stand: Muslims Oppose Proposed Anti-Terror Laws' (Press Release, 27 September 2005).

19 Dennis Shanahan and Samantha Maiden, 'PM bids in terror law deal', *The Australian*, 27 October 2005, 1.

20 For example, the ACNielson/Herald poll conducted in 2005 found that two-thirds of Australians were willing to sacrifice privacy and civil liberties for protection from terrorist attacks: Mike Seccombe and Louise Dodson, 'Safety before liberty, say most voters', *Sydney Morning Herald*, 3 August 2005, 2.

21 ABC Television, 'Muslims prepare for backlash', *Lateline*, 11 July 2005; Channel 9, *60 Minutes*, 24 July 2005.

22 See, for example, Janet Albrechtsen, 'It is time we banned Hizb ut-Tahrir', *The Australian,* 8 July 2007 <http://blogs.theaustralian.news.com.au/janetalbrechtsen/index.php/theaustralian/comments/it_is_time_we_banned_hizb_ut_tahrir/> at 30 August 2007.

23 Miranda Devine reported that the comments were made on 18 March 2005 at an address to more than 1000 people in Bankstown Town Hall: 'Raped women have themselves to blame, says dissident cleric', *Sun Herald*, 24 April 2005, 7. The documentary, 'Undercover Mosque', screened on the British Channel 4 program *Dispatches* on 15 January 2007.

19

News Media Responsibilities in Reporting on Terrorism

Tanja Dreher

The detention of Dr Mohamed Haneef in July 2007 provided a litmus test, not only of Australia's counter-terrorism measures, but also of news reporting of the domestic front in the so-called 'war on terror'.[1] While there was some evidence of diversity of opinions and of independent and investigative reporting in the enormous volume of news coverage of the Haneef affair, overall there remains considerable cause for concern. This chapter outlines the most significant critiques of news reporting of the case and indicates the action required of professional journalists and of concerned citizens in order to develop more responsible journalism in the area of national security.

A rush to judgement

Initial reports of Dr Haneef's detention followed a pattern of sensationalised reporting that has become typical of news coverage of terrorism-related events and investigations in Australia and around the world. Despite Australian Federal Police (AFP) Commissioner Mick Keelty's statement that Haneef 'may have done nothing wrong and may at the end of the day be free to go',[2] reports of his detention appeared under headlines such as 'Those who cure you will kill you', 'Doctor member of sleeper cell' and 'Were these young Gold Coast doctors living sinister lives?'. Journalism researchers have criticised Western news reporting for too readily accepting a 'war' framing in their coverage of the events of 11 September 2001 – a framing that has served to heighten the sense of threat and that can also be used to justify repressive measures in order to safeguard 'national security'. The reporting of Mohamed Haneef's detention was consistent with this trend in being placed within a news frame of global threat and urgency which diminished the possibilities for a careful weighing of evidence and measured assessment of risk.

Much of the most sensationalist coverage was characterised by a scant regard for the privacy of those detained. Photographs taken inside Dr Haneef's Gold Coast unit were published and neighbours were interviewed about his relationships and his routine. When Haneef's colleague, Dr Mohammad Asif Ali, was also questioned by police, a half-page photo of his face appeared on the front page of Sydney's *Daily Telegraph* under the 'Enemy Within' headline. After Dr Ali's swift release and AFP assurances that he was not under any suspicion, journalists continued to stake out his home and Queensland authorities speculated that he would be unable to return to work at the Gold Coast hospital following the intense media scrutiny.[3] While the consequences for Dr Ali of his involvement in this episode have been reported, these brief reports do not outweigh the initial sensational coverage and there has been no news media apology.

Despite the high profile of the Haneef story and its potential both to heighten public fears and to damage reputations, there were significant inaccuracies in the news coverage. Some journalists displayed a lack of understanding of the detention proceedings, repeatedly referring to Haneef in interviews as 'the suspect' before any charges were laid. Weeks into his detention, some News Limited papers published a report that Haneef was suspected of plotting to blow up a residential skyscraper at Surfer's Paradise.[4] The story featured a colour photograph of Dr Haneef and his wife posing in front of the building and alleged that police had found documents referring to 'the destruction of structures'. The AFP took the extraordinary step of contacting Haneef's lawyers as well as the press to correct the record: Haneef had never been suspected of plans to bomb the tower. Calls from media commentators for an apology from the journalists behind the story went unheeded.

The combination of inaccuracies, sensationalist reporting and intrusions into privacy produced an overall rush to judgement that has been described as a 'trial by media' or a 'witch hunt' bound by neither the rules of evidence nor the presumption of innocence. The initial tendency to position Haneef as 'guilty until proven innocent' was exacerbated by the lack of legal protections for individuals detained without charge – without the restrictions imposed by the law of contempt, news media are able to report all manner of speculation and hearsay while the detainee is unable to respond or represent her or himself directly.

The racialised frame

The rush to judgement in early news reporting of Haneef's detention was facilitated by the racialised frame that dominates media coverage of the war on terror and serves to criminalise Muslims and 'third-world looking migrants' in Australia. Racialised news reporting of terrorism, border protection and crime over several years has produced a climate of suspicion in which Arabs and Muslims in Australia are regularly understood as threatening.

The racialised frame came to dominate reporting over several months in mid-2001 with news reports that linked the local story of 'ethnic gang rapes' in Sydney to the broader national story of asylum seekers, the *Tampa* and the 'Pacific Solution', and then to the global news reporting of 9/11 and the subsequent war on terror. Media researchers have argued that the naming and framing of these events in news reporting has contributed to 'the emergence of the "Arab Other" as the pre-eminent "folk devil" of our time' and the production of refugees, Arab and Muslim Australians as 'the new "Others"'.[5] The crucial element in the 'othering' of Arab and Muslim communities was the racialised framing, whereby race, culture or religion is used to explain events. Where biological racism posits genetic hierarchies, racialised understandings assume cultural incompatibility or the 'clash of civilisations' to be the source of conflicts and threat. This racialised framing has been central to the linking of news reporting of a wide range of issues including local crime, immigration, national security and the war on terror.

One feature of the racialised frame is that news reporting regularly focuses on Islam in seeking explanations for terrorist activity – and an interest in jihad or in sharia law is commonly depicted as evidence of support for terrorism. Another is the recurring use of dehumanising imagery – from comparing the 'Lebanese gang rapists' to animals, to describing terrorists as madmen and fanatics, and reporting asylum seekers arriving by boat as 'human cargo' and civilian victims of the invasion of Iraq as 'collateral damage'. The recurrence of such imagery pathologises Islam and Arab culture as beyond rational human understanding – a process described as 'criminalising ethnicity and ethnicising crime'.[6]

The accumulation and convergence of racialised reporting has served to position whole cultures as threatening, criminal, foreign, even barbaric, amplifying the scrutiny of Arab, Muslim and refugee communities. Complex events have been explained in terms of essentialised Arab or Muslim 'cultures'. Racialised news reporting also privileges a moral frame of 'good and evil', 'us and them', rather than a focus on social causes. The production of 'the new Others' thus legitimises politics and strategies of exclusion and control and obscures the possibilities of complex interrelationships and negotiations.

Research has also found that racialised news reporting in 2001 to 2002 contributed to heightened intercommunal tensions and an increase in racist violence, discrimination and harassment.[7] Data collection is inconsistent, but community organisations continue to report backlash incidents following news of terrorism-related events, and on 4 July 2007 the *Sydney Morning Herald* reported that 'a man of Egyptian descent was beaten up in a Sydney pub last night after his attackers suggested he was a suicide bomber'.[8]

The racialised framing, which has cast suspicion on Arab and Muslim Australians since 2001, forms the backdrop to the reporting of Mohamed Haneef's detention under new counter-terrorism laws. While there has been considerable evidence of greater caution and attempts to avoid racialised reporting in the Australian news media in recent years, initial reports did include headlines such as 'Oath of Evil' and 'Enemy Within'. More commonly, reporting of Haneef's detention was linked to debates over immigration and the possible need for tougher visa checks for overseas doctors. As racialised public debate has created a climate of insecurity and fear of foreigners, representatives of overseas-trained doctors were immediately asked to comment on the case and to reassure the public. Before any charges were laid against Haneef, journalists began to question policymakers about the implications for immigration policy, and the 457 sponsored working visa in particular. Once the Minister for Immigration, Kevin Andrews, intervened by revoking Dr Haneef's visa to prevent him going free on bail, reportage of the case was increasingly linked to wider debates about changes to the so-called 'character test' requirement for permanent visas – a trend exemplified by discussion of this topic appearing under the banner 'National Security' in the *Sydney Morning Herald*.[9] In Andrews' media appearances even after Haneef's return to India, there was an overlap between his defence of the cancellation of the doctor's visa and his support for a citizenship test and a requirement for potential immigrants to Australia to make a commitment to 'integrate'.

The discursive linking of national security, the threat of terrorism, immigration and Islam in news reporting reflects the extent to which migration and the transnational lives of professionals from the 'Muslim world' have become understood as a potential threat in public debate. This climate of heightened fear explains why Australian journalists would be so willing to report as suspicious details of Haneef's activities which are actually typical of transnational migrants and expatriates – the global networks of family communications and connections, the informal sharing of resources (including SIM cards) and financial transactions, and the dispersal of domestic relationships and subsequent international travel. While many Australians inhabit transnational networks in which these activities are familiar, mainstream Australian journalists for the most part framed the details of Haneef's life as strange and questionable.

Leaks and spin

Following Dr Haneef's release from detention without charge, criticism of the news media has focused on the effects of leaks, spin and media manipulation on reporting. Australian journalists have been highly dependent on AFP and ASIO leaks in reporting counter-terrorism raids and investigations. While leaked information provides crucial access to stories, it can also be difficult to verify or to critique. It enables the source to determine the level and the nature of any threat or danger against which specific events will be reported. The Haneef case saw a highly politicised and calculated use of leaks to the point that the news media were described as a 'battleground' in a 'propaganda war'.[10] Some of these leaks worked in Haneef's favour – his defence team's leaking of the transcript of the first police interrogation encouraged journalists to look more critically at the handling of the matter. A report in *The Australian*, 'Reasons to hold Haneef stretch thinner by the day', relied on 'top-level documentation' and shifted the news agenda decisively towards detailed scrutiny of the detention and questioning proceedings.[11] Weeks later, the Immigration Minister selectively quoted from a police brief of edited snippets of internet chatroom conversation in order to explain his decision to revoke Haneef's work visa,[12] while the AFP steadfastly refused to release the transcript. At each of these vital developments in the affair, news reporting has been dependent on selective access to, and disclosure of, information by parties with an interest in promoting their case.

The reporting raised further questions about the relationship between the news media and the AFP. News Limited papers have been previous recipients of juicy AFP leaks, such as precise details of the Melbourne homes raided in June 2005.[13] When homes in Sydney and Melbourne were raided in November 2005, an advocate for the families suggested that sections of the media were leaked information before the raids.[14] After news reporting of the leaked Haneef interview transcript sparked intense scrutiny of the AFP operation and speculation as to the source of the leak, AFP Commissioner Mick Keelty called the Editor in Chief of *The Australian*, Chris Mitchell, at 6.30 am to discuss the leak.[15] To the concern of media commentators, Mitchell publicly denied the AFP were the source of the leak – greatly narrowing the field of potential sources.

Challenges for journalists

While there is much to criticise in the reporting of the war on terror in the Australian news media, it is vital to acknowledge the considerable challenges faced by Australian journalists. The racialised frame of understanding is deeply entrenched in public debate in Australia and very difficult to counter within news reporting. Even where news outlets have made an effort to present a more complex picture of communities under scrutiny – as in reporting a 'good news' story of Indian doctors working in a NSW country town – this does not necessarily disrupt the expectation that racialised communities need to explain and justify themselves and their presence in Australia. Some have argued that efforts to report on the 'moderate Muslim community' in Australia contributes to the effect of 'convicting' or demonising those positioned as 'extremist' or 'fundamentalist' Muslims during the war on terror.

Australian journalists face significant restrictions on the reporting of counter-terrorism measures. The news media cannot report that someone has been detained under terrorism prevention powers by ASIO, and stiff penalties apply.[16] The Media Entertainment and Arts Alliance (MEAA) has complained that the trials of accused terrorists are closed to the media for days at a time over evidence sensitive to national security.[17] Constraints also apply in reporting Australian troops in the war on terror, and on access to immigration detention centres. Restrictions on information and on access to courts leaves journalists heavily reliant on official sources – particularly in regards to counter-terrorism raids and investigations as discussed above.

The fetters placed on reporting counter-terrorism measures can be understood as part of a wider anti-disclosure culture in government and the corporate world. Several commentators have documented the increasing use of media management and spin doctors along with controlled access to information across political parties, government departments and commercial interests. According to the MEAA, 'the media are increasingly managed and marginalised by public affairs personnel, their requests for information are refused and their professional obligations criminalised'.[18] Clive Hamilton and Sarah Maddison have also identified processes of 'silencing of dissent' among non-government organisations such that advocacy groups have become reluctant to speak out on a range of issues, including human rights, immigration, antiracism and social justice.[19]

Additionally, it must be recognised that Australian journalism operates in one of the most concentrated media markets in the OECD, a situation which is hardly conducive to genuine competition or to independent and investigative journalism. At the same time, the ability of the national public broadcasters to provide high quality journalism has been steadily eroded through chronic underfunding, creeping commercialisation and continuing attacks on the ABC over bias, particularly in its reporting on the invasion of Iraq. Federal communications ministers have lodged numerous formal complaints with the ABC and the question of bias has been referred to Senate Estimates. Media Monitors have been called in to constantly assess coverage and new editorial guidelines on balance were adopted in late 2006.

The influence of talkback radio, however, stands in stark contrast to the intense scrutiny of public broadcasting. Many of the most sensationalist and inflammatory examples of media coverage of the war on terror come from high profile shock jocks in commercial radio who are not bound by the journalists' Code of Ethics. Many professional journalists are themselves dismayed at the excesses of tabloid journalism and frustrated at the commercial logics which support 'infotainment' and populist commentary over well researched, balanced news reporting.

One of the most significant challenges for professional journalists is their dependence on sources and, in particular, their close relationships with institutional sources such as police, the courts, legislators and policymakers. Research indicates that media professionals 'index' the range of views presented according to the range of views expressed in mainstream government debate. This means that news media will usually reflect elite political consensus, accessing a wider range of views when there is elite disagreement.[20] As news regularly presents elected officials and law enforcement agencies as legitimate 'primary definers' of issues and their significance, journalists are largely dependent on shifts in the political field in order to present robust debate on questions of policy and law. During the Haneef affair, independent and critical journalism was spurred on by outspoken criticism from within the legal profession and mounting evidence of bungling by the authorities.

Campaigning for robust, democratic news media

Given the scale of the challenges facing professional journalism in Australia, it is vital that demands for more responsible news reporting are located within a wider campaign for robust democratic debate. Any such campaign must acknowledge and build on the efforts of mainstream newsmakers to produce high quality journalism and to avoid the excesses of alarmist reporting, racialised rhetoric and media manipulation. While there is much to criticise in the early reporting of the Haneef affair, there were also efforts to report the story behind the story and, particularly after revelations of the scant evidence against Haneef, journalists did question the handling of the case by both the AFP and the Minister for Immigration. Investigative reporting attempted to piece together the precise details of the evidence against Haneef, while a background feature described his life as 'an ordinary life'.[21] Feature and commentary pieces discussed the role of spin and leaks. News outlets also provided space and airtime for a diversity of opinions and critiques from academics, community leaders, the judiciary and civil liberties advocates, including opinion pieces and broadcast interviews.

Australian journalists are well aware of the many criticisms of the news media, and 'journalism on journalism' such as ABC TV's popular *Media Watch* program have popularised a degree of media literacy and critique. Yet media scrutiny has produced little sustained campaigning for a genuinely robust and democratic media. This is a task for anyone concerned with the possibilities for democracy and justice in Australia, and not simply for mainstream journalists. While those working for media reform are usually energised by their participation in social movements, people involved in campaigns for social justice and democratisation will rarely take part in media reform activities. For advocates, educators, activists and those who speak in the media as expert commentators, there is much that can be done.

Individuals and organisations interested in a robust and democratic media should support professional journalists when they protest against restrictions on access to information. Recent years have seen a number of extraordinary examples of news institution complaints against government control of information, including the Canberra Press Gallery's submission to the 'SIEV X' Senate Inquiry, a 2003 letter to the Attorney General from a number of media organisations in regards to counter-terrorism legislation, and the formation in May 2007 of the cross-industry 'Right to Know' campaign. Working for improved media might also include support for the public broadcasters against political interference, and demonstrating that there is an interested public for those programs and outlets which do maintain a commitment to high quality journalism.

In addition to supporting encouraging developments in the Australian news media, it is important to develop positive conceptions of what can be expected of journalists beyond media critiques. Hopeful but realistic expectations are needed. Those interested in vigorous debate in the news media must also demand diversity from institutional sources and political leaders. This means encouraging dissent and rigorous scrutiny of power in all areas of public debate. A campaign for robust media can also support alternative and critical media, and contribute to media advocacy projects that seek to shift entrenched news frames and diversify the range of voices reported. All of these measures will contribute to a public culture that both demands and supports informed, robust democratic debate.

News media responsibilities

In the absence of such a public culture, the many criticisms that may be made of Australian journalism during the war on terror are likely to have little effect. However, in the context of a wider campaign for democratic media, there is much that can be expected of news reporting of terrorism.

Responsible news media could be expected to apologise when significant mistakes or inaccuracies in reporting are discovered. Journalists certainly have a responsibility to protect the privacy of individuals who have not been charged with any offence and to resist the rush to judgement in order to respect the principle of 'innocent until proven guilty'. News reporting should also make clear the conditions under which information is obtained and any restrictions. In the highly politicised and polarised context of the war on terror, professional journalists should exercise caution, particularly in the use of emotive and alarmist imagery. A public culture which demands rigorous informed debate requires a sober account of events in order to assess the risks associated with terrorism. Responsible journalism should not heighten fears and insecurity unnecessarily.

Alternative frames are required to put the fears produced by narratives of 'us and them' into perspective. Journalists have a responsibility to interrogate the rhetorics of war, good and evil, and law and order used by elite sources. News professionals must analyse rather than simply adopt the language of the 'war on terror'. This also means challenging news values and news agendas that highlight conflict and assume the worst of audiences. Rather than playing to prejudice and fear, a robust news culture might explore alternative conceptions of security based, not on force, but in connection and justice. Responsible journalism seeks to fully humanise those who are racialised or othered, and explores the complexities of Islam, of concepts such as 'jihad' and 'sharia', and of 'terrorism' itself.

Only by shifting the racialised frame can terrorism be brought into alternative frames of social and political explanation. Rigorous news reporting moves beyond easy assumptions of links between Islam and terrorism to explore explanations and understandings of conflict as based in injustice, inequality and oppression – and considers possibilities for conflict resolution. A public culture that scrutinises the politics of fear in order to demand complex understandings and robust debate provides the vital impetus for such rigorous and responsible journalism to thrive.

Notes

1 See Chapter 20 of this book for more details of the Haneef affair.

2 ABC Television, 'Police Commissioner discusses alleged terrorism arrests', *7.30 Report*, 3 July 2007.

3 Cosima Marriner and Damien Murphy, 'Friend's life turned upside down', *Sydney Morning Herald*, 5 July 2007, 4.

4 Paula Doneman and Lincoln Wright, 'Picture Puzzle', *Sunday Mail* (Brisbane), 22 July 2007, 1. The same story also appeared in other papers on the same day: 'Terror riddle: Australian plot probed by Haneef cops', *Sunday Herald Sun*, 1; 'Doctor terror plot theory', *Sunday Tasmanian*, 2; 'Doctor terror link checked', *Sunday Times*, 9; 'New Haneef inquiry – Probe into pictures of buildings', *Sunday Telegraph*, 4.

5 Scott Poynting, Greg Noble, Paul Tabar and Jock Collins, *Bin Laden in the Suburbs: Criminalising the Arab Other*, Sydney Institute of Criminology Series (2004); Liz Jacka and Lelia Green (eds), *The New 'Others': Media and Society Post-September 11*, Themed Edition (2003) 109 *Media International Australia incorporating Culture & Policy* 7.

6 Jock Collins, Greg Noble, Scott Poynting and Paul Tabar, *Kebabs, kids, cops and crime: youth ethnicity and crime* (2000).

7 Anti-Discrimination Board of NSW, *Race for the Headlines: racism and media discourse* (2003); Human Rights and Equal Opportunity Commission, *Isma – National consultations on eliminating prejudice against Arab and Muslim Australians*, (2004); Tanja Dreher, *Targeted: Experiences of Racism in NSW after September 11, 2001*, UTS Shopfront Monograph Series, No 2 (2006).

8 Ben Cubby, 'Bomb jibe, then bashing', *Sydney Morning Herald*, 4 July 2007, 6.

9 Connie Levett, 'Immigrants face tougher character test', *Sydney Morning Herald*, 17 July 2007, 6.

10 Cosima Marriner and Craig Skehan, 'The spin they're in', *Sydney Morning Herald*, 4 August 2007, 26.

11 Hedley Thomas, 'Reasons to hold Haneef stretch thinner by the day', *The Australian*, 13 July 2007, 1.

12 Kevin Andrews, 'Dr Haneef – Advice from Solicitor-General' (Press Release, 31 July 2007).

13 ABC Television, 'ASIO gags media', *Media Watch*, 4 July 2005.

14 *Arrests made in counter-terrorism raids* (2005) ABC News Online, 8 November 2005 <http://www.abc.net.au/news/newsitems/200511/s1499839.htm> at 30 August 2007.

15 ABC Radio, 'Leaked Haneef transcript could affect court: Keelty', *AM*, 18 July 2007.

16 *Australian Security Intelligence Organisation Act 1979* (Cth) s 34ZS.

17 Media, Entertainment and Arts Alliance, *Official Spin: Censorship and Control of the Australian Press 2007* (2007) 6.

18 Above n 17, 24.

19 Clive Hamilton and Sarah Maddison, 'Non-government organisations' in Clive Hamilton and Sarah Maddison (eds), *Silencing Dissent* (2007) 78.

20 Simon Cottle, 'Rethinking Theories of News Access', (2000) 1(3) *Journalism Studies* 427.

21 David Marr, 'Just an ordinary life', *Sydney Morning Herald*, 21 July 2007, 25.

PART VII

Terrorism and the Rule of Law

20

Achieving Security, Respecting Rights and Maintaining the Rule of Law

Andrew Lynch

It is clear that terrorism is a danger in the modern world that we cannot ignore. But what should be the role of law in shaping our responses to this threat? Is law a tool that we can marshal in our efforts to ensure that dangerous extremists are thwarted in their attempts to intimidate governments and the public by violent means? Almost certainly this is so – even if one believes that such a function may be performed through judicious application of existing criminal offences, without the need for specific anti-terrorism laws. But the more demanding question is just how far the law may be employed in a preventative capacity before it produces poor outcomes – both for individuals and our collective security goals – and erodes its moral and philosophical core.

This is the trap that terrorism lays for democratic nations committed to the rule of law. In seeking to defend ourselves from those who would cause us harm, our commitment to law as a restraint on power – the essence of constitutional governance that defines such nations – is sorely tested. It is tempting to accept that the state needs enhanced powers in order to preserve security and order. Additionally, individuals may agree that some sacrifice of their rights is also necessary to this end. But the very liberties that are prone to curtailment at such a time are those that are most vital to the health of our democracy – freedoms of association and speech, the right to a fair trial by an independent judicial system, and protection from far-ranging executive discretion.

So, the twin goals of effective counter-terrorism and fidelity to constitutionalism pose a difficult challenge for governments committed to both (it need hardly be said that states with a peripatetic attraction to the rule of law suffer little anxiety over the introduction of powers that achieve security through oppression). Overwhelmingly, this challenge was met, in the wake of the attacks of 11 September 2001, by appeals to 'balance' national security with human rights.

The problem of 'balance'

More recently, there has been a reconsideration of this approach in two distinct ways. First, Australia's Attorney-General, Philip Ruddock, has drawn on the views of Canada's former Attorney-General, Irwin Cotler, to argue that national security and human rights should not be seen as mutually exclusive, and that the Commonwealth's anti-terrorism laws should properly be seen as giving 'primacy, amongst other matters, to the responsibility of governments to secure a person's right to life – a person's entitlement to live in a situation of safety and security'.[1] This may counter 'the false assumption that counter-terrorism legislation is inevitably at odds with the protection of fundamental human rights',[2] but its value beyond that is difficult to appreciate, particularly when those assumptions are borne out by an examination of some of the laws in question. Cotler argued that reframing the relationship between security and rights in this way did not obviate concerns about civil liberties,[3] but, at least as a matter of political rhetoric in a country without a charter of rights, this seems often to be its intended effect.

Second, the metaphor of 'balance' has been attacked more fundamentally as crude and misleading. This is so for a number of reasons. For example, Dr Christopher Michaelsen points out that it is routinely employed to prioritise security as a precondition to the liberty of individuals despite these two goals having a more complex relationship, in which liberty actually legitimates the existence of the state. Human rights are central, he argues, to the 'very idea of modern liberal democracy' and should not be 'reduced to a mere variable in the government's security policy'.[4] Repackaging security as the ultimate human right – the right to life – does not overcome this objection. In short, there can be no justification for laws that seek to promote security by diminishing the enjoyment by its citizens of essential rights.[5] A similar degree of respect for the position of non-citizens is supported on several grounds. As a practical consideration, the promotion of social cohesion amongst all members of a society, as well as positive relations with other nations, is a crucial counter-terrorism strategy ill-served by executive heavy-handedness of aliens without just cause. Additionally, as Professor David Dyzenhaus and Rayner Thwaites argue in the conclusion to their chapter in this book, the design of preventive terrorism measures so as to apply to both citizens and aliens provides a strong inducement for governments to ensure those initiatives are consistent with the ideals of the rule of law.

Inevitably, the idea of balancing our existing rights against assessments of the danger posed to us by terrorism suffers from a lack of parity, and is more likely than not to cause us to overreact. As Professor Lucia Zedner has said, 'precisely because it is unknowable, prospective risk always threatens to outweigh present interest'.[6] When one combines this natural wariness with the perception of many in the community (whether correct or not) that they will not personally be required to sacrifice much, if anything, for security, it is clear that the mythical scales by which any 'balancing' is to take place are heavily weighted in one direction from the outset.

In light of these complaints, it is tempting to simply discard the rhetoric of balancing rights against security as unhelpful. But a more constructive response would be to invert it. Instead of viewing the two as existing in direct competition or alternatively, and as the Attorney-General would have it, subsumed within the pre-eminence of 'human security' as a human right, it should be acknowledged that a commitment to a range of human rights helps, rather than hinders, the objective of security.

This approach should be acknowledged as operating in two contexts – the international and the domestic. It is beyond the scope of this chapter to fully explore the former beyond a submission that respect for human rights should be a major consideration in the development of foreign policy, particularly our willingness to deploy Australian troops in overseas military endeavours and our attitude to those nations – especially our allies – whose treatment of their enemies is an affront to human dignity or may even involve acquiescence in torture. To take just this last point as an example, it is striking that pragmatism and principle often point to the same conclusion.[7] As discussed in the earlier chapters of Neil James and Professor Sarah Joseph, it is clear that adherence to the commitments in the United Nations *Convention Against Torture* is not only respectful of human life but also focuses our security efforts away from strategies which, by all accounts, are patently unreliable.

Acknowledging the importance of human rights in making foreign policy choices must be expected to have some bearing on the depth of hostility and enmity directed to the nation. This is not to argue that Australia should conduct its international relations cowed by fears of possible reprisals. Nor is it to suggest that a country can ever be comprehensively insured against terrorist attack – undoubtedly extremist groups who wish us harm will always exist. But it is to recognise that the appeal of terrorism is dealt a major blow by the promotion of global justice, the pursuit of diplomacy over armed conflict, and according value to the lives and aspirations of other peoples of the world.

The remainder of this chapter considers the significance to domestic anti-terrorism law of building our security upon, rather than in diminishment of, civil liberties. Recent events, specifically the treatment under Australian law of (former) terror suspect Dr Mohamed Haneef, provide a striking demonstration of this.

The Haneef affair

On Saturday, 30 June 2007, the day after two car bombs had been discovered in central London, two men drove a jeep laden with explosive material into the doors of Glasgow International Airport in an attempted terrorist attack. Although the jeep failed to explode, it did catch fire and the driver, Kafeel Ahmed, suffered severe burning. He died several weeks later.

A number of people were arrested in relation to these events, including Kafeel's brother, Sabeel Ahmed, who was in Liverpool at the time. It was initially reported that he had been charged with failing to disclose information that could have prevented an act of terrorism. However, it has since emerged that Sabeel did not have foreknowledge of the Glasgow attack, having not opened the email sent to him earlier by his brother claiming responsibility until 90 minutes after the incident took place.[8] His charge is simply one of withholding information that could have assisted police to secure the apprehension, prosecution or conviction of the perpetrator of a terrorism crime.[9]

Dr Mohamed Haneef is the second cousin of the Ahmed brothers and was arrested at Brisbane International Airport on 2 July over suspicions about his involvement in the UK plot. Haneef had been working for several months at a hospital on Queensland's Gold Coast. He was the first person to be detained under new anti-terrorism powers which enable Australian police to hold a suspect without charge for an extended period of time during which questioning up to a maximum of 24 hours may occur.[10] While the 'period of arrest' cannot exceed 24 hours this does not include, amongst other things, 'reasonable time' during which the questioning of the person is 'reasonably suspended or delayed' and that is approved by a magistrate on application by the investigating officers. The justifications for approving extra detention on the basis of this so-called 'dead time' include the need to collate and analyse information, the fact that officials are waiting on relevant information from a place outside Australia in a different time zone or the need to arrange translation of materials.[11]

At the time this scheme was introduced in 2004, concerns were raised at the open-ended nature of the detention period with calls for an absolute limit of 48 hours. In response, Attorney-General's Department staff assured the Senate inquiry into an earlier version of the law that such a limit was not necessary and it would be surprising if the powers were used to detain anybody for even a period of that duration.[12]

Mohamed Haneef ended up spending 12 days detained in the Brisbane watchhouse until the Australian Federal Police (AFP) laid charges. The central fact upon which the charge depended was the provision by Haneef, when he departed England for Queensland one year earlier, of his mobile phone SIM card to his cousin Sabeel so the latter could make use of its remaining free calls.

Haneef was charged under s 102.7(2) of the *Criminal Code* (Cth), which makes it an offence to 'intentionally provide to an organisation support or resources' that would help it engage in planning or preparing a terrorist act. The charge does not require the person to have actually known that the organisation she or he is supporting is a terrorist one – it is enough simply to have been 'reckless' as to this fact.

The Code defines a person as being reckless when he or she is aware of a 'substantial risk' that a particular circumstance exists or will exist – in this case that the 'organisation' to which Haneef gave the SIM card (if giving the card to his cousin can be said to amount to giving it to an organisation) was a terrorist organisation. A successful prosecution would have had to show that the circumstances were such that it was 'unjustifiable' for Haneef to take the risk of supporting the group.

On Monday 16 July, Mohamed Haneef was granted bail by a Brisbane magistrate subject to his meeting certain conditions and payment of a $10,000 bond. The result was surprising since Haneef faced strong opposition from the Commonwealth, which asserted facts later shown to be incorrect – namely that the SIM card was recovered from the wreck of the jeep at Glasgow airport. Additionally, there is a statutory direction that terrorism suspects should only be granted bail in 'exceptional circumstances'.[13]

Just hours later, before Haneef had a chance to regain his freedom, the Minister for Immigration, Kevin Andrews, invoked his discretion to revoke Haneef's visa because he failed the 'character test'. Section 501 of the Commonwealth *Migration Act 1958* gives a number of grounds on which this may occur. Andrews resorted to what is unquestionably the weakest – that Haneef had associations with persons whom Andrews 'reasonably suspects' of involvement in criminal conduct. The alternative grounds under which an individual may fail the character test focus squarely on his or her personal criminal conduct or the risk they pose to the Australian community.

This development provoked a storm of protest. Its immediate effect was to ensure that even if Haneef met his bail conditions he would be placed in immigration detention.[14] Minister Andrews said that cancellation of the visa was in the 'national interest', which, under the *Migration Act*, removed the need for natural justice – essentially depriving Haneef of an opportunity to satisfy the Minister that he did in fact pass the character test.[15]

The case against Haneef now seemed to operate on two fronts, not easily separable despite Andrews' insistence that his actions were entirely removed from the AFP investigation. The consequence of his intervention, based as it was on advice from the AFP, was to intensify the spotlight on the elements of the case being alleged against Haneef.

This was greatly assisted by the decision of Haneef's barrister, Stephen Keim SC, to release the first record of police interview to *The Australian* newspaper on 18 July. Keim claimed he was moved to act in response to the negative inferences which he felt were being made about his client by politicians and the police via the media. This attracted condemnation from a range of figures, including the Prime Minister and Attorney-General. In retort, Keim criticised the double-standards applied to leaks and complained that the legal team had repeatedly requested, without success, the transcript of the final interview his client gave just prior to charges being laid.[16]

Comparison of the interview transcript with the claims made by the prosecution at the bail hearing and the advice on which the Immigration Minister had acted exposed a number of inconsistencies.[17] Authorities had claimed that Haneef had resided with the two Ahmed brothers in the United Kingdom. But in the interview Haneef listed the persons with whom he shared a particular house – none being either of the Ahmeds. He admitted only to having stayed with Kabeel Ahmed at the latter's Cambridge house for just a few weeks in 2004. Additionally, the prosecution had said that Haneef was unable to explain why he had purchased a one-way ticket to return to India yet the transcript recorded a very plausible explanation he gave about his shortage of funds, his father-in-law's assistance in buying the ticket and his intention to arrange his return flight from India.

These inconsistencies indicated the police case was thin, but it fell apart dramatically with the revelation that the SIM card – the hook on which the charge against Haneef hung – had actually been found by UK police several hundred miles from the site of the terrorist attempt in Glasgow.[18] In the face of mounting public pressure, a swift review by the Director of Public Prosecutions led to the withdrawal of the charge against Dr Haneef on 27 July.

Almost a month after he was taken into detention, Haneef was released from police custody and allowed to fly home to India to be reunited with his wife and newborn daughter. Calls to reconsider the revocation of Haneef's visa were rejected by Minister Andrews who stood by advice from the Solicitor-General that the grounds supporting his original decision under the legislation were still valid. Andrews proceeded to selectively release passages from the second record of police interview in an attempt to justify his stance, while claiming he was unable to release the full record on the basis that it might prejudice ongoing police investigations.

The quotes which the Minister released were open to interpretation as implicating Haneef in the recent UK plot, but were far from conclusive even without their surrounding context. The Minister's suspicions over Haneef's efforts to leave Australia quickly in early July were difficult to reconcile with the verified fact that he had telephoned the Metropolitan Police several times after learning his cousins had been arrested over the plot in order to explain why his SIM card was with them. Although he had failed to get through to the detective he was trying to reach and his calls were not returned, this action was hardly consistent with an attempt to flee the authorities. On 22 August Haneef's lawyers released the transcript of his second police interview in order to counter the continuing 'innuendo and selective release of information' by the government and police.[19]

The day before, Spender J of the Federal Court of Australia overturned the Minister's decision to revoke the visa saying that he was wrong in not requiring a link between Haneef's association with his second cousins in the United Kingdom and any possible criminality on his own part.[20] Haneef could not be taken to have failed the character test when the facts relied on to show the necessary association failed to disclose that it was anything other than an innocent one. At the time of writing the government had announced its intention to appeal this decision.

The lessons from Haneef

The events surrounding Dr Haneef highlight many of the concerns about Australia's anti-terrorism laws which, until now, existed only in the abstract. In particular, they demonstrate the fallacy which lies at the heart of arguments that security is enhanced when the rights of individuals are sacrificed.

Before being charged, Haneef was detained for a period of almost two weeks – well in excess of the time the government's staff had suggested, and the Senate Committee inquiry had understood, the questioning power would extend when it was introduced a few years earlier. Legislative machinery that confers strong powers on police and investigative agencies must be drafted very carefully, on the assumption that such tools will be readily employed once available. Although the committee's recommendation that additional periods of detention require judicial approval is a welcome feature of the law as enacted, it clearly suffers from some defects. In particular, the limited information to which the detainee's lawyers are able to be privy so as to challenge police applications, as well as a tendency for judicial deference when issues of national security are at stake, mean that there is a benefit in providing clear safeguards in the legislative scheme itself, such as a maximum amount of detention regardless of 'dead time'.

Having detained Haneef for so many days, it is not unreasonable to assume the AFP would have felt under some pressure to produce a result rather than simply let him go. This is not difficult to achieve under Australian law. As Professor Andrew Goldsmith discussed earlier in this book, terrorism offences tend to be drafted far more expansively than traditional crimes in order that they fulfil a preventative purpose. While that function is certainly legitimate, where to draw the line remains the central difficulty. The criminalisation of preparatory activity may produce some surprising results. Many members of the public expressed alarm that the seemingly innocuous act of giving a cousin your SIM card when you leave the country could lead to your being charged with supporting a terrorist organisation if yet another relative engages in terrorist activities several months after your departure. Plenty of Australians buy a local SIM card when they arrive in a new country for a stay of a few weeks or months. They may well leave it behind for friends or relatives to use when they move on. This is hardly unusual or sinister.

The criminal law should be enacted with precision so as to catch only those acts – whether of 'support' or otherwise – that are crucial to the furtherance of terrorist plans. Overly broad preparatory offences run the risk of being applied to persons whose conduct may be entirely innocent. As Professor Clive Walker has said, 'penalizing equivocal actions … will leave room for claims of people being victimized for their views or even their stupid curiosity'[21] – or, in Haneef's case, the conduct of his relatives.

Another lesson from the Haneef affair is that the criminal justice system should be let to run its course. The one point at which an orthodox process was followed – the bail application – stands in distinct contrast to the extended pre-charge detention and the Immigration Minister's later intervention, demonstrating the benefits of an open hearing of both parties before an independent judicial officer. Had the grant of bail been respected by the Commonwealth and Haneef allowed his liberty to return to the community, the injustice he suffered would not have seemed quite as grievous as it did when the charges against him collapsed two weeks later.

The decision by Minister Andrews to revoke Haneef's visa appears to have been the tipping point in the case. The use of immigration law as a general tool of counter-terrorism has been identified as a worrying trend in the wake of 9/11.[22] But the exercise by the Minister of his discretion here was especially unsatisfactory given his preparedness to act against an individual regardless of whether that person's conduct tainted his good character. The idea that law would punish a person for a familial or indeed any innocent association is a significant denial of a basic right. The Federal Court's decision that the relevant legislation cannot support such a wide discretion is an important assertion of the rule of law over expansive executive power.

Although Spender J found no evidence of Minister Andrews acting for an improper purpose so as to frustrate the magistrate's grant of bail by ensuring detention,[23] the public appearance of intervention at this point, combined with the failure by the Commonwealth to pursue an appeal against the bail decision, upped the stakes markedly.

The perception of Haneef as a man cornered by a relentless executive arm of government, in possession of enormous statutory powers and discretions and contemptuous of the judicial process, was cemented by this development.

This was only further strengthened by Andrews' repeated attempts to justify his actions by insinuating he knew far worse things about Haneef than were available on the public record. Spender J succinctly described the Minister's strategy as follows:

> [T]he Minister has chosen to give a selected part of what is said to be protected information to the public by way of press release, but has not sought to divulge to the Court any part of the protected information under s 503A(3) of the Act. The Minister is, in a sense, presenting one case in the public arena, a case the accuracy of which cannot be challenged in any meaningful way, and a smaller and not the same case in the Court, in a way which does not permit explanation or challenge by way of cross-examination.[24]

As this passage indicates, and as discussed by Dr Tanja Dreher in the preceding chapter, another significant feature of the matter was the vital role played by the media throughout. The investigating authorities, the government and the defence lawyers all used leaks and statements to the press to promote their own version of the case. Despite consternation caused by the many leaks, the importance of a free press was made abundantly clear in exposing the operation of the anti-terrorism laws on an individual in Haneef's position. This experience fuels existing concerns about the significant restrictions on speech imposed by the Commonwealth in respect of schemes such as those for preventative detention orders and ASIO questioning and detention and more generally as discussed by Dr Katharine Gelber in this book.

Finally, the actions of the government and its agencies were met with deep cynicism across the community. This is hardly a helpful development in a security climate that depends on people to trust their leaders and their assessment of the threat facing the nation. This unease must surely be compounded in our Muslim communities, whose fear of persecution under the anti-terrorism laws was described by Waleed Aly in his chapter. The promotion of social cohesion is integral to stopping terrorism in its tracks. More specifically, the cooperation and good relations between police and intelligence agencies and Australian Muslims are a crucial resource in unearthing and preventing potential terrorists. The pursuit of Haneef over little more than his familial association with the UK plotters will have alarmed those in close-knit ethnic communities and undone efforts to reassure Australia's Muslims they have nothing to fear from these laws.

Rights, law and security

The idea that we need to curtail individual rights to be more secure is not borne out by the Haneef case. At numerous points this young man's rights –

to liberty, to know the case against him, to a fair hearing, to the presumption of innocence – were disregarded. But there was nothing to indicate that the Australian community was made even the slightest bit more secure as a consequence.

The political obsession with enacting 'tough' anti-terrorism laws seems only to produce legislation drafted with alarming width, instead of laws that are effectively targeted so as to prevent and criminalise unambiguous terrorist activity. Clearly, wide laws can easily result in executive overreach. This does not make us safer. It may even make us less so by fostering cynicism and division in the community, and wasting police resources on investigations that are trivial or baseless.

In addition to informing the scope of terrorism offences, the objective of prevention has led to the creation of even more novel laws – most notably those allowing control orders, which Australia adopted with several modifications from the United Kingdom. Chief amongst the differences is that Australian control orders are issued by the courts rather than a member of the executive. Australian judges have had some experience in issuing similar preventive orders based on an assessment of future risk, and Justice White's chapter gives a frank judicial perspective on the application of such powers.

While the involvement of the judiciary may seem a preferable mechanism, ensuring a better protection of the individual's rights, the counter-argument is that the courts are compromised by their exercise of powers which may substantially deprive people of their liberty despite not having been found guilty of a crime. As Dr James Renwick's contribution to this book explains, concerns of institutional integrity can potentially invalidate laws due to the Australian Constitution's strict separation of judicial power, though recent case law has endorsed the view that judicial power may legitimately be exercised for purposes beyond the traditional focus on punishment.

That courts may exercise powers conferred on them by the legislature for the purpose of protecting the community – absent a simultaneous purpose of punishing an individual for breach of the law – is now beyond doubt. Coinciding with the ordeal of Dr Haneef was the High Court's decision in *Thomas v Mowbray*[25] in which five of the seven Justices upheld the constitutional validity of the control order regime in Division 104 of the *Criminal Code*. The majority rejected the arguments of Jack Thomas that the interim control order issued over him after he won his appeal against conviction for terrorism crimes in the Victorian Court of Appeal was unconstitutional by virtue of incompatibility with judicial power.[26]

Quite aside from the jurisprudence underpinning the *Thomas* decision,[27] it is a clear signal – in addition to the Haneef affair and the specific issues discussed by all the contributors to this book – that the Australian legal system, in common with many others around the world, is undergoing a rapid readjustment in order to respond to the post-9/11 world. Regardless of cynicism which may exist in some quarters about the need for these changes and the true extent of any ongoing threat, it is beyond dispute that very real shifts are taking place in the law as all three arms of government adapt to this new paradigm.

As the law is increasingly called on to play its part in the attainment of security and prevention of violence, a commitment to the preservation of individual rights and constitutional constraints on government is imperative. Safeguarding our defining civil liberties and the presumption of innocence under Australian law is neither a hindrance nor a luxury, but instead the only certain way to ensure that in responding to the threat of terrorism we do not allow those who would do us harm to dictate what kind of people we are and our relationship to the state. Doubtless the debates contained in this book will continue for some time ahead and the current period of legal experimentation is surely far from over. But an approach to security which is built upon, rather than dismissive of, civil liberties should mean that we are still able to recognise ourselves when the dust settles.

Notes

1 Commonwealth, *Parliamentary Debates*, House of Representatives, 24 June 2004, 31,701 (Philip Ruddock). See also the chapters by both the Attorney-General and Secretary of the Attorney-General's Department, Robert Cornall, earlier in this book.

2 Philip Ruddock, 'Australia's Legislative Response to the Ongoing Threat of Terrorism' (2004) 27 *University of New South Wales Law Journal* 254, 255.

3 Irwin Cotler, 'Thinking Outside the Box: Foundational Principles for a Counter-Terrorism Law and Policy' in Ronald J Daniels, Patrick Macklem and Kent Roach (eds), *The Security of Freedom: Essays on Canada's Anti-Terrorism Bill* (2001) 111, 113. See also Clive Walker, 'Clamping Down on Terrorism in the United Kingdom' (2006) 4 *Journal of International Criminal Justice* 1137, 1146-48.

4 Christopher Michaelsen, 'Balancing Civil Liberties Against National Security? A Critique of Counter-Terrorism Rhetoric' (2006) 29 *University of New South Wales Law Journal* 1, 6.

5 Fernando R Tesón, 'Liberal security' in Richard Ashby Wilson, *Human Rights in the 'War on Terror'* (2005) 62.

6 Lucia Zedner, 'Securing Liberty in the Face of Terror: Reflections from Criminal Justice' (2005) 32 *Journal of Law and Society* 507, 516.

7 This is a central theme of Kent Roach, 'Must We Trade Rights for Security? The Choice Between Smart, Harsh, or Proportionate Security Strategies in Canada and Britain' (2006) 27 *Cardozo Law Review* 2151.

8 Peter Wilson, 'Timing of email supports Haneef', *The Australian*, 21 August 2007, 9.

9 *Terrorism Act 2000* (UK), s 38B(1)(b).

10 *Crimes Act 1914* (Cth) Pt 1C, Div 2.

11 *Crimes Act 1914* (Cth) s 23CB(5).

12 Senate Legal and Constitutional Legislation Committee, Parliament of Australia, *Provisions of the Anti-Terrorism Bill 2004* (2004) para 3.25.

13 *Crimes Act 1914* (Cth) s 15AA.

14 The issuing by the Attorney-General of 'criminal justice certificate' under s 147 of the *Migration Act 1958* (Cth) meant that Haneef would not be deported until criminal proceedings against him had concluded.

15 *Migration Act 1958* (Cth) s 501(5).

16 Andrew Fraser and Hedley Thomas, 'Tell us all you know: accused's lawyer', *The Australian*, 19 July 2007, 1.

17 Hedley Thomas, 'Haneef Dossier Flawed', *The Australian*, 20 July 2007, 1.

18 Hedley Thomas, 'Pressure on Ruddock to explain "sloppy" Haneef case', *The Australian*, 21 July 2007, 1.

19 Tom Allard, Connie Levett and Craig Skehan, 'Brother told Haneef to call police', *Sydney Morning Herald*, 23 August 2007, 5.

20 *Haneef v Minister for Immigration and Citizenship* [2007] FCA 1273, [230].

21 Walker, above n 3, 1145.

22 Kent Roach, 'The criminal law and terrorism' in Victor V Ramraj, Michael Hor and Kent Roach (eds), *Global Anti-Terrorism Law and Policy* (2005) 129, 142-4.

23 *Haneef v Minister for Immigration and Citizenship* [2007] FCA 1273, [311].

24 Above, [326]-[327].

25 *Thomas v Mowbray* [2007] HCA 33.

26 *Director of Public Prosecutions v Thomas* [2006] VSCA 165.

27 The decision and its significance for the rule of law is subjected to analysis by Dyzenhaus and Thwaites in Chapter 2 of this book.

Index